A History of Modern Ethiopia 1855–1991

SECOND EDITION

Bahru Zewde

Professor of History
Addis Ababa University

James Currey
OXFORD

Ohio University Press
ATHENS

Addis Ababa University Press
ADDIS ABABA

Addis Ababa University Press
Addis Ababa, Ethiopia
PO Box 1176
Tel. + 251-1-23 97 46
Fax. + 251-1-23 97 29
E-mail: aau.press@telecom.net.et

James Currey Ltd.
73 Botley Road
Oxford
OX2 0BS

Ohio University Press
Scott Quadrangle
Athens, Ohio 45701, USA

First published 1991
Reprinted 1994, 1995, 1996, 2001
Second edition 2002
Reprinted 2005

Originally published in the UK, 2001 by James Currey Ltd.

1 2 3 4 5 05 04 03 02 01

British Library Cataloguing in Publication Data

Bahru Zewde

  A history of modern Ethiopia, 1855-1991. -2nd edn.-
    (Eastern African studies)
  1. Ethiopia. History - 19th century 2. Ethiopia - History -
  20th century
  I. Title
  963'.05

ISBN 0-85255-786-8 (James Currey paper)

Library of Congress Cataloguing in Publication Data available

ISBN 0-8214-1440-2 (Ohio University Press paper)

Maps by Katherine Kirkwood
Typeset in 10/12pt Baskerville by Colset Pte Ltd Singapore
and revisions to second edition by Longhouse Publishing Services, Cumbria

Printed and bound in Ethiopia
by Addis Ababa University Printing Press

EASTERN AFRICAN STUDIES

EASTERN AFRICAN STUDIES

A History of
Modern Ethiopia
1855–1991

AAUP BOOKS CURRENTLY IN PRINT

* አሌሳንድሮ ትሪዩልዚ. እና
ተስማ ታ·ባ ፣ ፲፱፻፺፮ ዓ.ም::
የወለጋ የታሪክ ሰነዶች:-
ከ1880ዎቹ እስከ 1920ዎቹ
(እ.ኢ.ኢ.)
    Br. 65.00
* አማኑኤል አብርሃም ፲፱፻፺፱
ዓ.ም:: የሕይወቴ ትዝታ
    Br. 32.00
* Andargatchew Tesfaye, 2004.
*The Crime Problem and Its
Correction, Vol. II*
    Br. 55.00
* Bahru   Zewde,   2002.
*Pioneers   of   Change   in
Ethiopia: The   Reformist
Intellectuals   of   the   Early
Twentieth   Century,   Co-
published   with   James
Currey Publishers, Oxford
& Ohio University Press,
Athens
    Br. 40.00
* Balsvik, R., 2005. Haile
Sellassie's   Students: *The
Intellectual   and   Social
Background   to   Revolution,
1952 1974,*   Co-published
with   Michigan   State
University
    Br. 40.00

* Crummey,   Donald,   2000,
*Land & Society in the
Christian   Kingdom   of
Ethiopia,   from   the
Thirteenth to the Twentieth
Century,* Co-published with
the   University   of   Illinois
Press and James Currey
Publishers, Oxford
    Br. 50.00
* Fekade   Azeze,   1998.
*Unheard Voices: Drought,
Famine   and   God   in
Ethiopian Oral Poetry*
    Br. 20.00
* Gutt, Eeva and Hussein
Mohammed,   1997.   *Silt'e-
Amharic-English Dictionary*
    Br. 50.00
* Ketema   Alemu,   2003.
*Digital   and   Analogue
Communication Systems*
    Br. 60.00
* ሚሊዮን   ነቅንቅ ፣   ፲፱፻፺፪
ዓ.ም::   ትልቋ ኢትዮጵያ ፣
የብዙ ነገዶች ማህበረሰብ ፣ a
translation   of   Donald
Levine's *Greater Ethiopia,*
2000
    Br. 20.00

* Rubenson, S. (ed.), 2000.
*Internal   Rivalries   and
Foreign Threats: 1869–1879,
Acta   Æthiopica   Vol.   III,*
Co-published   with   Rutgers
University
    Br. 50.00
* Rubenson, S. (ed.), 1994.
*Tewodros   and   His
Contemporaries   1855–1868,
Acta   Æthiopica   Vol.   II*
Co-published   with   Lund
University Press
    Br. 65.00
* Taffara Deguefé, 2003. *A
Tripping Stone: Ethiopian
Prison Diary*
    Br. 40.00
* Wolde-Ghiorgis, Woldemariam,
2004. *Principles of Electrical
and Electronic Instrumentation*
    Br. 55.00
* Yared Amare, 1999. *Household
Resources, Strategies and
Food Security in Ethiopia*
    Br. 20.00

Forthcoming

* ተክለሐዋርያት ዋይሕ ፣ 'አቶ ባዮግራፊ'
* Tsegaye Tegenu, 'Evaluation of the Operation and Performance of
Ethnic Decentralization System in Ethiopia: A Case Study of the Gurage
People, 1992–2000'
* Ezekiel Gebissa, 'Leaf of Allah'

NB: All prices are at local wholesale rate.

To Kaleb

To Kaleb

Contents

Introduction

1 The background

2 Unification and Independence 1855-1896

Contents

Illustrations

List of Illustrations

Maps

Sources of Illustrations

Art Gallery of the Institute of Ethiopian Studies, Addis Ababa: 3.29
Kurt Herzbruch. *Abessinien*. Munich, 1925, Fr. Seybold Verlag: 1.1, 3.23
Hormuzd Rassam. *Narrative of the British Mission to Theodore, King of Abyssinia*, II. London, 1869, John Murray: 2.1
Henry A. Stern. *The Captive Missionary*. London, 1868, Cassell, Petter & Galpin: 2 2
Photographic collection of the Institute of Ethiopian Studies, Addis Ababa University: 2.4, 2.8, 2.11, 2.15, 3.4, 3.6, 3.10, 3.11, 3.17, 3.19, 3.30, 4.1, 4.4, 4.9, 5.4, 5.5, 5.6, 5.7, 6.1, 6.3, 6.4, 6.5, 6.6, 6.7
– (Album of the British Expedition to Maqdala, 1867-1868): 2.3
– (Album Charles Michel-Cote, Ethiopie-Soudan, 1919-1920): 2.7
E. Canevari and G. Comisso. *Il generale Tommaso Salsa e le sue campagne coloniali*. Milan, 1935, A. Mondadori: 2.5
Achille Bizzone. *Eritrea nel passate e nel presente*. Milan, 1897, Società editrice Sonzogno: 2.6
Philipp Paulitschke. *Harar*. Leipzig, 1888, F. A. Brockhaus: 2.9
Lincoln de Castro. Nella terra dei negus, I and II. Milan, 1915, Fratelli Treves: 2.10, 2.13, 3.9, 3.20
Otto Bieber. *Geheimnisvolles Kaffa. Im Reich der Kaiser-Goetter*. Vienna, 1948, Universum Verlagsgesellschaft: 2.12, 3.2
Das ist Abessinien. Berne, Leipzig, Vienna, 1935, Wilhelm Goldmann Verlag, GmbH: 2.14, 3.5, 3.7, 3.14, 3.21, 3.34
Leopoldo Traversi. *Let Marefià*. Milan, 1931, Edizioni 'Alpes': 3.1
Kabbada Tasamma. *Ya Tarik Mastawasha*. Addis Ababa, 1963 Ethiopian calendar, copyright YMCA Ethiopia: 3.3, 3.25, 3.27, 3.28, 3.31
Carlo Annaratone. *In Abissinia*. Rome, 1914, Enrico Voghera: 3.8, 3.22, 3.33
Max Gruehl. *Abyssinia at Bay*. London, 1935, Hurst & Blackett: 3.12
Merab. *Impressions d'Ethiopie*, III. Paris, 1929, Editions Ernest Leroux: 3.13
Courtesy of *Ato* Kabbada Bogala: 3.15, 5.8
Courtesy of Hakim Warqenah family: 4.10
Courtesy of *Tsahafe T'ezaz* Walda-Giyorgis family: 5.3
Courtesy of Denis Gérard: 6.2
Felix Rosen. *Eine deutsche Gesandtschaft in Abessinien*. Leipzig, 1907, Verlag von Veit & Comp: 3.16
Arnold Holtz. *Im Auto zu Kaiser Menelik*. Berlin, 1908, Vita: 3 18
National Geographic Magazine: June 1925, 3.24: August 1928, 3.32: June 1931, 4.2
G.K. Rein. *Abessinien* Berlin, 1920, Dietrich Reimer (Ernst Vohsen) A-G: 3.26
Luigi Goglia. *Storia fotografica del Impero fascista 1935-1941*. Rome-Bari, 1985, Giuseppe Laterza & Figli, SpA: 4.3, 4.5, 4 6, 4 7, 4.8
John H Spencer. *Ethiopia at Bay A Personal Account of the Haile Sellassie Years*. Algonac, 1984, Reference Publications: 5.1
Bringing Africa Together: The Story of Ethiopian Airlines. Addis Ababa, 1988, copyright Ethiopian Airlines: 5.2
Hezbawi Wayana Harenat Tegray (Tegray People's Liberation Front), *Ya Hewahat Hezbawi Tegel* ('The Popular Struggle of TPLF') (Addis Ababa, 1992 Ethiopian Calendar): 6.8

Acronyms

CADU   Chilalo Agricultural Development Unit
CELU   Confederation of Ethiopian Labour Unions
COPWE   Commission for Organizing the Workers' Party of Ethiopia
EAL   Ethiopian Airlines
EDU   Ethiopian Democratic Union
ELF   Eritrean Liberation Front
EPLF   Eritrean Popular Liberation Forces (Front)
EPRDF   Ethiopian Peoples' Revolutionary Democratic Front
EPRP   Ethiopian People's Revolutionary Party
ESUE   Ethiopian Students Union in Europe
ESUNA   Ethiopian Students Union in North America
HVA   Handelsvereenging Amsterdam
IBRD   International Bank for Reconstruction and Development
IHA   Imperial Highway Authority
Ich'at   Amharic acronym of Ethiopian Oppressed Peoples' Revolutionary Struggle
Imaledeh   Amharic acronym of Union of Ethiopian Marxist-Leninist Organizations
Ma'ison   Amharic acronym of All Ethiopia Socialist Movement (AESM)
Malerid   Amharic acronym of Marxist-Leninist Revolutionary Organization
NDR   National Democratic Revolution
OLF   Oromo Liberation Front
PDRE   People's Democratic Republic of Ethiopia
PMAC   Provisional Military Administrative Council
POMOA   Provisional Office for Mass Organizational Affairs
PPG   Provisional People's Government
TPLF   Tigray People's Liberation Front
WPE   Workers' Party of Ethiopia

Preface

For far too long, the absence of a general history of Ethiopia has been acutely felt by specialists engaged in Ethiopian studies, by educators in institutions of higher learning, and by many readers interested in Ethiopia. Yet few historians have turned their attention to the writing of such a general history, although Ethiopian historiography has made remarkable advances in the last two and a half decades. The dramatic changes that Ethiopia has been going through, particularly in the last two of those decades, have made the need for a background history leading up to those events more urgent.

The genesis of this present book is to be sought in considerations of the above nature. The book addresses itself to what historians of Ethiopia have come to regard as the modern period of the country's history, the nineteenth and twentieth centuries. No attempt has been made to go to earlier periods, except in the brief remarks in the Introduction, nor do the events of the post-1974 period find coverage here, because the time for a dispassionate and documented historical analysis of those occurrences has not yet arrived.

The pitfalls of writing a general history are obvious. As one tremendous exercise in precis-writing, it glosses over too many intricate processes. To dispense with the detailed acknowledgements that a general history would entail leaves me with a sense of guilt. Yet no one is more aware than I myself of the great value of the lists of books, articles and theses appended to the chapters as sources for the writing of this book. I would like to draw special attention to the sound scholarship embodied in Sven Rubenson's *The Survival of Ethiopian Independence*, and to the BA and MA theses which have made possible a much fuller reconstruction of the recent Ethiopian past than could have been hoped for in previous decades.

To the Department of History of Addis Ababa University, which initiated me into the basic canons of historical investigation, I owe almost everything in my training as a historian. Here I have found an ambience combining warm co-operation and academic stimulation that has sustained me through the years, some of them difficult. The Institute of Ethiopian Studies has been my second academic home, and the rich collection of Ethiopiana in its Library has provided a vast basis of sustenance. The Research and Publications Office of the University has been an unfailing source of financial support for my research endeavours, and the preparation of this manuscript for offering for publication was made possible by a grant from that office.

The Background

A number of colleagues at Addis Ababa University read the manuscript in full or in part, and made many useful suggestions for its improvement. In this respect, I would like to thank Daniel Ayana, Daniel Gamachu, Eshetu Chole, Hussein Ahmed, Merid Wolde Aregay, Shiferaw Bekele, Shumet Sishagn, Taddesse Tamrat, and Tekalign Wolde Mariam. I am also indebted to Donald Crummey of the University of Illinois at Urbana-Champaign for his comments, and to Terence Ranger of St Antony's College, Oxford, for encouragement in the initial stages of the manuscript's preparation. I record with gratitude the generous assistance of Denis Gérard, who devoted a great deal of his time and his financial resources to preparing some of the illustrations. Thanks are also due to Kabbada Bogala for processing the remaining illustrations, to Metasebia Demessie for drawing the maps, and to Manna Zacharias for typing the manuscript.

Finally, I am very grateful to the General Editor of Addis Ababa University Press, the person next to myself who is most closely associated with this book, for dedicated application to editing the manuscript.

Preface
to the Second Edition

Since its publication in 1991, *A History of Modern Ethiopia (1855–1974)* has had a gratifyingly favourable reception. It has managed to capture a wide readership and its impact both inside and outside Ethiopia has far exceeded my expectations. The academic reviews have also been generally encouraging. A recurrent source of disappointment has been, however, the fact that the story stops in 1974. This new edition, which brings the narrative to 1991, has been prepared primarily to address that concern.

'Contemporary history' is a treacherous ground and historians generally fear to tread it. In the preface to the first edition of the book, I justified the terminal date on the ground that 'the time for a dispassionate and documented historical analysis of those occurrences [i.e. of the period 1974–1991] has not yet arrived'. Those two impediments exist now to a much lesser degree than when the book was first written. Now that Darg rule is over, a requiem of that past has become possible. Although Darg officials are still on trial, the passion of the revolutionary years has subsided considerably. Moreover, in addition to the many secondary works that have been written on the period, we have also seen a sizeable number of testimonials by active participants of the period. Chapter 6, which is the major innovation of this new edition, has now been made possible because of these developments.

Yet, the chapter can not be anything but a synopsis of that complex period. While the importance of that period certainly merits wider treatment and the wealth of data invites it, I have striven as much as possible to maintain the balance of the whole book. After all, the revolutionary period lasted only seventeen years, a small fraction in a narrative that has the span of a century and a half. Revisiting the manuscript has also enabled me to rectify minor errors pointed out by the reviewers as well as to attune certain phrases to the contemporary setting.

I am grateful to my colleagues Shiferaw Bekele and Taddesse Tamrat for reading an earlier draft of the sixth chapter and making suggestions for improvement. My thanks are also due to Douglas Johnson of James Currey Publishers for the gentle pressure he has been exerting on me to expedite the writing of the revised edition. As so often, I am indebted to my loyal friend, Denis Gérard, for preparing the photographs. The first edition was criticized by some for not having a decent photograph of Emperor Hayla-Sellase. I have now rectified that omission, which was induced not by any personal antipathy I might have had for the sovereign but by a conscious decision not to cloud the fate of the whole book for the sake of one photograph.

*A session of Ethiopia's first parliament being addressed
by Emperor Hayla-Sellase I, 1935 (see Chapter 3)*

Introduction

Ethiopia is an ancient country located in north-east Africa, or, as it is generally known, the Horn of Africa, so called because of the horn-shaped tip of the continent that marks off the Red Sea from the Indian Ocean. It is bounded by Sudan in the west, Eritrea in the north and north-east, Kenya in the south, Somalia in the south-east, and Djibouti in the east. To the outside world, it has long been known by the name of Abyssinia. This appellation apparently derived from 'Habashat', one of the tribes that inhabited the Ethiopian region in the pre-Christian era.

The term Ethiopia is of Greek origin, and in classical times was used as a generic and rather diffuse designation for the African land-mass to the south of Egypt. The first known specific application of the term to the Ethiopian region is found in the Greek version of a trilingual inscription of the time of Ezana, the Aksumite king who introduced Christianity into Ethiopia towards the middle of the fourth century AD. This adoption of the term continued with the subsequent translation of the Bible into Ge'ez, the old literary language. The *Kebra Nagast* ('Glory of Kings'), written in the early fourteenth century, which gave the 'received' account of the story of the Queen of Sheba and King Solomon, not only linked the Ethiopian kings to the House of Israel, but also sealed the identification of the term Ethiopia with the country: since the thirteenth century, when a dynasty that claimed to represent the restoration of the Solomonic line came to rule the country, its rulers have styled themselves 'King of Kings of Ethiopia'. While it is not uncommon for Ethiopians to refer to themselves, particularly in informal circumstances, as 'Habasha' (Abyssinians), officially they prefer to be called Ethiopians.

Present-day Ethiopia is located between longitudes 33° and 48°E, and latitudes 3° and 15°N. Although thus lying very near the Equator, the country on the whole is far from 'tropical' in the accepted sense of the term. On the contrary, the elevated nature of its highlands, rising to over 1,500 metres, gives it a decidedly cooler climate than its geographical location seems to suggest. The highlands are criss-crossed by numerous river valleys, and, on an even grander scale, divided by the Rift Valley. The valley is part of the great geological fault that cuts across large parts of eastern Africa, including Kenya and Tanzania. It diagonally slashes Ethiopia into two unequal parts. The bigger part contains the mountainous north, where the country's highest peak, Ras Dashan (c. 4620 metres), is located, and the gentler plateau of the south-western highlands. The smaller part includes the south-eastern highlands of Bale, Harar, Arsi and Sidamo, and tapers down to the lowlands inhabited by the Oromo (formerly known as the Galla) and the Somali. With the exception of the south-western tip of the country, the highlands are surrounded by an almost uninterrupted ring of lowlands. A steep escarpment abruptly descends from the northern highlands to the Red Sea plains; elsewhere, the descent from highland to lowland is relatively more gentle.

The northern highlands are dotted with hills and mountains, often flat-topped, known as *amba*. These *amba* have had an important place in the historical evolution of the country, serving as sites for churches, prisons (like the royal prison of Amba Geshen in Wallo) and battles (Amba Alage in 1895 and Amba Aradom in 1936). Ethiopians divide their country topographically into three major zones: *daga* (the rather cool highlands where the annual average temperature is about 16 °C), *wayna daga* (the intermediate zone where most of the settled population lives) and *qolla* (the hot valleys and plains attaining their hottest and lowest levels in the desert conditions that prevail in the north-eastern end of the Rift Valley). Although originally climatic designations, these terms have come over time to assume broader meaning, denoting differing modes of life and character.

The country is watered by four major river systems. The first consists of the Takkaze, the Abbay and the Baro, known respectively as the Atbara, the Blue Nile and the Sobat in Sudan; they all flow westwards into the Nile. Of these, the Abbay (Blue Nile) is certainly the most famous; its source, Lake Tana, for long exercised the imagination of travellers and geographers, until the Scottish traveller James Bruce settled the issue in the second half of the eighteenth century. To the second group belong the Ganale (known as the Juba in Somalia) and the Wabe Shabale; they both flow towards the Indian Ocean. The Gibe (Omo in its lower course) originates and ends in the south-western highlands, with Lake Rudolf (also known as Turkana) on the Ethio-Kenya border as its terminus. The Awash sets off from the highlands west of Addis Ababa, Ethiopia's capital, and streams along in a leisurely loop, for the most part across the Rift Valley, until it vanishes in its north-eastern sands.

It is also in the Rift that the country's major chain of lakes is located. Three parts are discernible in the chain: the northern cluster (including Lakes Zway, Langano, Abyata, Shala and Awasa), Lakes

1. Relief map of Ethiopia

Abbaya and Chamo in the middle, and Lake Rudolf at the southern tip. There is also a string of volcanic crater lakes around the town of Dabra Zayt, formerly named Beshoftu, some 31 miles (50 km) to the south of Addis Ababa.

The rains that fill these rivers and lakes come twice a year. The main rainy season in Ethiopia falls between June and September and is known as *keramt*. The 'heavy rains', as they are also known, are caused by moist air from the high pressure area of the South Atlantic and the Indian Ocean moving into the low pressure area of the Sahara desert and Arabia. The south-westerly nature of the wind means that south-western Ethiopia gets the heaviest dose of these rains, which progressively decrease as we move northwards and eastwards. The 'little rains', also known as the *balg* ('autumn' in the Ethiopian context, but spring in Europe), generally occur between March and May. They are caused by monsoon winds blowing from the Indian Ocean. Rains in Ethiopia, whether 'heavy' or 'little', are characterized by torrential downpours. The long rainy season has historically been marked by a hiatus in military activity, as flooded rivers and wet ground made campaigning difficult.

The rainfall pattern has had a direct bearing on the vegetation scene. The heavy and almost year-round rains in the south-west have given rise to a dense concentration of tropical broad-leaf forests, particularly in the administrative regions of Illubabor and Kafa. Although deforestation has reduced the wooded area to about a tenth of its original size, the south-west still accounts for some 65% of the country's total forest resources. It is this region which has traditionally been the source of most of the natural products of commerce, ranging from elephant tusks to coffee. The northern and central parts of the country were initially covered with coniferous forests and temperate grasslands; currently, less than 1% of the original forests remain, the result of intense human activity attended by an even more disastrous rate of deforestation than in the south-west. We can say that, over the years, the country's vegetation has generally been characterized by a decrease in the forest area and an increase in the area covered with grass and scrub. Of late, the even faster degradation of land has brought about the recurrent droughts which have made the country so notorious.

Keramt is the main growing season in Ethiopia, although the *balg* rains are also crucial for some parts of the country. The temperate conditions of the northern and central highlands have permitted the growing of a wide variety of food crops. Of these, the most important is *tef* (*Eragrostis tef*) a small cereal indigenous and peculiar to the country; it is processed into the distinctive bread, *enjara*, the staple diet of a large proportion of the country's population. *Tef*'s equivalent in the southern parts of the country is the root-crop *ensat* (*Ensete ven-*

4

tricosum). The country's abundant grasslands have also supported a large livestock population, reputedly the largest in Africa. The possession of livestock is not confined to the lowland pastoralists. Highland farmers also keep a fair proportion of livestock for their food value, as transport animals and, in the case of oxen, as draught-animals to pull the plough.

Like many other African societies, Ethiopia presents a mosaic of nationalities speaking a multiplicity of languages. Linguists have divided these languages into four groups, three of them tracing a common ancestry to a parent language called proto-Afroasiatic. From this parent language sprang not only the languages spoken in Ethiopia but also a number of languages spoken in the northern half of Africa and in south-western Asia. The three language groups of the proto-Afroasiatic family spoken in Ethiopia are known as Cushitic, Omotic and Semitic. Cushitic and Omotic are the most ancient in the Ethiopian region; the Semitic languages are the most recent. A fourth group of languages belong to an independent family known as Nilo-Saharan.

The Nilo-Saharans are situated in a more or less continuous line along the western fringes of the country. The Kunama in south-western Eritrea form the northernmost group. Further south, in Matakkal in western Gojjam, are to be found the Gumuz. They spill over into the adjoining region of Wallaga, home of the Barta and the Koma. The southern end of the Nilo-Saharan corridor is composed of the Majangir, on the escarpment leading from the Oromo-inhabited highlands to the Baro plains, and the Anuak and Nuer, who dwell in the plains; some sections of the Anuak and even larger sections of the Nuer are to be found on the Sudanese side of the boundary.

Of the Cushitic-speaking peoples of Ethiopia, historically the most important in ancient times were the Agaw and the Beja. The Agaw have now been largely assimilated into the dominant Semitic culture, with a pocket waging what looks like a rearguard fight for survival in the Gojjam administrative region. An Agaw pocket, the Belen or Bilen, is also found in the Karan district in Eritrea. The Beja are now to be found largely in Sudan. The Oromo now constitute the largest single nationality in Ethiopia; they began to migrate from the south in the sixteenth century, and later settled over large parts of the country. Linguistically closest to the Oromo are the Somali, a predominantly pastoralist people now found scattered in Ethiopia, Djibouti, Somalia and Kenya. Other Cushitic-speaking peoples are the Afar, inhabiting the hostile environment at the north-eastern end of the Rift, the Saho on the escarpment to the north, the Hadiya and Kambata in Shawa administrative region and the Gedeo (Darasa) and Konso further to the south.

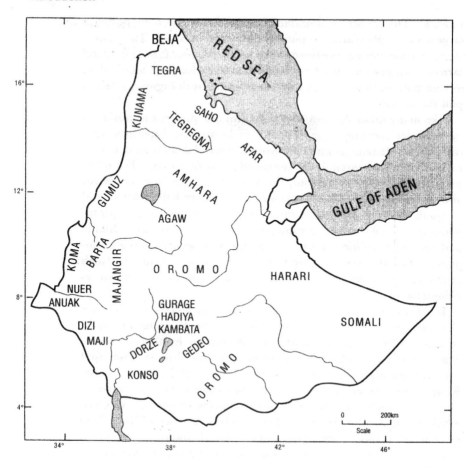

2. Linguistic map of Ethiopia, showing the distribution by the nineteenth century

The Omotic-speaking peoples derive their name from their location on both sides of the Omo river. Situated exclusively in south-western Ethiopia, they have been distinguished by two important features: the large-scale cultivation of *ensat* and the evolution of highly organized polities. The Dorze, Janjaro, Kafa and Walayta were of particular significance in the latter regard. Showing comparative levels of complexity were the Dizi (Gimira) and Maji, found in the extreme south-west.

The Semites have played the most dominant role in the country's history. The kingdoms and empires that successively emerged in the region have invariably been under their control, particularly that of the Tegregna- and Amharic-speaking peoples of northern and central Ethiopia. The oldest of the Semitic languages, Ge'ez, now confined to ecclesiastical use, has served as a sort of lingua franca of the Semitic-speaking peoples. The most akin to Ge'ez is Tegra, spoken by the inhabitants of northern and eastern Eritrea. The Tegregna-speakers are found in highland Eritrea and in Tegray. Amharic, which is the official language of the country, is the native tongue of most of the inhabitants of the north-central and central highlands. Two Semitic language pockets in a predominantly Cushitic environment are Gurage in south-central Ethiopia and Harari in the east.

Conventionally, Ethiopian history began with the visit of the Queen of Sheba, allegedly from Ethiopia, to Solomon, King of Israel, in the tenth century BC: hence the reference to Ethiopia's 'three thousand years of history' that we hear and read so often. Aside from the fact that this association has scarcely any scientific basis, it represents too short a view of the Ethiopian past. Archaeological and linguistic research in recent years has made possible and necessary the adoption of a longer and more scientific perspective. On this basis, the beginnings of the Ethiopian past are to be sought not in the historical but in the prehistoric period.

Archaeological discoveries of the late 1960s and early 1970s have lent this past more than national significance. The discovery in 1974 of the earliest hominid in Hadar, in the Afar desert, has focused international palaeontological research on the country. Named 'Lucy' by foreigners, and 'Denqenash' ('You are Marvellous') by Ethiopians, this female ancestor of the human race was dated to three and a half million years ago. In the Omo valley in the south-west, too, human fossils dating from one to two and a half million years ago have been found. Much nearer in time, there are other manifestations of prehistoric culture: the neolithic site of Malka Qunture, some 31 miles (50 km) to the south-west of Addis Ababa, and the cave paintings found in Eritrea in the north, Sidamo in the south and Harar in the east. An important facet of this prehistoric culture was the domestication of plants and animals, believed to have started some six thousand years ago. *Ensat* was cultivated in the Omotic south-west and *tef* and

7

dagusa (*Eleusine corocana*, finger millet) in the northern and eastern highlands. Barley and wheat were subsequently introduced into the region. The emergence of the ox-drawn plough signalled a revolution in agricultural production, and at the same time gave the country one of its distinctive marks over the centuries.

The developments described above constituted the basis for the emergence of states in the Ethiopian region. Not much is known about the predecessors of the Aksumite kingdom, which has been the focus of much of the historiographical attention. But such centres as Yeha, to the north of Aksum, attest to the flourishing of a rich civilization which appears to have been an amalgam of the indigenous culture and external influences, notably from South Arabia. Aksum flourished from the first to the seventh century AD. Its elaborately carved stelae and the ruins of palaces and other edifices attest to high attainments in building technology. Its towns included the eponymous capital and Adulis, a Red Sea port of international repute. Aksum was above all sustained by trade, both inland and maritime. The latter not only made it an integral part of Mediterranean commerce and culture but also brought it into contact with India and the Far East. Military expansion, as so often, followed trade. At the height of its power, the Aksumite state controlled large parts of northern Ethiopia and the Arabian coastline across the Red Sea. The conversion of the Aksumite king Ezana to Christianity in the 330s ushered in a new chapter in the country's history. The creed, in its Orthodox form, came to express the cultural identity of a large section of its highland population. Ideologically and diplomatically, the Ethiopian church and state were thenceforth tied up with the Alexandrian patriarchate in Egypt, who had sole authority to consecrate a bishop for the Ethiopian church, the *abun*.

From about the middle of the seventh century, Aksum entered a process of decline. The rise of Islam and the subsequent disruption of the Red Sea trade sapped Aksum's source of life. Beja pressures from the north combined to force the Aksumite state to recoil further inwards. It was in these circumstances that the Agaw, hitherto subjugated, seized state power and inaugurated their almost eponymous dynasty, Zagwe. While the origins of this dynasty are shrouded in obscurity, the period for which we have some reliable documentation lasts from about 1150 to 1270. The Zagwe left their deepest imprint on Ethiopian history through the construction of eleven monolithic churches in Lalibala, named after one of the more famous of their kings.

In 1270, the Zagwe were overthrown by Yekunno-Amlak, a chieftain of one of the subject peoples, the Amhara (then inhabiting the Wallo region). He inaugurated a dynasty which called itself 'Solomonic', to emphasize its legitimacy as opposed to the Zagwe, who were portrayed as usurpers. Yekunno-Amlak and his successors, notably Amda-Tseyon (r. 1314–1344) and Zar'a-Yaeqob (r. 1434–1468), built an empire which matched, and in some respects surpassed, its Aksumite predecessor in military might and territorial extent. The period also witnessed a further expansion of Christianity to the south, as well as to the Lake Tana region and Gojjam. But Islam posed a serious challenge in the south-east. The bid to control the vital trade route linking the Gulf of Aden port of Zeila to the southern interior, even more than religious divergence, pitted the Christian state against a string of Muslim principalities that had emerged since the turn of the ninth century. By the end of the fifteenth century, the supremacy of the Christian kingdom over these principalities had become an established fact. Simultaneously, the quest for 'Prester John', a legendary Christian king of superlative wealth and power believed to rule somewhere beyond the Muslim crescent which shut Europe off from Asia, brought the Portuguese to Ethiopia. An important Portuguese mission visited the country in 1520, and established the basis for future co-operation.

In 1527, the tide began to turn against the Christian kingdom. Galvanizing for his own ends an irresistible population movement of the nomadic Afar and Somali, a military genius by the name of Ahmad ibn Ibrahim, more popularly known as Ahmad Gragn or Gragn ('the Left-Handed'), led the Muslims in a series of sweeping victories over the Christian kingdom. In 1529, at Shembera Kure, a site about 44 miles (70 km) to the south-east of what is now Addis Ababa, Gragn scored his first major victory over the Christian forces led by Emperor Lebna-Dengel (r. 1508–1540). Harried from one part of his realm to another by the conquering foe, the king died a fugitive in 1540, after sending a desperate request for Portuguese military assistance. A force of some 400 Portuguese, led by Christopher da Gama (son of Vasco da Gama, discoverer of the route round South Africa to India), arrived the following year, and helped to defeat Ahmad Gragn at the Battle of Wayna Daga, to the east of Gondar, in 1543.

But the damage had already been done. The Christian kingdom could not easily recover its former might. Indeed, like two exhausted gladiators, both the Christian kingdom and the Muslim state of Adal in the Harar region, whence Gragn had launched his phenomenal assault, lay prostrate as the Oromo swept across the highlands like a tidal wave. This was the most significant population movement in the country's recent history, changing its demographic shape and its political geography. The political centre steadily retreated to the north. In the mean time, the Jesuit missionaries, who had come to Ethiopia hoping to make religious capital out of the atmosphere of friendship generated by the Portuguese military support of the

Christian state, made continued attempts to convert the kings and their country to Catholicism. They nearly succeeded in doing so with Emperor Susneyos (r. 1607–1632), who embraced the new creed in the hope of strengthening the declining power of the monarchy. Nobility, clergy and peasantry rose against him. Appalled by the ensuing civil war, he gracefully abdicated in favour of his son, Fasiladas (r. 1632–1667). The first act of the new king was to expel the Jesuits.

Fasiladas is also famous in Ethiopian history for founding Gondar as the imperial capital in 1636. Coming as it did after a long period when Ethiopian kings had ruled from roving royal camps, the establishment of Gondar marked a new chapter in the country's urban history. Fasiladas led the way in the construction of a number of impressive castles and churches in and around the town. But this flourishing of urban culture did not check the decline of monarchical power. The power of regional lords continued to grow at the expense of the monarchs. By the second half of the eighteenth century, the emperors in Gondar merely reigned; they did not rule. This period of Ethiopian history is known as the *Zamana Masafent* ('Era of the Princes'). It forms the prelude to the modern history of Ethiopia.

Sources, Introduction

Anfray, Francis. 'The Civilizations of Aksum from the First to the Seventh Century', in G. Mokhtar, ed., *General History of Africa. II. Ancient Civilizations of Africa.* Berkeley, California, 1981.

Bender, M.L., Bowen, J.D., Cooper, R.L., and Ferguson, C.A., eds. *Language in Ethiopia.* London, 1976.

Fattovich, Rodolfo. 'Remarks on the Late Prehistory and Early History of Northern Ethiopia', in Taddese Beyene, ed., *Proceedings of the Eighth International Conference of Ethiopian Studies*, Volume I. Addis Ababa and Frankfurt-on-Main, 1988.

Johansen, Donald C., and Edey, Maitland, A. *Lucy: The Beginnings of Mankind.* New York, 1981.

Kobishanov, Yuri M. *Axum.* University Park and London, 1979.

Merid Wolde Aregay. 'Southern Ethiopia and the Christian Kingdom, with Special Reference to the Galla Migrations and Their Consequences.' PhD thesis (University of London, 1971) (available in the Department of History, Addis Ababa University).

Mesfin Wolde-Mariam. *An Introductory Geography of Ethiopia.* Addis Ababa, 1972.

Taddesse Tamrat. *Church and State in Ethiopia, 1270-1527.* Oxford, 1972.

1 The Background

1. The internal scene in the first half of the nineteenth century

The northern principalities

The year 1769 symbolizes the initiation of the period in Ethiopian history known as the *Zamana Masafent*. It was in that year that a Tegrean prince named *Ras* Mikael Sehul (the second name being an epithet to describe his astuteness) made a bloody intervention in royal politics in Gondar. He killed the reigning emperor, Iyoas, and put his own favourite, Emperor Yohannes II, on the throne. Before a year was out, Yohannes himself incurred *Ras* Mikael's disfavour, and was in turn deposed and replaced by Emperor Takla-Haymanot II.

This making and unmaking of kings by *Ras* Mikael marked the nadir of imperial power. While the intervention of other members of the nobility was not to be so dramatic, the long-standing struggle for power between the monarchy and the nobility had been decidedly resolved in favour of the latter. Until 1855, when Kasa Haylu became Emperor Tewodros II and restored the power and prestige of the imperial throne, the successive emperors were little more than puppets in the hands of the forceful nobility. An emperor had practically no army of his own. In the 1830s and 1840s, his annual revenue was estimated at a paltry 300 Maria Theresa silver dollars, the Austrian currency then in use in Ethiopia, whereas *Ras* Walda-Sellase of Tegre had 75,000 thalers at his disposal, and *Negus* Sahla-Sellase of Shawa had some 85,000 thalers.

Ras Mikael's domination of Gondar politics was itself short-lived. In the last quarter of the eighteenth century, a strong man by the name of Ali Gwangul had emerged as a powerful figure and kingmaker. He initiated what came to be known as the Yajju dynasty, after their place of origin in present-day northern Wallo. From their base in Dabra Tabor, successive members of this dynasty controlled the throne for about eighty years. Although Muslim and Oromo in origin, they had become Christianized, and followed other Amhara customs. The power alignments for or against them were dictated less by ethnic and religious considerations than by self-interest and regional aggrandisement. Yajju power may be said to have reached its peak in the 'reign' (1803–1825) of *Ras* Gugsa Marsu.

On the southern side of the Bashilo river, where Islam is believed to have had establishment previous to the Ahmad Gragn period, the Muslim and Oromo elements were more pronounced. Known as Amhara in medieval times, the region came to be identified by the name of Wallo, after the most important tribe that had settled in the area. Towards the end of the eighteenth century, a dynasty known as the Mammadoch and based at Warra Himanu established its hege-mony over the whole region. The name of the dynasty was apparently derived from its founder Muhammad Ali (more popularly known by his 'horse-name', Abba Jebo, 'father of Jebo', his war-horse). The death of his grandson Abba Jerru Liban in 1825 marked the decline of Mammadoch power, as his descendants began to fight among themselves for supremacy. This state of affairs gradually reduced Wallo to a buffer zone which invited the expansion and interference of its more powerful neighbours.

In Tegre, a term denoting the Marab Melash ('the land to the north of the Marab river') and the Red Sea coastal region, as well as present-day Tegray, a strong ruler emerged in the person of *Ras* Walda-Sellase, at about the beginning of the nineteenth century. By reason of his region's proximity to the sea, he was the first Ethiopian ruler to come into contact with European travellers of the nineteenth century. With total obliviousness to the Ethiopian reality, the British traveller and artist Henry Salt, who met Walda-Sellase at his capital Antalo in 1805, described him as the 'Prime Minister' of Ethiopia. Such a flattering appellation did not move Walda-Sellase into allow-ing Salt to pass on to the imperial seat in Gondar, which was then controlled by Walda-Sellase's bitter opponent, *Ras* Gugsa Marsu.

Some years after the death of *Ras* Walda-Sellase in 1816, *Dajjach* Subagadis Waldu of Agame in eastern Tegre established himself as the lord of Tegre, and continued his predecessor's bid for control of the imperial throne. This led him into a bloody clash with the Yajju lord, *Ras* Mareyye Gugsa of Bagemder, at the Battle of Dabra Abbay (14 February 1831). Both leaders lost their lives: Mareyye fell in the course of the battle, and Subagadis was executed by Mareyye's vic-torious troops. The man who picked up the pieces was *Dajjach* Webe Hayla-Maryam of Semen, head of another important area of regional power consolidated by his father and predecessor, *Dajjach* Hayla-Maryam Gabre. The most significant results of the battle were the end of Tegrean autonomy and the extension of *Dajjach* Webe's over-lordship to that region. By the mid-nineteenth century, Webe had emerged as perhaps the most powerful regional lord of northern Ethiopia. The Battle of Dabra Tabor (7 February 1842) between him and *Ras* Ali Alula, known as Ali II, the Yajju ruler of Bagemder, was an outcome of Webe's eventually abortive bid to wrest supreme power from the Yajju princes. This was another strange battle of the *Zamana Masafent*, in which, as he was celebrating his victory, Webe was captured by Ali II's vassals.

Two principalities which were to dominate the history of southern Ethiopia in the latter half of the nineteenth century were somewhat peripheral to central politics. They were Gojjam and Shawa. Although both principalities were to have, as their distinctive feature, territorial expansion in neighbouring Oromo lands, Gojjam was not totally unaffected by the imperial politics at Gondar. Its most famous ruler, *Dajjach* Goshu Zawde, actively engaged in the bid for preeminence among the northern princes. Yet such was the political anarchy of the *Zamana Masafent* that his power in Gojjam itself was challenged by his own son, *Dajjach* Berru Goshu, who managed temporarily to defeat his father in late 1841. As the *Zamana Masafent* comes to its close, we find *Dajjach* Goshu in a position of vassalage to the Yajju ruler, *Ras* Ali II, both bent on checking the rise of a new challenger, Kasa Haylu. But, as we shall see, Kasa Haylu, afterwards Tewodros II, defeated Goshu, who died in the Battle of Gur Amba (27 November 1852), and Ali II in the Battle of Ayshal (29 June 1853); the latter victory symbolized the end of Yajju hegemony.

South-east of the Abbay river (the Blue Nile), Shawa was comparatively insulated from the wars and politics of northern Ethiopia. Its successive rulers steadfastly worked towards the strengthening of the principality by conquering the neighbouring Oromo lands. The stability of the region and the relative prosperity of its inhabitants were well attested by European visitors. Yet this is not to say that Shawan rulers were totally unconcerned with developments in the north. Their affiliation to the imperial idea was evident in their concern to show their Solomonic descent. At the same time, this claim encouraged them to regard themselves as central rather than peripheral to the Ethiopian polity. Their titles also demonstrated progressive confidence. They started with the modest one of *abeto*, and, passing through *mar'ed azmach*, ended up with the elevated style of *negus*, or king. This last title was rarely claimed by any of the northern princes.

Yet even the adoption of the title of *negus* showed an element of restraint. Shadowy as the emperors in Gondar were, they still retained the aura of 'Solomonic' legitimacy. The title of *negusa nagast*, king of kings, thus emperor, was still regarded as their exclusive preserve. The ultimate ambition of regional lords was thus not to crown themselves *negusa nagast*, but to gain pre-eminence by securing the position of power signified by the title *ras bitwaddad*, which would enable them to manipulate the legally crowned emperor. It required the audacity of a Kasa Haylu to crown himself *negusa nagast*. Even then, he had to resort to the legitimizing name of Tewodros – the apocalyptic harbinger of a new and just order. The regional conflicts of the *Zamana Masafent* thus showed scarcely any centrifugal tendencies. The moves of the regional lords were to dominate the centre, not to go away from it.

This same dialectic of division and unity was manifested in the doctrinal controversies which rent Abyssinian Christian society from the seventeenth century to the middle of the nineteenth. The controversy was ignited by Jesuit theology, more specifically the doctrine of the nature of Christ. It was the absence of a unanimous response to the Jesuit doctrinal challenge that gave birth to the diverse doctrines that have continued to baffle students of Ethiopian history. The party which still claimed to espouse the orthodox doctrine preferred to call itself *Tawahedo* (Union), although its opponents gave it the more pejorative appellation of *Karra* (Knife). The variations on the orthodox doctrine were known as *Qebat* (Unction) and *Ya Sagga Lej* (Son through Grace). The latter was also more popularly known as *Sost Ledat* (Three Births), in contradistinction to the *Hulat Ledat* (Two Births) thesis of the *Tawahedo*.

These doctrinal disputes had a political significance that exceeded their intrinsic value. The various doctrines came to be associated with the different regions, and thus abetted and sharpened the political divisions of the *Zamana Masafent*. *Qebat*, for instance, was a distinctively Gojjame doctrine, whereas *Karra* was associated with Tegre, and *Ya Sagga Lej* with Gondar. It is also significant that the first major attempt to resolve these differences was made by the same man who tried to forge Ethiopian unity, Tewodros. But final resolution of the doctrinal question had to await the Council of Boru Meda (1878), presided over by Emperor Yohannes IV (r. 1872–1889).

While the nobles fought amongst themselves and the priests engaged in over-refined theological disputes, the social order was sustained by the peasantry, practically the only productive class in society. Through a combination of a long-established plough agriculture and animal husbandry, the peasant supported the whole social edifice. Thanks to a lineage system of land-ownership known as *rest*, the peasant could claim a plot of land as long as he could trace his descent. But his control over his produce and his labour time was limited by the claims of the nobility, both lay and clerical. A system of surplus appropriation, the *gult*, gave the nobility rights of collecting tribute, often of an arbitrary nature, from the peasant. Hence the term *gabbar* (from *geber*, tribute), often used interchangeably with *balagar*, peasant. In addition, the peasant had to undertake corvée

14

(forced labour) such as farming, grinding corn, and building houses and fences. This claimed up to one-third of his labour time. One of the nineteenth-century travellers elaborated the theme:

The imposts are numerous, but vary according to the traditionary customs of each village. They [the peasants] pay a certain portion in kind to the Ras, or other great chief, and sometimes a regular tax in money; besides this, they must furnish oxen to plough the king's lands. Their immediate governor then takes his share in kind of every grain (say a fifth), and feeds besides a certain number of soldiers at the expense of the householder: he has rights to oxen, sheep, goats, butter, honey, and every other requisite for subsistence; he must be received with joy and feasting by his subjects whenever he visits them, and can demand from them contributions on fifty pretexts – he is going on a campaign, or has just returned from one; he has lost a horse or married a wife; his property has been consumed by fire or he has lost his all in battle; or the sacred duty of a funeral banquet cannot be fulfilled without their aid.

(Plowden, 137–138)

Inasmuch as the *gult* was given as a reward for military service, the whole system tended to foster a military ethos. To be an armed retainer of a lord freed one not only from the drudgery of farming but also from the harassment and persecution of the soldier. Conversely, the life of the peasant became increasingly precarious. Perennial victim of the vagaries of nature – such as drought and locust invasions – the peasant was simultaneously at the mercy of the marauding soldiery. The wars of the *Zamana Masafent* were particularly destructive in this respect. The system of billeting or quartering soldiers in peasant households subjected the latter to numerous exactions and indignities. Mansfield Parkyns, a British traveller of the early nineteenth century, has given us gruesome details of the fate of a peasant who was roasted alive as a penalty for having hidden some butter from the insatiable soldiers billeted in his house.

Although detection entailed such frightful punishments as the one just described, hiding grain was one of the ways by which the peasant tried to ward off the human locust. Burning grain was another, although such measures were no less wasteful socially. Often, too, the peasant abandoned farm and homestead and fled for security – either to a place of less insecurity or to join one of the many bandits who mushroomed in this period. Commenting on the despoliation which such a situation created in one of the northern provinces, the missionaries Isenberg and Krapf had this to say:

[T]he Wag country . . . is decidedly one of the most important and interesting provinces of Eastern Abyssinia. It would admit a larger population and a high degree of cultivation of the soil, if a better government ruled this country. It would be necessary, however, for such a government to do away with the system of annually plundering their subjects, as this is the very means to destroy commerce, order, cultivation of the ground, and every improvement of human society. At present the Governor comes annually with his troops

15

and takes away what he pleases; and the consequence is that the inhabitants conceal their treasures and take to flight to the mountains; whereupon the Governor destroys their houses and fields.

(Isenberg and Krapf, 486–487)

States and peoples of southern Ethiopia

The history of early nineteenth-century Ethiopia would not be complete without a description of the peoples and principalities of the southern half of the country. It was the unification of these two parts in the second half of the nineteenth century that gave birth to modern Ethiopia. The peoples of southern Ethiopia had attained varying degrees of social and political organization. The term 'southern' is used here not in the strictly geographical sense, but as a convenient category embracing those states and peoples which did not directly engage in or were peripheral to the imperial politics of Gondar. Their organizations ranged from communal societies to states with powerful kings and elaborate mechanisms for the exercise of authority. Examples of the latter kind were the kingdoms of Kafa, Walayta and Janjaro. They are often known by the generic linguistic term of Omotic, because of their location in the vicinity of the Omo river.

The kingdom of Kafa traced its origins back to the fourteenth century. The economy, as in both Walayta and Janjaro, as well as among a number of Cushitic and some Semitic peoples of the south, was based on the cultivation of *ensat* ('false banana', *Ensete ventricosum*). A class of peasants, holding their own land but being forced to give labour service, formed the human base. They were supported by slaves acquired through raiding or trading, or as payment for debt. The first written reference to the kingdom goes back to the sixteenth century, and the state reached the apogee of its power at the turn of the eighteenth century. At the apex of the political and social hierarchy was the king, the *tato*, assisted by an advisory council of nobles, the *mikrecho*. While Orthodox Christianity had managed to win many adherents among the ruling class, possession cults, headed by the *ibede gudo*, the supreme spiritual leader, predominated among the masses. The state obtained its revenue from taxation and customs dues on the prosperous trade with the Oromo states which emerged to the north of Kafa towards the end of the eighteenth and the beginning of the nineteenth century. Slaves constituted the main item of export trade, followed by ivory, coffee and honey.

The kingdom of Walayta to the east also had equally remote origins, its beginnings being associated with Motolomi, of medieval fame, who according to tradition was converted to Christianity by *Abuna* Takla-Haymanot, the Shawan saint. Motolomi is said to have

16

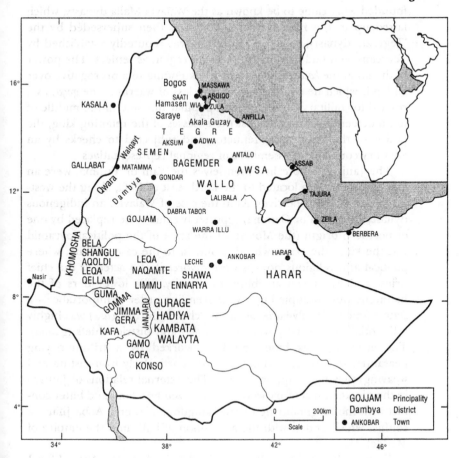

The map shows towns and districts, with labels including:

Bogos, MASSAWA, SAATI, ARQIQO, Hamasen, WIA, ZULA, Saraye, Akala Guzay, ANFILLA, TEGRE, AKSUM, ADWA, Wacayt, SEMEN, ANTALO, KASALA, GALLABAT, MATAMMA, BAGEMDER, AWSA, ASSAB, Qwara, Dambya, GONDAR, WALLO, LALIBALA, TAJURA, DABRA TABOR, ZEILA, GOJJAM, WARRA ILLU, BERBERA, KHOMOSHA, BELA, SHANGUL, AQOLDI, LEQA, LEQA NAQAMTE, LECHE, ANKOBAR, HARAR, QELLAM, SHAWA, LIMMU, ENNARYA, Nasir, GUMA, GOMMA, JIMMA, GURAGE, GERA, JANJARO, HADIYA, KAFA, KAMBATA, GAMO, WALAYTA, GOFA, KONSO

GOJJAM	Principality
Dambya	District
● ANKOBAR	Town

0   200km
Scale

3. Ethiopia in the nineteenth century

founded what came to be known as the Walayta Malla dynasty, which lasted up to the fifteenth century. It was then superseded by the 'Tegrean' dynasty, so called because it was reputedly established by Tegreans who had initially come to the region as settlers. The power of the king, the *kawa*, was autocratic, extending to a prerogative over all land, which he could grant to the class of warriors, the *goqa*, as a reward for military service. After a popular uprising in the middle of the nineteenth century against the excesses of the reigning king, the power of the *kawa* was attenuated and subjected to checks by an advisory council and assemblies of regional representatives.

The Janjaro, who called themselves the Yam or Yamma, were an agricultural people located to the north-east of Kafa, along the western edges of the Gibe river. As in the case of Walayta, an indigenous dynasty (the Dida or Gamma) reportedly came to be replaced by one of northern origin (the Mowa). At the apex of the political pyramid was the king, the *amno*, who (in contrast to the case of Kafa, where political and religious powers were divorced) also acted as the chief priest and was given attributes of divinity. The lower tiers of the hierarchy were occupied by – in descending order of importance – a state council of twelve *astessor*, whose chairman (the *waso*) was highly influential, provincial governors (*erasho*) and district chiefs (*ganna*). The economy was based on land worked by a tribute-paying peasantry, with trade and crafts (more particularly iron-casting and weaving) playing a supportive role. The external relations of Janjaro in the nineteenth century were characterized by a long and bitter conflict with the neighbouring Oromo kingdom of Jimma Abba Jifar – a conflict which ended with the absorption of both into the empire of Menilek II.

Jimma Abba Jifar itself, named after its founder Abba Jifar I (r. 1830-1855), was an example of the Oromo states which emerged in south-western Ethiopia in the eighteenth and nineteenth centuries. In one of the most interesting processes of social transformation in Ethiopian history, the Oromo, who initially had an egalitarian and republican system of socio-political organization based on age-groups and known as the *gada*, developed monarchical institutions. The main factors for such a transformation were the changes that the Oromo underwent from a pastoral to an agrarian mode of life, and the class differentiation that this brought about. The continuous wars of expansion that the Oromo waged in the course of their migrations and settlement also tended to strengthen the powers of the *abba dula* (the war-leader in the *gada* system) at the expense of the *abba boku* (the traditional titular head of the Oromo community). This evolution towards monarchical power was manifested in two regions. The first was in the area of the Gibe river, hence the name 'Gibe monarchies'. The second was in present-day Wallaga, in western Ethiopia.

Five such kingdoms emerged in the Gibe region: Limmu-Ennarya, Jimma, Gomma, Guma and Gera. As its name suggests, Limmu-Ennarya was an Oromo state established on the remains of the medieval kingdom of Ennarya, which had existed in a state of tributary relationship to the Christian kingdom. Initially Limmu-Ennarya was the most important of the Gibe states, primarily by reason of its control of the long-distance trade that linked the region with the north. The reign of its most famous ruler, Abba Bagibo, (r. 1825–1861), marked the peak of Limmu-Ennarya ascendancy. Jimma's successful challenge of this ascendancy resulted in its supremacy in the second half of the nineteenth century. A distinctive feature of the Gibe states, in contrast to the other Oromo states which were established in Wallaga, was their conversion from traditional religions to Islam in the first half of the nineteenth century.

There were two main centres of monarchical power in Wallaga. A leader called Bakare established the state of Leqa Naqamte, which grew even more powerful under his successors Moroda and Kumsa Moroda, later known as Gabra-Egziabher, 'slave of God', after his conversion to Christianity, following the incorporation of his principality in the Ethiopian empire by Menilek II in 1882. In southwestern Wallaga, a ruler named Jote Tullu emerged in the second half of the nineteenth century, combining ruthless military power with successful exploitation of trans-frontier trade.

Jote Tullu's kingdom was in constant interaction, both hostile and peaceful, with the sheikhdoms that had emerged to the north, particularly with that of Aqoldi, more commonly known as Asosa. Like the other two sheikhdoms, Khomosha and Bela Shangul (or Beni Shangul), Aqoldi grew out of the imposition of an Arabic-speaking mercantile aristocracy of Sudanese origin on the indigenous inhabitants, the Barta. To be more precise, this new ruling class was superimposed over an earlier aristocracy of Funj origin, or at least association with the Funj, from the kingdom of Sennar in Sudan. A similar process of superimposition was duplicated on the other side of the Abbay or Blue Nile, and led to the rise of the sheikhdom of Gubba, on the Gumuz-inhabited western fringes of Gojjam. By virtue of their Sudanese origin, all these sheikhdoms were Muslim and fostered the propagation of Islam in the region.

The emirate of Harar, in the eastern part of the country, represented another important centre of Islamic power and influence. Battered by the Oromo, this successor state to the medieval kingdom of Adal, the homeland of Ahmad Gragn, had dwindled to a fraction of its medieval power and glory. Surrounded by the Qottu Oromo, the city state led a rather precarious existence, symbolized by the wall that has remained its distinctive feature to this day. Over a period of time, however, the Harari and Oromo peoples established a *modus*

*1.1 . The city of Harar as it appeared in the first decade
of the twentieth century*

vivendi marked by trade, some intermarriage and the Islamization of
the Oromo by Harari missionaries. But the growing weakness of the
Harar emirate tended to invite foreign intervention. In 1875, an
Egyptian force led by Muhammad Rauf Pasha occupied the city, in a
bloody imposition of authority which involved the murder of the
emir and the massacre of the Oromo representatives gathered in
response to the summons by the invader. Egyptian rule lasted a
decade.

Elsewhere in southern Ethiopia, a much lower level of socio-
political organization prevailed. In the south-west, the Nilo-Saharan
Anuak, led by their village headmen (*kuaari*), had an economy which
combined agriculture with hunting and gathering. Their neighbours,
the Nuer, were pastoralists who developed a rather complex spiritual
culture around their cattle. Both were linked with the Oromo of the
highlands by trade. The southern and south-eastern peripheries were
inhabited by the Borana and Somali clans respectively, all pastoralists
recognizing no boundaries. The pastoralist outer ring was continued
by the Afar in the Danakil desert; their proverbial ferocity, coupled
with their inhospitable terrain, safeguarded their independence for a
long time. Independence did not rule out interaction, however, for
the town of Bati, for instance, developed as a commercial rendezvous
for highlander and lowlander. Neighbouring the Afar on the north,
the Saho lived in somewhat similar circumstances, although they had
a much narrower margin of operation because of the shorter distance
between the coast and the highlands.

In the present-day region of Gamo Gofa in the south-west, the Cushitic Konso developed a distinct culture characterized by terraced farming, wooden carvings and stone enclosures, while the two kingdoms that eventually gave their names to the administrative region (Gamo and Gofa) were further examples of the advanced sociopolitical organization prevalent among the Omotic peoples.

With the exception of the lowlands, the distinguishing feature of the southern peoples of Ethiopia was the predominance of the *ensat* culture (in contrast to the cereal culture of the north). To this culture also belonged the Gurage (fragmented into a number of tribes and hence easy victims of the slavers of the nineteenth century), the Hadiya and the Kambata. Political fragmentation was the rule among the Shawan Oromo as well. This state of affairs facilitated the expansion of the kingdom of Shawa, a process which gained impetus in the reign of *Negus* Sahla-Sellase (r. 1813-1847) and reached its climax under Emperor Menilek II. The Arsi to the south had an economy combining agriculture and pastoralism, and a more pronounced sense of regional identity fostered by the leadership of their hereditary *abba dula*.

The link: long-distance trade

The two spheres of the Ethiopian polity, which for the sake of convenience have been dichotomized into northern and southern, did not exist in mutual isolation. The unity of interest that long-distance trade created between them tempered the political and cultural heterogeneity depicted above. The network of trade routes that united north and south was one of the main bases of the process of unification that took place in the second half of the nineteenth century.

Although the trade routes which linked south-western Ethiopia to the coast had medieval antecedents, it was in the nineteenth century that they attained particular prominence. This was partly because of the revival of external trade in the Red Sea region; partly, too, their prominence reflects the better documentation we have for this period, because of a number of European travellers who penetrated the interior. Ethiopian long-distance trade in the nineteenth century had two major routes. Of these, the more important at the outset was the link between south-western Ethiopia and the north. Beginning from Bonga in Kafa, this route linked such important commercial centres as Jiren in Jimma, Saqa in Limmu-Ennarya, Assandabo in Horro-Gudru, Basso in Gojjam and Darita in Bagemder with the imperial capital, Gondar. From there, it bifurcated, one branch going to Matamma on the Ethio-Sudanese frontier, and another, via Adwa, to Massawa on the Red Sea coast.

The second major route ran from west to east. While initially of secondary importance, its fortunes rose with those of Shawa in Ethiopian politics. By the end of the nineteenth century it had become the most important artery of commerce in the Ethiopian region. From Jiren and Saqa in the south-west, this route passed through such commercial landmarks as Soddo and Rogge (near Yarar mountain, visible to the east of present-day Addis Ababa), to Alyu Amba, the commercial capital of Shawa, near Ankobar, then Shawa's political capital. Thence, the route continued to Harar, political and commercial centre of the east, and on to the coastal Somali towns of Zeila and Berbera.

The directions of trade routes were also indicative of the origins and destinations of the items of trade. If we were to single out two commodities which dominated the long-distance trade of the nineteenth century, they would be salt and slaves. The salt, originating in the Taltal plains of Tegre, was carried to the south-west, its value increasing in direct proportion to its distance from the source. Not only was it used as a consumption item, but, in its bar form (*amole*), it also served as currency. Goods of foreign origin, such as glass, beads, cloth and ironware, also penetrated from the coast to the south-west.

In the opposite direction, slaves of south-western origin found their way to the north-west and east. A few were destined for internal use, but the majority were exported to Sudan and the Arabian peninsula. The modes of acquiring slaves varied: some were captives of war, others were victims of slave-raids, still others had been sold into slavery by parents rendered destitute by famine or financial stress. The prosperous long-distance trade in slaves created such towns as Yajube, near Basso in Gojjam, and Abdul Rassul, near Alyu Amba in Shawa, which specialized in the sale of slaves, often by auction. Other items which originated in the south-west and were mostly exported were ivory, gold and musk. In the second half of the nineteenth century, coffee, the commodity that was to be the main product of the south-west in the twentieth century, came to the forefront.

Long-distance trade was conducted through the agency of caravans. The leader of the caravan was known as the *naggadras* (head merchant), and he was entrusted with ensuring the safety of the group under his leadership. The merchants were exposed to the hazards of both man and nature. Not only did they have to cross deserts and ford rivers, but they also had to endure the whims and caprices of petty and big chiefs. The innumerable toll-stations along the route had a particularly negative effect on the trade. Conversely, the control of trade routes to augment their revenue was a matter of prime importance to political authorities.

In addition to the two main arteries of trade, there were three other types of interaction. The first was localized trade in the highlands.

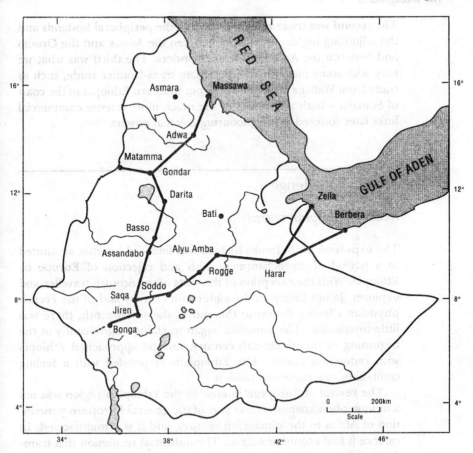

4. *Trade routes of the nineteenth century (adapted from M. Abir,* Ethiopia: The Era of the Princes, *London, 1968, and Guluma Gemeda, 'Gomma and Limmu: The Process of State Formation among the Oromo in the Gibe Region* c. 1750–1889', *MA thesis, Addis Ababa University, 1984)*

The second was trade relations between the peripheral lowlands and the adjoining highlands, such as between the Anuak and the Oromo and between the Afar and the highlanders. The third was what we may with some anachronism designate trans-frontier trade, such as trade from Wallaga to Sudan and from southern Ethiopia to the coast of Somalia – both precursors of the much more intense commercial links later fostered by neighbouring colonial powers.

2. The external challenge

Renewed European interest

The expulsion of the Jesuits in 1632 was followed by what amounted to a period of disenchantment with and rejection of Europe by Ethiopia. With the exception of the visits of the Scottish traveller and explorer, James Bruce, in the eighteenth century and of the French physician Charles Poncet at the end of the seventeenth, there was little interaction. This situation began to change significantly at the beginning of the nineteenth century. Europe approached Ethiopia with redoubled energy. The Ethiopians responded with a feeling combining eagerness and caution.

The revival of European interest in the Ethiopian region was not a unique phenomenon. It was part of the general European penetration of Africa in the nineteenth century, and it was multifaceted. In essence it had economic origins. The industrial revolution that transformed European society, starting from the end of the eighteenth century, at the same time ushered in a new pattern of relationship between Europe and Africa. The revolution in production could not be contained within the confines of Europe. The manufacture of industrial goods far in excess of what Europe itself could consume made the conquest of the African market imperative. Thus, in Ethiopia, as elsewhere in Africa, the European officials who came into contact with Ethiopian rulers were above all ambassadors of commerce. This was clearly the case with the first European official to set foot on Ethiopian soil in 1804: Sir George Annesley, later Viscount Valentia, from Britain. The promotion of commerce was the dominant theme of the first treaties concluded between European officials and Ethiopian authorities, such as those between *Negus* Sahla-Sellase and the British Captain W. Cornwallis Harris (1841) and the French Rochet d'Hericourt (1843), and between *Ras* Ali II and the British Walter Plowden (1849).

A second dimension of European interest in Ethiopia, as in the rest of Africa, was a resurgence of missionary activity. In spite of the bitter legacy of the Jesuit experiment of the sixteenth and seventeenth centuries, Europeans applied themselves to the task of proselytizing Ethiopians with renewed zeal. Nor was this activity confined to the Catholics. It was the Protestants, mainly of the Church Missionary Society (CMS) of London, who pioneered this new phase of evangelical activity in the nineteenth century. Samuel Gobat was active in the north, in Tegre and Bagemder, while C.W. Isenberg and J.L. Krapf operated mainly in Shawa. On the Catholic side, the path was cleared by Giuseppe Sapeto and was followed by Giustino De Jacobis, who in 1839 founded the Lazarist mission in northern Ethiopia. Seven years later, the founder of the Capuchin order in Ethiopia, Cardinal Massaja, arrived.

Side by side with the official envoys and the missionaries came the scientists and explorers. Among the pioneers were the German Eduard Rueppell and the two French brothers Antoine and Arnauld d'Abbadie. The d'Abbadie brothers have now come to occupy a prominent place in Ethiopian studies, thanks to their prolific writings. European scientists investigated the country, ranging from its botany to its ethnography. They did so with such energy and perseverance that *Dajjach* Webe Hayla-Maryam of Semen is reputed to have commented: 'One collects our plants, another our stones; I do not know what you are looking for, but I do not want it to be in my country that you find it' (Rubenson, *Survival*, 54).

These facets of European interest in Ethiopia – the commercial, the official, the missionary and the scientific – were very much interconnected and reinforced each other. The scientists were not disinterested academics, but often engaged in political affairs. The missionaries enjoyed moral, and sometimes material, support from their states. Both missionaries and those who came on official missions dabbled in scientific or pseudo-scientific studies of the country. The missionary Krapf was actively involved in the negotiations for the treaty between Shawa and Britain. Sir George Annesley, who had come to Massawa with the aim of conducting botanical and geographical investigations, readily engaged in exploring ways of promoting trade with Ethiopia. Nor was missionary activity totally divorced from commercial matters. Proselytization, it was hoped, would promote trade and capitalism.

Egyptian expansion

Yet, compared with the desperate scramble that was to characterize European penetration of Africa in the last quarter of the century, these early European sallies into Ethiopia were of a tentative nature. Expansion of a more vigorous kind came from nearer home. It was Egypt, the country with which Ethiopia had had the longest foreign

25

contact in its history, that presented the initial challenge. At the dawn of the nineteenth century, Egypt was undergoing a significant process of change which was to have an enduring effect both on its internal shape and its foreign policy. The short-lived Napoleonic occupation of Egypt (1798–1801) was not uneventful. While it lasted, it undermined the Mamlukes, who had ruled the country for nearly six centuries, and brought distant echoes of the French Revolution to the banks of the Nile. Its termination under a combined Anglo-Ottoman assault had two lasting consequences – the beginning of British interest in Egypt and the Red Sea, and the emergence of Muhammad Ali, the Albanian adventurer in the Ottoman army who established the dynasty that was to rule Egypt for a century and a half.

Muhammad Ali's first task was to deal the final blow to the tottering Mamluke power. Then, after establishing a secure economic and military base for his own power, he turned his attention outwards. His expansion in the direction of Syria was frustrated by the British; but it was his southward expansion which was to have a lasting impact and pose a threat to Ethiopia. The defeat of the Funj kingdom of Sennar in 1821 inaugurated Egyptian rule in Sudan. At the same time, it ushered in a period of border skirmishes between the Egyptians, who were vigorously pushing eastwards, and the Ethiopian rulers of the borders, ranging from *Dajjach* Webe of Semen to *Dajjach* Kenfu of Dambya. The latter's half-brother, Kasa Haylu, inherited these skirmishes – a situation which had considerable effect both on his rise to power as Emperor Tewodros and in the shaping of his personality.

Further, with Muhammad Ali's conquest of Arabia, Egypt was emerging as the new power on the Red Sea, replacing the moribund Ottoman empire. This had the salutary effect of reviving the Red Sea trade. For Ethiopia, however, it meant – as in the western borderlands – the implantation of a more dangerous neighbour. Although the Ottoman Turks had occupied Massawa as early as 1557, and continued to maintain the fiction of a principality known as Habasha (Abyssinia) as part of their domain, by the beginning of the nineteenth century Ottoman authority on the coast was non-existent. Local power was exercised by their one-time viceroys, the *naibs* of Arqiqo, who had established over the years a mode of peaceful co-existence with the highland rulers of Ethiopia, more exactly those of Tegre. Egyptian occupation of Massawa in 1841, ostensibly on the grounds of legal right to former Ottoman possessions, changed the situation. In Ethiopian parlance, nevertheless, both Ottoman and Egyptian continued to have an identical appellation: 'Turk'.

The sources for Chapter One are included with those at the end of Chapter Two (pp. 79–80).

2

Unification and Independence 1855–1896

1. The first response: Kasa – Tewodros

The man who represented the first effective response to both the internal and the external challenge – to the squabbling princes as well as to the 'Turk' – was Kasa Haylu, who, on his coronation in 1855 as Emperor Tewodros II, inaugurated the modern history of Ethiopia. Kasa became Tewodros largely by dint of his own personal qualities: his sense of mission, his military skill and valour and his extraordinary intelligence. He was essentially a self-made man. Kasa the *shefta* (bandit) became Tewodros the emperor. Although his career was initially formed within the politics of the *Zamana Masafent*, finally he proved to be its antithesis.

Yet it would be drawing too idealized a picture if we ignored his family background in discussing Kasa's rise to power. It was this background which gave him both his territorial base on the Ethio-Sudanese border – Qwara – and a taste of conventional politics. Kasa was related, if at a considerable distance, to *Dajjach* Maru of Dambya (south-west of Gondar), one of the leading participants in the *Zamana Masafent*. Maru in turn was a relation by marriage to both the Yajju dynasty and *Dajjach* Webe Hayla-Maryam of Semen. Ironically, though perhaps not surprisingly in the context of the period, it was fighting against these relatives that Maru met his death at the Battle of Koso Bar in October 1827. But his name survived in the fief which was grudgingly given to *Dajjach* Kenfu Haylu of Dambya by the Empress Manan Liban, mother of the Yajju *Ras* Ali II. The fief was known as Ya Maru Qammas (literally 'What has been tasted by Maru', a collective name for the scattered possessions of

27

Dajjach Maru, which included Qwara). Kasa himself, who went to Qwara after the Battle of Koso Bar, was sometimes called Kasa Maru.

In Qwara, Kasa grew up in the family of Kenfu of Dambya, who was developing a reputation as a stalwart defender of the Ethiopian frontier against Egyptian encroachment. In 1837, Kenfu moved to the offensive when he defeated an Egyptian force at Wad Kaltabu, deep inside Sudanese territory. But the association between Kasa and Kenfu was not entirely a happy one, as the latter was apprehensive of Kasa's claim to Ya Maru Qammas, which Kenfu wanted to reserve for his own sons. But his concern was all in vain. On his death in 1839, neither his sons nor Kasa could lay their hands on Qwara; it was appropriated by Empress Manan. The path of legitimate succession thus blocked, Kasa became a *shefta* in the plains of Qwara. He soon came to head a group of bandits composed of other disgruntled persons and ordinary robbers.

Kasa's *shefta* days were probably the most formative period of his life. It was then that some of the enduring features of his personality were confirmed. Two of these were his simplicity and disdain for pomp. He lived the life of his followers, taking part even in ploughing and sowing. Another feature was his concern for social justice. His distribution of money that he had acquired by robbery to the peasants, so that they could buy ploughs, had an element of Robin Hood about it. It presaged his fateful decision to expropriate the Orthodox Church of some of its land to feed his soldiers.

Most significantly, his *shefta* life in Qwara brought him into direct conflict with the Egyptians. This conflict was at the root of his lifelong obsession with the 'Turk', and his wild dream of liberating Jerusalem from their rule. At the same time, it brought about the only major military defeat of his career. At the Battle of Dabarqi in 1848, Kasa's troops, whose only advantage lay in their blind courage, were mown down by the artillery wielded to deadly effect by the disciplined Egyptian troops. Kasa came out chastened from the whole experience. At the same time was born his abiding interest in discipline and artillery. The former he tried to instil in his troops, with the assistance first of some Egyptian advisers and then of his trusted British friend John Bell. Tewodros's interest in artillery culminated in the forging of his overvalued mortar, 'Sebastopol', whose final ineffectualness symbolized the futility of his life.

Kasa's growing prominence in Qwara attracted the attention of the Yajju lords. In a desire to tame him, they resorted to diplomacy. Qwara, which Kasa had already come to control by dint of his military force, was formally given to him, and the daughter of *Ras* Ali, Tawabach, was also given to him in marriage. While his love for the daughter endured, the *rapprochement* with father and grandmother was short-lived. Embittered by the humiliation and contempt that seemed

2.1 Emperor Tewodros II's mortar 'Sebastopol' being dragged up the slopes of Maqdala: the emperor is outlined in the background

to have been reserved for him in the Yajju court, Tewodros resumed his *shefta* life. The campaign to subdue him ended in humiliating defeats, firstly of *Dajjach* Wandyerad, who had boasted to his Yajju overlord that he would haul back 'the *koso*-vendor's son' (for there was a common gibe that Kasa's mother sold *koso* flowers for tapeworm treatment), and secondly of Empress Manan herself, who spent some time in ignominious captivity.

These early victories of Kasa foreshadowed the major and even more decisive victories of the 1850s. In a series of battles which demonstrated his extraordinary talent as military leader and strategist, he defeated one major leader of the *Zamana Masafent* after another. In the Battle of Gur Amba (27 November 1852), the Gojjame war-lord and one-time patron of Kasa, *Dajjach* Goshu Zawde, was crushed fighting under orders from *Ras* Ali. The day-long battle claimed many casualties, including Goshu himself. The proximity of the battle-site to Gondar, the capital city of the north, was an indication that Kasa was no longer content to roam in the borderlands and that he was staking out his claims to control the centre. Some five months later, on 12 April 1853, Kasa defeated four of *Ras* Ali's and

29

Dajjach Webe of Semen's vassals, each ranking as *dajjazmach*, of whom two were killed in battle. The turn of the masters themselves was not long in coming. Ali's force was routed at the Battle of Ayshal (29 June 1853), and he was forced to flee to Yajju territory. This victory of Kasa over the last of the Yajju princes in effect symbolized the end of the *Zamana Masafent*. Between Kasa and the imperial throne, there remained only one obstacle, *Dajjach* Webe, the last of the warring princes. On 8 February 1855, Kasa defeated Webe at the Battle of Darasge, north-west of Gondar; and in the church that Webe had constructed for his own anticipated coronation, at the hands of the very same *abun* (*Abuna* Salama) that Webe had brought from Egypt, Kasa became Tewodros II, King of Kings of Ethiopia.

It is a mark of the breadth of Tewodros's vision that he did not see his victories over the northern regional rulers as the fulfilment of his goals. Soon after the Battle of Darasge, he turned his attention to the south – to Wallo and Shawa. With that action, he brought to an end the northern focus of the *Zamana Masafent*. One of the ultimate results of this turning southward of Tewodros's aims was that Shawa was now irreversibly drawn into the orbit of imperial politics – a process which was to culminate in the coronation of Menilek II as emperor of Ethiopia, and the evolution of Shawa as the geopolitical centre of the empire.

By Ethiopian standards, the campaign in Wallo was prolonged, and presaged the chronic problem, partly of his own making, of insubordination which Tewodros was to face in that region. Started in March 1855, in the middle of the arduous fasting season of Lent, nearly two months long, hostilities continued – in defiance of Ethiopian military tradition – during the rainy season, and ended only towards the middle of September. In the process, Tewodros matched the fierce resistance of the Wallo people with a ruthless policy of terror, marked by the amputation of limbs that was to become proverbial. Tewodros's seizure of the stronghold of Maqdala on 12 September 1865 terminated his Wallo campaign – for the time being. With that event, there was established a place which was to have great significance, both actual and symbolic, in the life of Tewodros. Maqdala became the centre of his model government. It was the den to which he retreated in his final hours of distress. It was the site where, in 1868, in a dramatic act of defiance that was to captivate the minds of future generations of Ethiopians, he committed suicide as British troops rushed in to capture him.

As in Wallo, the overlapping campaign in Shawa lasted some five months. There, Tewodros met a mixed reaction. Some of the regions, such as Manz, Gedem and Efrata, submitted without resistance. Led by Sayfu Sahla-Sellase, the fiery younger brother of *Negus* Hayla-Malakot, others resisted Tewodros's march into Shawa. The *negus* died in the middle of the campaign. Tewodros then directed all his attention to capturing Hayla-Malakot's son, Menilek, who had become the rallying-point of Shawan resistance. With this objective achieved at the Battle of Barakat in November 1855, Tewodros returned to Gondar after appointing another brother of Hayla-Malakot, Hayla-Mikael, to govern Shawa. Never ready to countenance the existence of a *negus* under him, Tewodros resuscitated the old Shawan title of *mar'ed azmach* to bestow it on his Shawan vassal. But Sayfu continued to challenge Tewodros's authority. Elsewhere, too, as for example in Gojjam and Semen, rebellion was already boiling. Thus, the termination of the Shawan campaign, marking as it did the peak of Tewodros's power, was also the beginning of the end for him.

Tewodros as modernizer

Tewodros has been described as 'Ethiopia's first monarch with a concept (however vague) of modernization' (Crummey, 'Tewodros', 457). Given the breadth of vision and the energy that he brought to the Ethiopian scene, this is a fair assessment. The parenthetical qualification contained in the above characterization is highly appropriate, however. Not only was Tewodros's concept of modernization vague, but his reforms also lacked consistency and method. Ultimately, they remained tentative gestures rather than comprehensive programmes of lasting importance. The social and political edifice of the *Zamana Masafent* proved too strong for Tewodros's modernizing efforts. The military and administrative reforms he envisaged were bereft of economic and technological bases. The foreign assistance that he sought so avidly was not forthcoming. In the end, Tewodros remained a lone and somewhat confused prophet of change.

The lack of consistency and the force of inertia of the *Zamana Masafent* were also evident in his administrative policy. Tewodros did not make a clean sweep of the local dynasties. In many instances, he confirmed them in their regional bases, at best appointing those he considered pliant members of the dynasties. Thus, in Tegre, he appointed *Dajjach* Kasa Subagadis, the son of the Agame chief who had died fighting against *Ras* Mareyye of Bagemder in 1831. In Wallo, Tewodros placed first *Dajjach* Liban Amade and then Amade Ali, son of Warqit, an important female leader. It was later that Tewodros entrusted Maqdala to one of his most loyal followers, *Grazmach* Alame. In Shawa, while the resuscitation of the old title of *mar'ed azmach* was probably a calculated blow to Shawan royal pretensions, *Mar'ed Azmach* Hayla-Mikael in effect continued the Shawan dynastic

31

line. It was only in Gojjam that, from the outset, Tewodros appointed one of his own commanders, *Ras* Engeda.

While such an appointment policy would appear to perpetuate the divisive tendencies of the *Zamana Masafent*, in actual fact it turned out that being Tewodros's 'own man' was not synonymous with loyalty, nor did having a dynastic base inevitably lead to rebellion. Both Engeda and Alame eventually fell out with Tewodros. The defection of Alame, one of the Emperor's most trusted followers, was a particularly bitter pill for him to swallow. Conversely, *Mar'ed Azmach* Hayla-Mikael dutifully paid his annual tribute. *Dajjach* Kasa Subagadis of Agame made a dramatic demonstration of his loyalty by sending the tongue of a follower of the rebel, Agaw Neguse of Semen; the unfortunate victim had bragged in front of his master that he would bring him the severed head of Tewodros. As a man who had been liberated from *Dajjach* Webe's prison by Tewodros, Kasa Subagadis was understandably grateful to the emperor. Conversely, he was implacably opposed to Webe's successors; after all, he had come out hunchbacked from prison.

Tegre's loyalty to Tewodros had even more concrete manifestations than the dramatic gesture by *Dajjach* Kasa Subagadis. The largest portion of royal revenue came from Tegre, including, that is, the regions of Hamasen, Saraye and Akala Guzay. It amounted annually to about 200,000 Maria Theresa thalers (compared with the less than 50,000 thalers from Bagemder). Of this, over 35,000 thalers, some 18%, was paid by *Dajjach* Baryaw Pawlos, the governor of the northern part of present-day Tegray, who was married to Aletash, daughter of Tewodros. About 32,000 thalers, or over 16%, came from *Dajjach* Haylu Tawalda-Madhen of Hamasen and Saraye, and over 17,000 thalers, or about 9%, came from *Basha* Gabra-Egzie of Akala Guzay.

Tewodros's commitment to military reform was less equivocal than his administrative policies. The army has generally been the first concern of any modernizing ruler of a country, because of its pivotal role in the conquest and maintenance of political power. Even in the case of Ethiopia's medieval rulers, their correspondence with European monarchs was dominated by requests for the fruits of modern military technology. To Tewodros, who owed his political power more to his military prowess than to his genealogy, the central role of the army must have been even more vital. He accordingly set out to remould the military structure of Ethiopia in three important respects: organization, discipline and armament. Yet, like almost all the other reforms of Tewodros, those in the military sphere were also vitiated by lack of consistency and of thoroughness.

What Tewodros attempted to do in the organizational sphere was to replace the regional armies of the *Zamana Masafent* with a national army which cut across local loyalties. Thus soldiers coming from different regions were formed into one regiment. A new hierarchy of command, with military titles which are still in use in the Ethiopian army – for example, *yasr alaqa*, *yamsa alaqa*, *ya shi alaqa*, respectively commander of ten, commander of fifty, commander of a thousand – was introduced. Tewodros also cut down on the traditional retinue of the army, which had retarded its mobility and at the same time presented logistical problems. Although there is no evidence as to the amount and manner of payment, Tewodros is also credited with replacing the vicious system of billeting by payment of salaries. At least at the outset, before his sense of justice fell prey to his indiscriminate violence, he was severe towards any of his soldiers caught looting. Yet, when Wallo rebels killed his night guard and stole some mules, he gave his soldiers permission to loot the locality in retribution. In another situation, the uncontrollable urge of his soldiers to plunder led him into a desperate consideration of abdication.

Discipline remained a lasting concern of Tewodros; one of the lessons that he had drawn from the Battle of Dabarqi in 1848 was of its value, but he proceeded to apply a harsh version of it. During his first Wallo campaign, he had the limbs of his own soldiers amputated for unauthorized fighting in which they had lost both men and firearms. In Shawa, when some of his soldiers mutinied because of strong rumours that he planned to send them on a campaign to Jerusalem, he punished them with a severity intended to prevent further such occurrences: forty-eight of them were hacked to death or shot. The two ringleaders first had their limbs amputated, and were then hanged. Yet such measures of primitive justice, far from reinforcing Tewodros's authority, only tended to spiral towards universalized violence. The very last letter of his life – written to Sir Robert Napier, the leader of the British military expedition, in the aftermath of the Battle of Aroge, which led to Tewodros's suicide in 1868 – was a pathetic admission of his failure to instil discipline in his subjects. 'My countrymen have turned their backs on me,' he wrote, 'because I imposed tribute on them, and sought to bring them under military discipline. You have prevailed against me by means of a people brought into a state of discipline' (Holland and Hozier, II, 42).

The third aspect of Tewodros's military reforms was his unrelenting drive to acquire modern arms. Although his stockpile grew largely through purchases and seizure from vanquished enemies, it was to arms manufacture that he applied himself with remarkable persistence. The first experiment came right after the Battle of Dabarqi: as Kasa Haylu, Tewodros improvised a rather crude explosive from the trunk of a tree. It was to be set off from a distance by means of a connecting thread. The whole experiment was aborted when one of Kasa's followers, captured by the enemy, divulged the secret under

33

torture. When Tewodros later sought foreign assistance, it was not so much the arms that he sought as the skilled manpower to manufacture those arms and to impart those skills to Ethiopians.

The upshot of this strategy appeared at Gafat, an area near Dabra Tabor which, more than any other place, symbolized Tewodros's modernizing drive. Gafat was at the same time a symbol of the uneasy relationship between Tewodros and the European missionaries. The latter came to Ethiopia to preach the gospel of love. They ended up being commandeered to manufacture weapons of destruction by a Christian sovereign who wanted from the Europeans their science, not their religion. At Gafat, a school was established where Ethiopian youths acquired literacy and some technical skills. By trial and error, and under the emperor's ceaseless prodding, the missionaries managed to manufacture some weapons.

At Maqdala, the first well-documented arsenal in Ethiopian history was established, with 15 cannon, 7 mortars, 11,063 rifles of different types, 875 pistols and 481 bayonets, as well as ammunition including 555 cannon-shells and mortar-shells and 83,563 bullets. But the objective of creating a trained Ethiopian cadre of technicians could hardly be realized when the apprentices were drawn from groups then regarded as social outcasts, such as the Muslims and Falasha, and from Oromo captives. Nor could the weapons forged at the Gafat foundry bring about any dramatic change in the military equation – as the fate of the highly prized mortar 'Sebastopol' demonstrated. This show-piece of Tewodros's arms manufacture was dragged in 1867 all the way up to the Maqdala massif at considerable sacrifice. But, when the moment came to empty it against the British, it misfired.

Tewodros also made the first attempt to put an end to the slave-trade which had become endemic in Ethiopian society. During one of his campaigns in Gojjam, he freed all the slaves at the Basso market and, in an impromptu wedding ceremony, he had all the male slaves married to the females. He followed this by an official ban on the slave-trade throughout his realm. In Qallu, Wallo, he forbade his soldiers to resell slaves they had captured. Such measures against the slave-trade did not extend to an abolition of the institution of slavery itself; perhaps understandably so, since slavery had come to be embedded in the Ethiopian social fabric. Indeed, later in his reign, we find Tewodros, exasperated by the guerrilla tactics of the Wallo rebel Amade Bashir, authorizing his soldiers to enslave the Muslim followers of his enemy.

Culturally, Tewodros's reign is significant because it witnessed the birth of a fairly well-developed literary Amharic. A world of stylistic difference separates the Amharic correspondence sent by Tewodros and that of previous correspondents such as *Dajjach* Subagadis.

Amharic prose attained even higher, almost poetic, elegance in the chronicle of *Dabtara* Zanab, the emperor's admirer.

Like all modernizing rulers, Tewodros realized that introducing far-reaching reforms was impossible without a secure financial base. It was in an effort to solve this problem that he came into collision with the Ethiopian Orthodox Church. That ultimately proved his undoing. His conflict with the clergy initially arose from two different levels of morality. With understandable exaggeration, Zanab draws a striking contrast between the virtues of Tewodros and the vices of the clergy of the *Zamana Masafent*: purity versus debauchery, chastity versus licentiousness, monogamy versus polygamy, and honesty versus dishonesty. Further, just as he sought to establish a unitary state, Tewodros wanted to see the church overcome its doctrinal divisions and emerge as a united institution. His 'concordat' with the Egyptian bishop *Abuna* Salama, whereby the latter gave his blessing to Tewodros's seizure of political power in return for his enforcement of the *Tawahedo* doctrine, appeared to have ushered in a new era of the unity of church and state.

But this spirit of co-operation was short-lived. The relationship between Tewodros and the clergy was soon beset with fundamental political and economic contradictions. As was revealed by the controversy over the *temtem*, the turban customarily worn by Ethiopian Orthodox Christian priests, Tewodros appears to have been bent on establishing absolute power over the clergy. He could not tolerate the fact that they appeared turbaned in front of him, whereas they had to take off their turbans in the holy of holies, the inner sanctuary of a church. It was the vital question of land, however, which made the church a sworn enemy of the emperor. In a question of striking directness, Tewodros enquired of the clergy in 1856: 'What shall I eat, and with what shall I feed my troops? You have taken half the land as *masqal maret* and the other half as *rim* and *gadam*' (Zanab, 28). (Tewodros was here referring to three of the various categories of church land.) The response of the clergy was as medieval as the emperor's question was modern. He was told to roam from one province to another and live off the land, 'as in the past'. Tewodros found the suggestion not at all attractive. After four years of procrastination in view of strong clerical opposition, he expropriated what he deemed was land in excess of the clergy's requirements and distributed it among tribute-paying peasants.

Tewodros and the foreigners

Interrelated with the broad vision which Tewodros brought to solve the internal problems of the country was his energetic response to the external challenge. This challenge had two elements: Egyptian and

European. But there was an intimate link between the two, just as the external and the internal elements were closely interconnected. The quest for European assistance could be regarded as the pivot of Tewodros's policy. It was with that assistance that he sought to eliminate the Egyptian danger (in his words, the 'Turkish' danger) and to bring about internal reforms. Knowledge of the alignments during the Crimean War of 1853–1856 (Christian Britain and France against Orthodox Christian Russia on the side of Muslim Turkey) must have been a shock to him. But it did not deter him from continuing to invoke the principle of Christian solidarity against Muslim Egypt. Conversely, the possibility of a Crimean-like collusion between the 'Turks' and the Europeans, particularly the British, perennially haunted him. Captain Cameron, the British consul appointed to Ethiopia in 1862, was finally imprisoned because, after his visit to Massawa, he failed to bring back a response to Tewodros's letter of that year to Queen Victoria, in which he asked for British assistance to help him break out of the Muslim blockade. Cameron also compounded his error by returning via Matamma, then under Egyptian control, and, so Tewodros suspected, by plotting with the 'Turks'.

Given his background of border clashes with the Egyptians, it is not surprising that Tewodros continued to harbour an ingrained suspicion of them. This was clearly seen in 1857, when he suddenly arrested the Coptic Patriarch Qerilos (then on a visit from Alexandria to Ethiopia) and *Abuna* Salama (head of the Ethiopian Orthodox Church) – both Egyptians – on discovering that they had sent a request for Egyptian military assistance on Tewodros's behalf, but without his knowledge. Simultaneously, he tried to undermine Egyptian authority in Sudan by using Sudanese refugees such as Wad Nimr, son of *Makk* Nimr, leader of a Sudanese revolt against Egyptian rule in 1821, to make inroads into Sudan and even collect taxes in Tewodros's name. But Tewodros the emperor, unlike Kasa the *shefta*, was preoccupied mainly with the coast rather than with the western borderlands. As he groped outwards for contacts with Europe, he found his outlet Massawa sealed off by the Egyptian presence. This feeling of insulation underlay his letter to Queen Victoria.

Although Tewodros sought to cultivate friendly relations with all European nations, it was towards the British that he manifested a special, almost affectionate, regard. It was to be one of his tragedies that this affection went unreciprocated. Such a special attitude may have been the result of his close association with John Bell, a British traveller who came to Ethiopia early in the 1840s and later won the favour of the emperor to such a degree that he became Tewodros's *liqa makwas* (an important court official who, among other things, acted as the emperor's double, with the aim of misdirecting possible assassination attempts), and with Walter Plowden, the first British consul to Ethiopia, who arrived in 1848. Tewodros went to great lengths to demonstrate his liking for the British. The killing of Plowden and then of Bell in 1860 by Garad, Tewodros's rebellious nephew, roused the emperor to a furious act of revenge against his own relatives. In the letters that he wrote to Hormuzd Rassam, the British envoy sent in 1864 to negotiate the release of the Europeans imprisoned in January of that year, Tewodros repeatedly expressed his 'love' for the British. At the same time, however, he could not conceal his dismay at the fact that, far from responding positively to his friendly overtures, the British appeared to be conspiring with his avowed enemy, the 'Turks'. This contradiction lay at the root of his quarrel with the British; hence the irony that the nation he had hoped would be his most reliable ally turned out to be his most bitter enemy.

Tewodros's unrelenting quest for European technical assistance arose from his acute realization of the backwardness of his country. Not only was he aware of this backwardness, but he was also not ashamed to publicize it. And he chose the most forceful language to do so: in his letters to Queen Victoria and Rassam, he called himself 'blind', 'ignorant', 'a blind ass'. He repeatedly contrasted the 'darkness' of Ethiopia with the 'light' of Europe. In the letter that he wrote in 1866 when he sent the Protestant missionary Martin Flad to Europe to recruit artisans, Tewodros was at pains to emphasize the favourable terms of employment that he envisaged for potential recruits:

I am sending Mr. Flad to Europe. I am seeking skilled artisans. I shall gladly receive all artisans who come to me. If they stay, I shall ensure that they live happily. If they wish to return to their country once they have taught their skills, I shall pay their salary and let them leave, happy and with an escort.
(Girma-Selassie and Appleyard, 336)

It was also Tewodros's eagerness to introduce European technology into his country that shaped his relations with the missionaries, particularly the Protestants. His relations with the Catholics were never happy. This was partly the result of the greater influence that Catholicism had come to exercise in northern Ethiopia, and the threat that this posed to Tewodros's own authority. Partly, too, it arose from the closer identification of the Catholics with a secular power, France. The conflict between Catholicism and Orthodoxy came to be dramatized in a personal antagonism between Giustino De Jacobis and *Abuna* Salama. Tewodros's 'concordat' with the latter inevitably placed him against the former. De Jacobis was expelled from Ethiopia in 1854, and his Ethiopian followers were persecuted. Thereafter the Catholics and the French became enemies of Tewodros and worked towards his downfall. In Agaw Neguse of Semen, nephew of the defeated *Dajjach* Webe who had been a patron of the Catholics, they found a domestic ally. Adopting the title of *negus* to bolster his pretensions, Agaw Neguse began a policy of active collaboration with Paris and the Vatican, going to the extent of offering the French the port of Zula, south of Massawa, in return for arms. The suppression of his rebellion and his own death in 1860 deprived the French and the Catholics of a strategically located and enthusiastic ally.

With the Protestants, Tewodros had more amicable relations. The influence of the Protestants Bell and Plowden and the educational background of *Abuna* Salama in the Church Missionary Society have been adduced as factors in this relationship. Protestant strategy, which aimed at the internal reform of the Orthodox Church rather than at conversion, also helped. The more practical orientation of the Protestant missionaries, such as their programme of introducing crafts like joinery and masonry, must also have made them more attractive to an emperor bent on introducing European artisanship. At any rate, the rapport between emperor and missionaries attained such degrees of intimacy as partaking together of holy communion. Two of the missionaries, J. Mayer and Theophil Waldmeier, married Ethiopians. Waldmeier, a steadfast admirer of Tewodros even when the ruler's later excesses made him a solitary figure, gave passionate expression to the Protestant image of Tewodros as a Reformation prince:

Where is another king to be found, who in spite of his power and greatness in self-denial disdains all comforts, luxury and good-living? . . . We all firmly believe that the Lord has proclaimed this man with His strength, and that subsequently He will use him still more as an extraordinary instrument for the physical and spiritual well-being of his entire people.

(Crummey, *Priests and Politicians*, 126)

Yet, however enthusiastic the Protestants might have been towards Tewodros, they were not prepared for the task that the emperor had in store for them: the manufacture of heavy armaments. They had to be coerced into it. As far as their evangelical activity was concerned, it was confined on the emperor's order to such non-Christian communities as the Falasha, although occasionally they could count among their converts such close associates of the emperor as his chronicler, the ecclesiastic *Dabtara* Zanab. In the end, the emperor did not spare the Protestant missionaries when he turned against the Europeans. It was indeed one of these missionaries, Henry A. Stern, who, because of his rather indecent references to Tewodros's parentage, fanned the flame of the emperor's anti-European fury. A number of the missionaries were subsequently among the captives at Maqdala.

THE CAPTIVES,

KERANS.   RASSAM.   STERN.   MR. AND MRS. ROSENTHAL,   BLANC.   PIETRO.   CAMERON.
PRIDEAUX.   AND CHILD.

2.2   *The prisoners of Emperor Tewodros II. Captain Cameron, the British consul, is first on the right; Hormuzd Rassam, the envoy who was sent to negotiate the release of the prisoners but ended up joining them, is seated second on the left; the missionary Henry Stern is standing first on the left*

The end of Tewodros

Both domestically and externally, therefore, Tewodros was confronted with a gloomy picture. Internally, he faced nation-wide opposition and rebellion. From the Europeans whom he had expected to come to his aid, he received only indifference or insolence. The frustration of his lofty objectives led him to seek extreme solutions. In exasperation, he spared neither friend nor foe. His indiscriminate violence aggravated his situation. At home, it multiplied his enemies. Abroad, it moved the British to action – against him. They were indifferent to his demands for assistance, but not to his imprisonment of Europeans.

    Internal opposition to Tewodros's authority had started as early as 1855. In the subsequent decade, Tewodros was to spend most of his time moving in haste from one province to another, faced with a fresh outbreak of rebellion before he had succeeded in putting down the

39

previous one. In Gojjam, Tadla Gwalu, a member of the local dynasty, remained a permanent thorn in the flesh. Closer to the emperor's seat of power, Tesso Gobaze of Walqayt threatened his authority to the extent of once even occupying Gondar. In Lasta, *Wag Shum* Gobaze – the future Emperor Takla-Giyorgis (r. 1868–1871) – raised the standard of rebellion after he had seen his own father executed by Tewodros. In Shawa, ever-defiant Sayfu Sahla-Sellase and also Bazabeh, the man whom Tewodros himself had appointed, rose against him. Likewise, the emperor's appointee in Wallo, *Dajjach* Liban Amade, was joined by an even more implacable opponent, Amade Bashir, to make that province Tewodros's political graveyard.

Both the reverses of his political fortune and his own spiralling violence depleted his own ranks. By 1866, as a result of desertions, his army, which had once numbered about 60,000, had been reduced to some 10,000 men. Tewodros had been forced to restrict his movements to the Dabra Tabor–Maqdala axis. Soon, even this stretch of territory was put at the mercy of the growing rebel forces. Towards the end of 1867, Tewodros was forced to abandon the old capital, Dabra Tabor, and establish his last stronghold in Maqdala. This retreat symbolized the ultimate frustration of his dream. The man who had dreamt of uniting all Ethiopia came to be confined to one isolated *amba*, a hilly stronghold. In his final letter to Sir Robert Napier, leader of the British and Indian forces in 1868, Tewodros himself called it 'this heathen spot' (Holland and Hozier, II, 42). Yet, although it marked the nadir of his political and military fortune, Maqdala also symbolized the spirit of defiance which was to endear him so deeply to future generations. Three places could be said to have epitomized his life: Qwara, Gafat and Maqdala. The first served as his initial political and military power base; the second symbolized his modernizing zeal; the third became his last refuge. It was in this refuge, in the act of suicide which has provided both traditional and modern artists with a popular motif, that the forlorn emperor denied the British the satisfaction of capturing the man against whom they had sent such a huge expedition.

The expedition itself had been sent after a fairly long parliamentary debate in Britain. Its objectives were the liberation of the European captives and the punishment of Tewodros. The force led by Sir Robert Napier was 32,000 strong. In historical writings, the exploits of the expedition have been given a prominence incommensurate with their historical importance. In actual fact, the fate of Tewodros had been sealed before the British started their journey to the interior. The war had been won by the British before a shot was fired. Not only was Tewodros deserted by his followers, but some of his enemies had decided to do everything possible to expedite the march of the British troops. The British thus obtained most valuable support from Kasa

Mercha of Tegre (the future Emperor Yohannes IV), who ensured that the expeditionary force would be supplied with the provisions and the means of transport essential for its march; indeed, the expedition proved to be the first army in Ethiopian history which was prepared to pay for its food. Kasa's collaboration with the British arose partly from the fact that he shared the almost universal disaffection from Tewodros; partly from a desire to strengthen his regional position, and thereby to present a stronger bid for the throne; partly also from his trust that the British would honour their promise to leave the country once their limited objectives had been achieved. At any rate, the result of such internal support for the invading force was that it was able to reach Maqdala from the coast in less time than it took Tewodros to traverse the distance between Dabra Tabor and Maqdala, although the invaders' journey was three times as long.

As it turned out, the British did keep their word to leave the country once their mission was accomplished. This prompt withdrawal of the British has remained somewhat enigmatic to students of Ethiopian history. Why, it is often asked, did the British withdraw after they had managed to penetrate to the very heart of Ethiopia? The puzzle ceases to be a puzzle when we recall the fact that the Napier expedition antedated the European scramble for African colonial possessions by almost two decades. The expedition was what we may describe as pre-colonial, in a country where Britain had not yet established vital interests worthy of defending by continued political and military presence. The British point of view was unambiguously put forward by Lord Stanley (later Earl of Derby), the British Foreign Secretary:

Her Majesty's government have no concern with what might befall Abyssinia from the removal of King Theodore from the country . . . it will in no way concern them what may be the future that awaits Abyssinia; what Ruler may hold power in the country; what civil wars or commotions may arise in it. On grounds of humanity Her Majesty's government would desire the country to be well governed, and the people to be contented and prosperous; but they do not consider it incumbent on them to set up or to support any form of government or any particular Ruler under which it shall be carried out, *in a country in which they have really no British interests to promote.*

(Rubenson, *Survival*, 275; emphasis added)

As for Tewodros, his last word to his countrymen and the world at large was contained in the letter he wrote to Napier on the day after the British victory on 10 April at the Battle of Aroge, which preceded the storming of Maqdala and the emperor's suicide. It is a document quintessentially Tewodrosian, crystallizing as it does his lifelong dreams and ambitions. Although it is addressed to the British general, the thrust of the message is a castigation of Tewodros's countrymen for their insubordination. It is a document that combines his compassion for the weak and the aged with lamentation for the frustration

41

of his dream of freeing Jerusalem; pride at his record of invincibility with regret for the discipline which he tried to inculcate among his countrymen and which eluded him to the end. It also has a poignant line about the artillery on which he had staked so much, and which ultimately proved so useless: 'Believing myself to be a great lord, I gave you battle; but by reason of the worthlessness of my artillery, all my pains were as nought' (Holland and Hozier, II, 42). In short, the letter is Tewodros's testament to posterity, indicating what he had set out to do and how and why he had failed to do it.

2. A new approach to unification

The death of Tewodros opened once again the issue of the throne. Three persons emerged as the chief contenders for it. *Wag Shum* Gobaze of Lasta had emerged as Tewodros's bitter opponent. *Wag Shum* Gobaze's victory over his rival, Tesso Gobaze of Walqayt, a few days before the British storming of Maqdala, had greatly enhanced his chances of supremacy in the historic centres of political power. But his lack of contact with the Napier expedition deprived him of access to the modern arms which were to prove so vital to his future rival, Kasa Mercha. Starting from his base in Tamben, an area bordering on Semen, this latter contender had extended his sway through a large part of Tegre by 1867, and had begun expanding beyond the Marab river. To the south, after managing to escape from the Maqdala prison in 1865, Menilek of Shawa had reasserted his claims as the lord of that province, and was expanding in the direction of Wallo, to the north.

But it is a measure of the new era ushered in by Tewodros that there was to be no return to the *Zamana Masafent*, to puppet kings controlled by one powerful *ras* after anothe The coronation of Tewodros in 1855 had symbolized the end of t e divorce between political power and political authority. Military muscle became as legitimate a ground for claiming the throne as Solomonic descent, if not a better entitlement. Thus, soon after the death of Tewodros, *Wag Shum* Gobaze had himself crowned as Emperor Takla-Giyorgis. Although Menilek had already started styling himself *negusa nagast*, he reached some kind of agreement with Takla-Giyorgis whereby the Bashilo river became the boundary between their respective spheres. The new strong man of Gojjam, *Ras* Adal Tasamma, also submitted to Emperor Takla-Giyorgis and, to cement the relationship, received the emperor's sister in marriage.

42   Marriage links, however, did not deter Kasa Mercha from chal-

2.3   A sketch of Dajjach *Kasa Mercha, the future Emperor Yohannes*
(r. 1872–1889)

lenging Takla-Giyorgis, who happened to be also his brother-in-law. Their rivalry culminated on 11 July 1871 in the Battle of Assam, near Adwa. Although outnumbered in the ratio of 5 to 1 (60,000 troops against 12,000), Kasa had the telling edge in armaments and discipline. The battle was over two hours after it began. The emperor's losses were estimated as 500 killed, 1,000 wounded and about 24,000 captured, including the emperor himself. Thus came to an end the brief and largely uneventful reign of Takla-Giyorgis. Six months later, on 21 January 1872, Kasa ascended the throne, with the name of Yohannes IV.

While the imperial idea so dramatically resuscitated by Tewodros was to endure, Yohannes nevertheless followed a policy of unification substantially different from that of his predecessor: his choice of the title of *r'esa makwanent* (head of the nobility) as he bid for the throne set the tune of his policy. He continued to regard himself as *primus inter pares* (first among equals), a *negusa nagast* (king of kings) in the strict sense of the word, not an undisputed autocrat. Tewodros had once styled himself 'husband of Ethiopia and fiancé of Jerusalem', and he was to prove himself a jealous husband indeed! Yohannes, in contrast, was ready to share Ethiopia with his subordinates, provided his suzerainty was recognized. In place of Tewodros's head-on collision with regionalism, Yohannes followed a more cautious approach, **43**

*2.4   Negus *Takla-Haymanot, hereditary ruler of Gojjam from*
1881-1901*

which amounted to a conscious toleration of it. While this more
realistic approach had the merit of recognizing the objective
impediments to establishing a unitary state, it had the disadvantage
of encouraging the latent centrifugal tendencies of the Ethiopian
polity.

Side by side with his policy of controlled regionalism, Yohannes
pursued another of maintaining a political and military equilibrium
between his two main vassals, Menilek of Shawa and Adal of Gojjam.
In view of the fact that the actual as well as potential challenge to the
throne came from Menilek rather than from Adal, this policy in effect
meant that the emperor found himself more often on the side of the
Gojjame rather than on that of the Shawan ruler.

Initially, however, relations between Adal and Yohannes were
anything but smooth. This is not surprising, as Adal had been Takla-
Giyorgis's protégé. But the emperor's campaigns to subdue the
Gojjame lord were frustrated by the latter's resort to guerrilla
tactics – a pattern of confrontation that was to be repeated in later
times. In an effort to undermine Adal's authority in Gojjam, the
emperor then made Dasta Tadla (son of the rebel Tadla Gwalu, who
had given Tewodros such a hard time) *ras* and governor of Gojjam.
Adal's victory over Dasta in July 1874 ensured his supremacy in
Gojjam, and induced both the emperor and Adal to seek a *rapproche-*
ment. After assurances from Yohannes that he would honour Adal's

legitimate rights to the throne of Gojjam, Adal submitted at Ambachara in October 1874.

Thereafter, Yohannes began to support Adal as a counterweight to Menilek. He also apparently gave his blessing to Adal's expansion south of the Abbay river in order to forestall the Shawan ruler. Adal reciprocated by suppressing rebellions in Bagemder and Semen in 1875–1876, while Yohannes was engaged with the Egyptians. In 1878, at Leche, as a member of the emperor's entourage, Adal had the satisfaction of witnessing the chastening of his rival, Menilek. The high point of the Yohannes–Adal accord came in January 1881, when the emperor made Adal *negus* of Gojjam *and* Kafa, thereby publicizing his desire to deprive Menilek of the resource-rich south-west, and to stifle his bid for imperial power. The Battle of Embabo one year later, when Menilek ensured for himself mastery of the south-west by defeating *Negus* Takla-Haymanot (as Adal had come to be called), was thus a source of serious alarm to the emperor, as it significantly upset his policy of equilibrium. The ultimate failure of this policy came in 1888, when the two vassals created a common front against Yohannes. The emperor reacted by devastating Gojjam, the land of his relatively more favoured vassal, with a fury which he himself found hard to explain: 'I do not know whether it is through my sin or that of the peasant, but I went on devastating the country' (Heruy, 83).

Menilek's challenge to Yohannes began soon after he returned in 1865 to Shawa from his ten-year captivity in Maqdala. He had inherited an area of relative prosperity, and it also had a tradition of strong autocratic leadership. With this secure base, he began to expand to the north, partly because this was a natural line of expansion at the time and partly to enhance his credentials for the throne. In the process, he founded the town of Warra Illu, north of the border between Shawa and Wallo. His expansion was challenged locally by Mastawat, one of the rulers of Wallo, and later by her son Amade Liban (alias Abba Wataw), and nationally by Emperor Yohannes himself. Soon, Wallo developed into a bone of contention between the emperor and Menilek. But they did not come into a direct clash over it. Instead they fought the war through the surrogates they had groomed from the two rival houses of Wallo: Abba Wataw for Yohannes and Muhammad Ali for Menilek. In the early 1870s, however, Yohannes was too absorbed in the Egyptian menace to give any meaningful help to his candidate. Towards the end of 1875, therefore, Menilek successfully captured the stronghold of Maqdala, imprisoned Abba Wataw and appointed Muhammad Ali as governor of Wallo.

Yohannes's victories over the invading Egyptians at Gundat (1875) and Gura (1876), both near the Marab river where it turns north into what is now Eritrea, changed the situation. In the aftermath of the battles, Yohannes moved south to deal with a problem that had been nagging him since his coronation, but which he had never previously had the time to solve. With the adroitness which was to be the hallmark of his political career, Muhammad Ali shifted allegiance from Menilek to the more powerful emperor. Yohannes kept on pushing southwards, determined to solve the problem of Menilek once and for all. In January 1878, he entered the district of Manz, in north-west Shawa. Menilek gave the order for mobilization. There were even some minor clashes, after which Menilek retreated to Leche. It was there that, urged by his advisers, he made his submission; with his supplies dwindling, the emperor was probably not unenthusiastic about a peaceful resolution of the conflict.

The Leche Agreement, as it has come to be known, took place on 20 March 1878, and forms a landmark in the history of the Ethiopian state. It resolved the political uncertainty of the post-Tewodros period. Yohannes's suzerainty was unequivocally recognized, and in very dramatic circumstances indeed. In the formal ceremony of submission, Menilek had to carry the traditional stone of penitence and prostrate himself in front of his overlord, as the *azmari* (minstrels) chanted songs chiding him for his ambition. The Shawan ruler also agreed to pay annual tribute to the emperor and to provide supplies for the imperial army when it passed through Shawa.

Yet the agreement was also a clear demonstration of the emperor's liberal approach to the issue of political power, his objective of being a feudal suzerain rather than an absolute autocrat. He left Menilek defeated but not shattered; he made him renounce the title of *negusa nagast* which he had paraded since the death of Tewodros; but he sanctioned Menilek's assumption of the title of *negus* with the following words:

You are accordingly king and master of a land conquered by your forebears; I shall respect your sovereignty if you will be faithful to the agreements decided between us. Whoever strikes your kingdom, strikes me, and whoever makes war on you, makes it on me. You are accordingly my eldest son.

(Marcus, *Life and Times*, 56)

On Menilek's side, too, his decision to submit was a mark of his tactical wisdom. Humiliated though he was, he came out militarily intact. The big lesson that he learned from the whole encounter was the need for patience. And, in the following decade, he was to work patiently, but assiduously, for the throne which he had earlier mistakenly thought to be within easy reach. After the Leche Agreement, Wallo was no longer his exclusive preserve. He was reduced to the role of a junior partner to the emperor, who began to subjugate Wallo with extraordinary ruthlessness. But, for Menilek, his frustra-

2.5   Ras *Alula Engeda, Emperor Yohannes's governor of the Marab Melash, and implacable opponent of Italian encroachment, shown in Arab costume, 1887*

tion in the north was to prove a blessing in disguise. It opened his eyes to the south. His southern campaigns were to provide him with the resources, hence the military power, to pose a more formidable challenge to the throne, so that, when Yohannes died at the Battle of Matamma against the Sudanese Mahdists in March 1889, Menilek's succession was an almost foregone conclusion.

While Yohannes was content to exercise only indirect control in Gojjam and Shawa, he could not afford to pursue a similar policy in the area most threatened by foreign intrusion – the Marab Melash, the territory north of the Marab river and stretching to the Red Sea. The defection in 1876 of its ruler, Walda-Mikael, to the Egyptian side spelt out the inherent dangers of indirect rule only too clearly. Soon after the Battle of Gura, therefore, Yohannes entrusted the administration of the Marab Melash to his trusted general, Alula Engeda, after promoting him from *shalaqa* (the Ethiopian army equivalent of major) to *ras*. Being of humble origin and owing his position entirely to the emperor, Alula showed steadfast loyalty. He executed his task as frontier governor with extraordinary energy and dedication. On   **47** the other hand, his meteoric rise provoked the disgruntlement of the Tegrean nobility. One of its members, *Dajjach* Dabbab Araya, a cousin of the emperor, was to provide as *shefta* a constant challenge to Alula's authority on the Massawa coast until his submission in 1888. Walda-Mikael himself did not easily acquiesce in the withdrawal of what he considered as his legitimate rights as governor. From his refuge in Bogos, encouraged and supported by his patrons, the Egyptians, he engaged in constant raids into Hamasen. Finally, in 1879, as Egyptian enthusiasm for his activities waned, Walda-Mikael made his peace with Alula and Yohannes, only to be imprisoned soon after.

Yohannes's policy of unification had also a religious dimension. In many ways, his religious policy lacked the liberalism and spirit of tolerance that he had shown in the political field. Here again, 1878 was the crucial year. The Leche Agreement in March, marking the apogee of the emperor's power, was immediately followed by the Council of Boru Meda, which brought to an end the doctrinal controversies that had rent the Orthodox Church since the seventeenth century. At a stroke, therefore, the ideological wings of the *Zamana Masafent* may be said to have been clipped. In a meeting presided over by the emperor himself, the *Tawahedo* doctrine was declared as the only doctrine, and adherents of other sects were told to conform. Those who still persisted in their old doctrines were persecuted; one man had his tongue cut out.

Apart from such methods of enforcing orthodoxy, the Council of Boru Meda was generally regarded as a positive measure restoring the unity of the church. The emperor's prestige accordingly grew. It grew even further when, for the first time in Ethiopian history, he succeeded in bringing four bishops from Egypt. The harsher aspects of Boru Meda in any case soon paled into insignificance in comparison with the intolerance, verging on fanaticism, that Yohannes showed towards Islam: it emerged that he was aiming not only at unity of doctrine, but also at unity of faith. There was no room for Islam in his ideological world. The thrust of his repression was directed against Wallo, the same province which had earlier been the main target of Tewodros's fury.

The Muslims of Wallo were told to renounce their faith and embrace Christianity or face confiscation of their land and property. The reactions were varied. The political leaders generally acquiesced. Thus, two prominent converts were Muhammad Ali, baptized into the Ethiopian Orthodox Church as Mikael, and Abba Wataw, who became Hayla-Maryam. Others conformed outwardly, praying to the Christian God in the daytime and to the Muslim Allah at night – thereby reinforcing the unique juxtaposition of Islam and Christianity that we find to this day in Wallo. Still others preferred exile, supporting or spreading Islam in such faraway places as Gurageland and Arsi, respectively south-west and south-east of central Shawa. But a large number of the inhabitants resisted, led by such sheikhs as Talha of Argobba. The repressive rule of Yohannes's son Araya-Sellase, to whom his father had entrusted the governorship of Wallo after 1882, helped to fan the flames of rebellion. The rebellion was finally suppressed by the intervention of both Yohannes and Menilek, and after a campaign characterized by devastation and massacre. *Ras* Mikael, who had made his political calculations and joined the campaign on the side of the emperor, emerged as the undisputed ruler of the whole of Wallo.

3. Intensification of the external challenge

After Maqdala, the British seemed to have washed their hands of Ethiopia. Their policy of disengagement was almost scrupulously observed. Overtures from their former ally, Kasa Mercha, for closer co-operation left them unimpressed. His request for military advisers was turned down. For the procurement of arms from England, he could manage to obtain the services of only a private firm, Messrs Henry S. King & Co. An Ethiopian mission sent with the objective of recruiting instructors in skilled crafts was left stranded in Alexandria, on orders from London. Even Kasa's seizure of the throne as Emperor Yohannes IV, after his victory over Emperor Takla-Giyorgis, Tewodros's immediate successor, could not move the British. They deigned to respond to Kasa's initial letter and gifts only two years after they had received his – with accompanying instructions to the British consul in Aden to inform Kasa that they were not interested in any future exchange of presents.

What made the Napier expedition something more than an episode was its indirect bearing on the internal power struggle in Ethiopia, and on the evolution of Ethiopia's foreign relations. In recognition of his services, the departing British had rewarded Kasa with 6 cannon, 850 muskets and rifles and a considerable supply of ammunition. In addition, although the British had refused any official secondment of military advisers, a member of the expedition, a certain J.C. Kirkham, had volunteered to help train Kasa's army along modern lines. It was the combination of British arms and Kirkham's rudimentary training which is generally believed to have been decisive for Kasa's victory over Emperor Takla-Giyorgis at the Battle of Assam in 1871.

Externally, the ease with which the British penetrated to the heart   **49** of Ethiopia and accomplished their mission helped to create a false idea as to Ethiopia's capability to withstand foreign aggression. Forgetting or unaware of the internal factors which had facilitated the British victory, other countries came to feel that the experience of the Napier expedition could easily be repeated. At this early stage, it was Egypt which showed the tendency to underestimate Ethiopia's strength to the greatest degree. In March 1871, the Swiss-born J.A. Werner Munzinger (then still French consul at Massawa), who in the future was to launch Egyptian expansion into Ethiopia, threatened Kasa Mercha with the fate of Tewodros unless he showed greater leniency towards the Catholic missionaries. The attempt to carry out this threat ultimately led to the Battles of Gundat and Gura, which ended with the crushing defeat of the invading Egyptian troops.

Munzinger's patron was Khedive Ismail. A man who, to all intents and purposes, considered himself a European, Ismail at the same time saw Egypt's destiny in Africa. Even more ambitious than his great predecessor, the Albanian Muhammad Ali, who, side by side with his expansions up the Nile in the early nineteenth century, had entertained territorial ambitions in the direction of the Middle East, Ismail pursued a policy of vigorous penetration of the African interior, more particularly of the Nile valley. With the help of such European explorers as Samuel Baker, he extended his sway to the equatorial regions of Sudan. The whole exercise was given the character of a crusade, as Ismail justified his expansion in terms of eradication of the slave-trade. It was the same abolitionist argument, so sweet to European ears, that Ismail evoked in his expansion into Ethiopian territory.

Ismail went about the job of realizing his dream of a north-east African empire systematically, combining military and diplomatic initiatives. He proceeded to encircle the newly crowned Emperor Yohannes territorially and to isolate him diplomatically. First to be occupied by the Egyptians was the northern territory of Bogos. The architect of this initial thrust was none other than Munzinger. The pretext was the alleged raids of a nearby Ethiopian governor into 'Egyptian' territory. Yohannes reacted immediately by sending a letter of protest to Ismail, and launching his first comprehensive diplomatic initiative in Europe. Kirkham, the military expert now doubling as the emperor's roving ambassador, was sent with letters to the monarchs of Britain, Austria, Germany and Russia, and to the President of France. The requests were identical: Christian solidarity with Ethiopia, who found herself under the threat of Islamization and enslavement by Ismail. The letter to Queen Victoria, however, in whom Yohannes was to continue to place so much trust, contained additional details about Munzinger's occupation of Bogos.

50   Yohannes's plea fell on deaf ears. Kirkham was greeted with a complete lack of interest in Russia, Germany and France. The British even took it upon themselves to vouch for Ismail's good intentions. Baffling as their reactions must have appeared to Yohannes, the European powers did not find the theme of Christian solidarity very convincing. To them, Muslim though it was, Egypt offered more opportunities for trade and investment than Ethiopia did, for in economic terms Ethiopia was a relatively unknown quantity. Particularly after the opening of the Suez Canal in 1869, the strategic as well as economic value of Egypt had risen considerably, and a fair amount of European finance had come to be invested in Egypt. It was therefore inconceivable that the Europeans would do anything to antagonize a country which offered them so many economic opportunities, for the sake of another which was still very much on the periphery of the international economic scene.

For Ismail to counter Yohannes's protests, therefore, it was enough simply to argue that, in occupying Bogos, Egypt was merely subduing a rebellious province. The Egyptians consolidated their hold by building a formidable fort at Sanhit (Karan). In an effort to make Egyptian rule attractive to the local population, taxes were waived.

The Egyptians followed a potentially even more insidious policy of internal disaffection in the south. In Menilek, the Shawan ruler who had yet to acknowledge Yohannes's suzerainty, they thought they had found the perfect internal ally against the emperor. Menilek himself had been putting out feelers for some kind of understanding with the Egyptians. But his interest did not seem to have gone to the extent of facilitating Egyptian invasion of northern Ethiopia, and even less of creating a southern front against the emperor. The Egyptians were more successful with *Dajjach* Walda-Mikael Solomon of Hamasen. After fighting them in the Battle of Gundat in 1875, he was persuaded to defect to their side.

In terms of Egyptian territorial occupation, Bogos was only the beginning. Eventually, the more serious menace to Ethiopia was to come, not from this inland foothold of Egyptian expansion, but from her coastal possessions. The transfer of Massawa and other Red Sea and Indian Ocean ports in the early years of the nineteenth century from the moribund Ottomans to the more energetic Egyptians foreboded trouble for Ethiopia. The Egyptians were not content with the kind of titular hold over the coast which was all the Ottomans could manage for centuries. From Zeila, an Egyptian force in the guise of a scientific expedition, led by Muhammad Rauf Pasha, penetrated the south-east Ethiopian interior and occupied Harar on 11 October 1875. Concurrently, Munzinger, the architect of Egyptian expansionism, led a force from Tajura, on the coast, in the direction of Shawa. His expedition came to grief on the sandy plains of Awsa, and Munzinger himself was killed in an ambush laid by the Afar. Earlier

51

in the year, however, the Egyptians had begun to probe the northern interior from their coastal bases of Massawa, Zula and Anfilla. Starting with the limited objective of controlling the lucrative Taltal salt plains, the Egyptian thrust accelerated into full-blown aggression.

Gundat and Gura: victory without peace

In the history of the Ethio-Egyptian wars of the mid-1870s, a persistent theme was the audacity of the aggressor and the moderation and self-restraint of the invaded. Thus, as late as September 1875, after the Egyptians had already mobilized for the march into the interior, Emperor Yohannes continued to seek a peaceful resolution of the conflict. He even ordered the retreat of the governors of Hamasen and Saraye to Adwa. In addition to the emperor's continuing hopes for European intervention, his retreat may have had behind it the objective of stretching the enemy's line of supplies. At any rate, it was only on 23 October, after the Egyptians had already reached Hamasen, that he issued the call to arms.

Two weeks after the mobilization order was given, Yohannes found himself at the head of over 20,000 troops. Almost all the northern chiefs had rallied to his call, including *Dajjach* Walda-Mikael Solomon of Hamasen, who was to change sides in the next battle, as previously stated, and who created endless trouble for Yohannes in subsequent years. The Egyptian invading force numbered some 2,000 men, led by a Danish commander, Colonel Arendrup. The two forces met at Gundat (Gudagude), just to the north of the Marab river, in the early hours of 16 November.

The battle turned out to be one of the shortest yet militarily most decisive in Ethiopian history. Lured into the steep valley by the tactical manoeuvres of the Ethiopian troops, the Egyptian army was almost wiped out. The hopeless situation in which the invading troops found themselves is narrated in the vivid words of the American Colonel Dye, himself to take part in the next battle as member of the Egyptian general staff:

No cry of quarter, no supplication to the Son or the Prophet, could stay the bloody hand. In vain, appeals were made to the conquering foe by upright or prostrate forms transfixed by lance or spear, by men with armless bodies or nearly headless trunks, their life blood pouring from every gashing wound. Nothing could stay the bloody carnage. Doomed, – doomed, as they are taught, – mercilessly fated was this little band. They escaped the bullet only to feel the scimitar, or resisted the club only to be lanced.

(Dye, 139)

Such a disaster called for either resignation or revenge. Ismail chose the latter. Before the year 1875 was out, he sent a much larger force (estimated at about 15,000) under his commander-in-chief, Muhammad Ratib Pasha. Veterans of the American Civil War introduced the latest techniques in the science of warfare. One of them, General Loring, was in fact chief of staff and second-in-command. Colonel Dye, as we have seen, was destined to be the impassioned chronicler of the Egyptian débâcle. The better preparation of the Egyptians made the Battle of Gura a relatively more protracted affair: it lasted three days, from 7 to 9 March 1876. The Egyptians fought from well-fortified positions; disaster began to strike them only when they came out of their forts. Still, Gura was less of an unmitigated disaster for them than the Battle of Gundat. The Ethiopian losses were correspondingly higher. But the end result was the same – yet another blow to Egyptian expansion.

For sheer valour in face of a far better-armed enemy, the Ethiopian performance at Gundat and Gura has few parallels in modern Ethiopian history. Dye's narrative gives an explicit picture of this valour:

Boom after boom was now heard along the entire line, and far over the plain went the echoing shell. Rockets, too, from the right and the centre, in awful concert, began their terrific flights. Battalion after battalion fired volley upon volley from right and left, sending death-dealing missiles at long range upon the swift-advancing foe. With steady tramp, the Abyssinians closed in upon the Egyptians. Riderless horses bolted their ranks in response to exploding shell; yet on the army came.

(Dye, 359)

In a way, the Gundat and Gura victories were even more remarkable than their famous successor, the Battle of Adwa, for, while Menilek was to lead a united Ethiopia against the Italians, Yohannes faced the Egyptians as the head of a divided house. For Egypt, the defeat had more deadly effects than was to be the case for Italy two decades later. The Ethiopian victory hastened Ismail's downfall and the subsequent British occupation of Egypt. Yohannes, on the other hand, came out of the conflict with material and psychological gains. The modern arms, including some twenty cannon that he captured from the enemy, strengthened his military position *vis-à-vis* his internal rivals like Menilek. The victory itself enhanced his prestige as the defender of faith and motherland.

Yet, in the immediate aftermath, the Gundat and Gura victories were to remain hollow. Ethiopia gained little in practical terms. The Egyptian conditions for peace soon after their defeat leave us uncertain as to who was the victor and who the vanquished. Not only did they demand the repatriation of the Egyptian prisoners and guarantees of free trade, but they also required the restoration of their captured arms and the cessation of Ethiopian troop movements in the Hamasen.

Conversely, Yohannes persisted in his policy of restraint. He   **53** followed up his victory not with a march to Massawa, but with letters to Victoria and Ismail once again suing for peace. He renounced the military option either because his army was in no condition to continue the fighting, or because he feared further military action would antagonize the European governments. Thus began Yohannes's diplomatic efforts to crown his victory with a peace treaty – something that was to elude him for almost a decade. He started by sending to Cairo a certain *Blatta* Gabra-Egziabher as envoy in the summer of 1876. His conditions for peace were basically two: restoration of occupied Ethiopian territory and free access to the sea. The detention of his envoy for over two months and his eventual return without any discussion of the issues did not augur well for the future of a negotiated settlement.

Early in 1877, Ismail in turn sent an envoy – the British governor-general of the Sudan, Colonel (later General) Charles Gordon. The conditions for peace that he brought with him were hardly acceptable to Yohannes. There were to be no changes in the boundary: Bogos was to remain in Egyptian hands. Although free trade and free passage of envoys and letters via Massawa were to be guaranteed, there was to be a limit on the vital import of arms and ammunition. Subsequent developments showed that the British, to whom Yohannes has repeatedly appealed for mediation, were not ready to give him the unrestricted access to the sea that was the corner-stone of his policy. Not even when he shifted his request from Massawa to Zula or Anfilla, minor ports to the south, were they ready to listen. The heart of the matter was that the British did not wish to see the consummation of the Ethiopian victory over the Egyptians. As early as 1879, they started grooming a power to replace the Egyptians on the Red Sea coast and at the same time serve as watch-dog of British interests. Gordon's parting recommendation for the cession of Zula to the Italians, who had already occupied Assab to the south, was a prelude to their installation in Massawa in 1885, through the good offices of Britain.

But, before that eventuality came about, developments took place which appeared to facilitate the realization of Yohannes's objectives. In 1881, the Mahdist movement, combining Muslim revivalism and nationalism, broke out in Sudan. In the following two or three years, it engulfed the northern and central parts of the country, and effectively cut off the Egyptian garrisons in the east. It therefore fell to the British, who with their unilateral occupation of Egypt in 1882 had assumed responsibility for her possessions, to try and extricate the imperilled Egyptian troops. It was then that they were forced to abandon their policy of indifference bordering on arrogance *vis-à-vis* Ethiopia and to start an assiduous soliciting of Ethiopian assistance. That was the setting for what has come to be known as the Hewett or Adwa Peace Treaty, named respectively after the British negotiator

Rear Admiral Sir William Hewett or the place where the treaty was signed on 3 June 1884.

On the surface, Yohannes obtained more or less what he had sought in vain for the preceding eight years. Free import of goods, 'including arms and ammunition', was guaranteed. Bogos was restored to Ethiopia. There were in addition clauses for the reciprocal extradition of offenders, and Egyptian facilitation of the appointment of bishops (*abun*) for Ethiopia. In real terms and in the long run, the peace treaty did Yohannes more harm than good. The retrocession of Bogos, which relatively speaking was the only positive gain, might well have been achieved without British intercession, as the Egyptian hold over the territory was becoming tenuous; Yohannes's governor of the Marab Melash, *Ras* Alula, had already been levying tribute in the region. The reciprocal extradition clause became meaningless when *Dajjach* Dabbab Araya, who had rebelled against his cousin the emperor, was given asylum in Massawa. As for the free transit of goods through Massawa, it failed to pass its first test when the Egyptians delayed delivery of a church bell ordered by Yohannes, on the grounds that duty had to be paid on it. More significantly, about three months after ratifying the treaty, the British entrusted Massawa to the Italians, who occupied it on 5 February 1885. It was a move which can be said to have been presaged by the ominous clause of the Hewett Treaty, that Massawa was to remain 'under British protection'. The British disposed of their responsibility the way it suited them best.

On the other hand, Yohannes was bound by Article III of the treaty to facilitate the evacuation of Egyptian troops from their posts at Kasala, Amideb and Sanhit, respectively in Sudan, near the Sudan border, and well within Bogos. This obligation Yohannes carried out with a faithfulness which provided a contrast to British duplicity. In the process, *Ras* Alula, who had been given the task of carrying out the relief operation, came into direct conflict with the Mahdists, inaugurating a period of bloody confrontation between Ethiopia and Mahdist Sudan that, in the end, was to consume the emperor himself. Ultimately, therefore, what Yohannes managed to achieve after two brilliant military victories and a belated peace treaty was, in the words of Sven Rubenson, to trade 'one weak enemy [Egypt] for two strong ones, the Mahdist state and Italy' (Rubenson, *Survival*, 362).

4. The road to Matamma

The years 1876-1878 might be said to have marked the apogee of Yohannes's power. Externally he had dealt a telling blow to Egyptian expansion. Internally, he had obtained the submission of his main rival. This double victory at the same time appeared to have resolved both the external and internal challenges that Ethiopia faced in the nineteenth century. Yet it was a victory which did not last. By 1885, we can say that Yohannes had reached the turning-point in his career, which was to end with his death at the Battle of Matamma. In that year the Italians occupied Massawa. In the same year, Ethiopian forces clashed with the Mahdists (or the Ansar, as they preferred to call themselves), initiating a period of hostility which was to reach its climax in 1889. Also after 1885, the latent insubordination of Menilek began to simmer until it burst out into the open in 1888. It was in that year that the triangular tension in which Yohannes had lived reached its ultimate limits. The following year, it was resolved, with his tragic death.

Italian colonialism in the Horn of Africa combined the vigour of youth with the desperation of the late-comer. This distinctive feature arose from the late arrival of Italy on the colonial scene: Italy became a unified state only in 1871. Italy's thrust was abetted by the British, who, themselves unwilling to get involved in Ethiopia, wanted someone to guard their interests in the region against their ancestral rivals, the French.

Nevertheless, Italy's first territorial acquisition antedated the completion of its unification. In 1869, the port of Assab, south of Massawa, was acquired for Italy by a team which symbolically included a missionary, Giuseppe Sapeto, and a navigational enterprise, Rubattino Company. But it was Massawa which provided Italy with the base for its penetration of the Ethiopian interior. And Massawa, as we have seen, was secured through the good offices of Britain in the wake of Egyptian evacuation from the Red Sea and Indian Ocean coasts. That evacuation had also secured Zeila and Berbera for the British and Tajura for the French. But while the British and French acquisitions were to terminate with narrow coastal colonies – British and French Somaliland – the Italians, from Massawa, were to make a bid for the whole of Ethiopia. Massawa, in short, led to Adwa.

With remarkable foresight, Yohannes recognized the connection. 'With the help of God,' he wrote to Menilek in late 1886, 'they will depart again, humiliated and disgraced in the eyes of the whole world' (Zewde, 199). When he wrote this, the Italians had already pushed further inland and occupied Saati, about 15 miles (24 km) west of Massawa, and Wia, 20 miles (32 km) to the south of the port. It had thus become evident that Yohannes's earlier hopes of containing the Italians within the coast were futile. Protests from *Ras* Alula, the governor of the Marab Melash, that the Italians should abandon their advance posts were ignored. It was in such circumstances that Alula opted to obtain by force of arms what he had failed to achieve through correspondence. On 25 January 1887, he attacked the Italian fort at Saati. He was repulsed, incurring considerable losses. The following day, at Dogali, between Saati and Massawa, Alula's force intercepted some 500 Italians sent to relieve the Saati garrison. The relief force was virtually destroyed.

News of the Battle of Dogali provoked a frenzied reaction in Italy. The call for revenge was heard in the streets as well as in the government chambers. Parliament voted for an appropriation of 20 million lire for the defence of Massawa and its environs. A special force of 5,000 men was organized to reinforce the existing troops. Roads and bridges were built and repaired in an effort to strengthen the infrastructure for future military action. Simultaneously, the policy of instigating Menilek to act against Yohannes was intensified.

In an initial attempt to solve the problem through diplomatic intervention, both Yohannes and the Italians turned to the British. Yohannes wrote to Queen Victoria complaining about the violation of the Hewett Treaty. The Queen's reply contained an implicit justification of Italian actions and a warning to Yohannes, suggesting that it was a pity that he was in disagreement with the Italians, who were powerful, though well intentioned. To the Italians, on the other hand, the British were once again obliging. A mission headed by Sir Gerald Portal was sent to Ethiopia, ostensibly to mediate between the belligerents, but in reality hoping to gain for the Italians what Dogali had denied them. Portal's proposals for peace included a public apology by Yohannes for the Dogali incident as well as Italian occupation of Saati, Wia, Karan and the territory of the Assaorta and the Habab peoples on the Red Sea coast. The 'mediator' was rebuffed, bluntly by Alula, diplomatically by Yohannes.

Under cover of this diplomatic ploy, however, the Italians had reoccupied Saati. Yohannes now took the field himself to resolve once and for all the Italian problem. At the head of a large army (80,000 troops), he went down to Saati in March 1888. Hope of an early victory vanished, however, when the Italians refused to come out of their fort. Faced with shortage of supplies, news of the Mahdist sacking of Gondar, and rumours of a conspiracy between Menilek and *Negus* Takla-Haymanot against him, Yohannes had no choice but to return without achieving anything. That was to be his last encounter with the Italians. One year later, he died on the battlefield at Matamma, and the Italians immediately marched on to the highlands.

Like the Italian occupation of Massawa, the bloody confrontation between Ethiopia and Mahdist Sudan was a legacy of Egyptian expansion. The Mahdist movement arose as a combination of religious revivalism and Sudanese nationalist opposition to Egyptian rule. As such it was primarily directed against Egypt, in Mahdist thinking

2.6   The port town of Massawa towards the end of the nineteenth century

regarded as both renegade and oppressor. But Yohannes's faithful implementation of the Hewett Treaty had the effect of redirecting Mahdist fury against Ethiopia. By coming to the relief of the beleaguered Egyptian garrisons, Ethiopia identified herself with the hated enemy. Simultaneously, the Egyptian buffer between her and Mahdist Sudan was eliminated, and the two countries were brought into direct confrontation.

The first battle was fought at Kufit (to the east of Kasala) on 23 September 1885. The Ethiopian troops were led by *Ras* Alula. The Mahdists or Ansar were commanded by a no less redoubtable general, Uthman Diqna. After two reverses, in the latter of which Alula himself was wounded, the Ethiopian side was victorious. About 3,000 Ansar lost their lives. The Ethiopian losses were about half that number killed, including Alula's lieutenant, *Blatta* Gabru.

Another arena of Ethio-Mahdist confrontation was in the south, in the present-day Wallaga region. In the sheikhdoms of Asosa, Bela Shangul and Khomosha, the Ansar had stepped into the shoes of the Egyptians, who had exercised some sort of paramountcy characterized chiefly by annual tax-gathering raids. Islam and trans-frontier trade had also prepared the ground for Mahdist penetration, although this did not mean that the Ansar were universally welcomed in the region. All the same, gaining influence over even some of the Oromo rulers, they had penetrated as far as the Najjo area, deep inside Oromo territory. It was there, at the Battle of Gute Dili (14 October 1888), that Menilek's general, *Ras* Gobana Dache, finally stopped them.

But the most decisive battles were undoubtedly fought on the Matamma front. Matamma, known as Gallabat to the Sudanese, had been historically the most important centre of contact, peaceful or hostile, between the two countries. It was therefore only fitting that the issue was finally resolved there. Significantly, too, trade continued even during the period of hostility, with traders often doubling as spies.

Mahdist forces occupied Matamma following the Egyptian evacuation, and initiated a period of border raids and counter-raids. It was in response to one such Ansar raid in Dambya, in the plains south-west of Gondar, that *Negus* Takla-Haymanot, Yohannes's general on this front, attacked and sacked Matamma in January 1887. One year later, the Ansar, led by another of their famous generals, Abu Anja, defeated Takla-Haymanot's troops at Sar Weha, in Dambya. They followed this up with the deepest incursion they had yet made in north-west Ethiopia, sacking the town of Gondar.

It was in the same year, 1888, that Yohannes's relations with his vassals entered a critical phase. Suspicious of Menilek's intentions, Yohannes had declined his offer of assistance during the Saati campaign. Instead, he had instructed him to position himself at Ambachara, to the south of Gondar, and watch the movements of the Mahdists. Menilek arrived too late to save Gondar from the Ansar attack. On his way back, he met *Negus* Takla-Haymanot of Gojjam, and the two vassals agreed to work together against the emperor. Hearing of the conspiracy, Yohannes opened a devastating punitive campaign against Gojjam soon after his return from his inconclusive Saati campaign.

He then prepared to wage a similar campaign in Shawa. Menilek turned to the Italians for closer collaboration, and to the people of Shawa to rise in defence of their region. Ethiopia stood on the verge of a bloody civil war. But Yohannes changed his mind and turned to deal with the Ansar. At the root of this decision was probably Yohannes's awareness that the Mahdist problem was the least complicated of the problems he faced. Having solved that once and for all, he could then turn his whole attention to the interrelated problem of Menilek and the Italians. But this was not to be. At the Battle of Matamma (9 March 1889), an initial victory turned into a rout when the emperor was fatally wounded. The following day he died.

59

5. The creation of the modern Ethiopian empire-state

Since the middle of the nineteenth century, the unification of Ethiopia had been a matter of utmost priority, although certainly this unification was conceived of differently at different times. For Tewodros, it meant the creation of a centralized unitary state. For Yohannes it signified the establishment of a loosely united Ethiopia, with autonomous regional rulers under an emperor exercising benevolent political suzerainty. By 1889, it had become clear that both approaches had failed to produce the desired result. This is not to deny the potency of the ideas and the traditions bequeathed by the two personalities. But, in the final analysis, it is difficult to overlook the fact that both failed in the objectives they had set out to achieve.

It was to be Menilek's main claim to historical distinction that he presided over the realization of an idea that had first been kindled in the fiery mind of Tewodros. Yet the final result bore little resemblance to the initial dream. Tewodros's vision of Ethiopia was limited to the central provinces, with Shawa marking the southern limit. Yohannes's conception, while extending further in the north, was broader in the south only by proxy, through the agency of his vassal Takla-Haymanot, who was made *negus* of Gojjam *and* Kafa. Menilek, on the other hand, pushed the frontier of the Ethiopian state to areas beyond the reach even of such renowned medieval empire-builders as *Negusa Nagast* Amda-Tseyon (r. 1314–1344). In the process, the Ethiopia of today was born, its shape consecrated by the boundary agreements made after the Battle of Adwa in 1896 with the adjoining colonial powers.

It was as Shawan ruler that Menilek started the process of expansion that was to culminate in the creation of modern Ethiopia. In this, he was following a tradition of territorial expansion that had marked the Shawan kingdom since its inception. In other words, Menilek completed a process begun by his ancestors, such as Asfawasan (r. 1775–1808) and Wasansaggad (r. 1808–1812), and continued by his grandfather *Negus* Sahla-Sellase (r. 1813–1847). But other elements lent Menilek's expansion newer and broader dimensions. Of these, the urge to control the source of the lucrative long-distance trade was probably the most important. It was this economic factor that ultimately pitted Shawa against Gojjam in the Gibe river region. Their competitive drives to control south-western Ethiopia, and thereby to direct as much trade as possible to their respective regions, culminated in the Battle of Embabo (6 June 1882), in present-day north-eastern Wallaga.

As the years progressed, it became clear that this process of territorial expansion was not an exclusively internal drama. On the contrary, it came to be more and more conditioned and shaped by external developments as well. Menilek's triumphant announcement of his Embabo victory to the outside powers was a clear demonstration of his awareness of the external implications of his internal expansion. Before his incorporation of Harar in 1887, Menilek also spelt out clearly to King Umberto I of Italy (and through him to his European audience) the historical and economic justifications of his campaign. In April 1891, in an effort to forestall the expansion of the colonial powers from their possessions adjoining Ethiopia, he defined in a well-publicized circular to European rulers what he considered to be the legitimate boundaries of the country. The race for territory became even more acute after the victory of the Battle of Adwa in 1896, as Menilek's troops pushed further outwards with reinvigorated *élan*, and the colonial powers, particularly Britain, rushed to check them.

The process of expansion

After the subjugation and incorporation by Menilek's predecessors of the Oromo groups (formerly called Galla) surrounding the Shawan state, it was the Gurage who found themselves on the line of Shawan expansion. The first campaigns to incorporate them were conducted in the years 1875-1876. The two poles of reaction that were to be evident in the years to come first manifested themselves here: peaceful submission and armed resistance. The northern Gurage, more precisely known as the Kestane, represented the former: their relative geographical proximity, and their religious affinity with Christian Shawa, together with the threat of the Oromo that surrounded them, rendered resistance impolitic. The western Gurage, on the other hand, were subjugated only after some fierce fighting. The subsequent rise of a Muslim revivalist movement led by Hasan Enjamo of Qabena, to the north-east of the Gibe river, posed a serious challenge to Shawan authority on the eastern side of the Gibe river. Inspired by Muslim refugees from Wallo, and with possible connections even with Mahdist Sudan, the movement swept across a large part of western Gurage, and was attended by a fast rate of Islamization. Hasan Enjamo's force, which had elements of a Hadiya–Gurage coalition, inflicted a number of defeats on the Shawan forces, until Menilek's general, *Ras* Gobana, took the field in 1888 and finally crushed the movement.

The western side of the Gibe river became a battleground for the rival states of Gojjam and Shawa. It was the Gojjame who had first established their ascendancy in the region. The Leche Agreement of 1878 had circumscribed Menilek's movements by the Awash river in the west. Conversely, *Negus* Takla-Haymanot of Gojjam had been recognized since 1881 also as *negus* of Kafa, which had the general connotation of the south-west. Thanks to the spirited drive of his general, *Ras* Darasso, the Oromo states south of the Abbay river had acknowledged Gojjam's overlordship: they paid tribute, and some of their subjects were recruited into the Gojjame army. The priests had followed the soldiers and had begun to spread Christianity in the region.

The advent of Menilek's general, *Ras* Gobana, in the region put this political and cultural ascendancy of the Gojjame to severe test. The Oromo states began to waver in their loyalty to Gojjam. The first armed confrontation between the rival forces, the dress-rehearsal for the Battle of Embabo, took place in January 1882. *Ras* Darasso's troops were forced to flee, leaving behind the ivory they had collected from the south-west. This was followed by an exchange of aggressive correspondence between Menilek and Takla-Haymanot – a kind of psychological warfare before the decisive clash of arms at Embabo on 6 June. In spite of their impressive fire-power, the Gojjame were out-manoeuvred by the Shawans, who won the day, thanks largely to their cavalry.

The Embabo victory was Menilek's passport to the south-west. With little or no resistance, the Oromo states submitted to Menilek one after another. In the years between 1882 and 1886, Menilek was able to obtain the submission of Kumsa Moroda (later *dajjazmach*, and baptized Gabra-Egziabher) of Leqa Naqamte, Jote Tullu (also made *dajjazmach*) of Leqa Qellam, Abba Jifar II of Jimma, and the rulers of the other Gibe river states, as well as of Illubabor, further to the west. The incorporation of the south-west had more than regional significance. It ensured Menilek a steady source of revenue to streng-then his political and military position in his ultimate bid for the throne. In short, the Battle of Embabo made Menilek the only serious candidate for the succession to Emperor Yohannes IV.

Things were not so easy much nearer home. The fierce resistance Menilek encountered among the Arsi people, south-east of Shawa, sharply contrasted with the ease with which he had extended his sway in the south-west. Attracted by his offers of autonomy in return for acknowledgement of his suzerainty, the Arsi leaders Suffa Kuso and Damu Usu had urged submission, but their idea was not acceptable to the other clan chiefs and elders. With levies from each clan, a sizeable army was organized to resist the incursion from the north. In terms of weapons, it was an unequal struggle: the Arsi matched spears and arrows against firearms. All the same, the campaign to subdue them proved a protracted one, lasting from 1882 to 1886. Menilek personally participated in many of the battles in Arsi. In one of them, in December 1883, he barely managed to escape with his life. The final decisive assault was led by his paternal uncle, *Ras*

2.7   Dajjach *Gabra-Egziabher (Kumsa) Moroda, seated,*
ruler of Leqa Naqamte

Darge Sahla-Sellase. Exploiting the internal division of the Arsi, and
employing a wily stratagem of luring the unsuspecting Arsi into a
position well defended by the Shawans, he inflicted a shattering defeat
on them at the Battle of Azule, in September 1886.

Arsi proved a stepping-stone to Harar, the commercial centre of
eastern Ethiopia. The evacuation by the Egyptians in 1885 had been
followed by the restoration of the emirate. Abdullahi, who was fated
to be the last emir of Harar, ushered in a period of Islamic revival,
and of renewed efforts to subdue the surrounding Oromo. For
Menilek, the Egyptian evacuation was a signal to step in before the
city fell to one or other of the European powers who were hovering
on the coast. The general insecurity that characterized Abdullahi's
rule and, more specifically, the killing of members of an Italian
expedition at Jildessa, to the north of Harar, in April 1886 provided
Menilek with arguments for European acquiescence in the extension
of his authority in that direction. The initial Shawan thrust, led by
his general, *Dajjach* Walda-Gabr'el, was vitiated by troop desertions
and easily repulsed. But in the final engagement, on 6 January 1887,
at Chalanqo, to the west of Harar, the Harari were outgunned,

63

2.8   Abba Jifar II, ruler of Jimma from 1875–1934

2.9   Emir Abdullahi, ruler of the Harar emirate from 1885-1887

outnumbered and outmanoeuvred. Menilek entered Harar in triumph. The emirate was turned into a province governed by his cousin, *Dajjach* (later *Ras*) Makonnen Walda-Mikael.

For nearly seven years afterwards, there was no significant territorial extension of Menilek's empire. This is probably attributable to the fact that he was too engrossed in the two overriding questions of imperial succession and Italian colonial ambitions. In 1894, however, the powerful southern kingdom Walayta was incorporated after one of the bloodiest campaigns of the whole process of expansion. *Kawa* (King) Tona had come to power on a tide of popular support as a result of his rejection of his predecessor's advice to submit, and led Walayta resistance. The proverbial fertility of the region was alluring to Menilek's troops in the wake of the Great Famine of 1888 to 1892, which covered large parts of Ethiopia. Tona's instigation of the Kullo and the Konta peoples, to the west of Walayta, to rise against Menilek's authority added fuel to the confrontation. Menilek personally led the campaign. Accompanying him were a number of his generals who were to be prominent at Adwa two years later: *Ras* Mikael of Wallo, *Fitawrari* Gabayyahu, *Liqa Makwas* Abata Bwayalaw and *Dajjach* Balcha. *Ras* Walda-Giyorgis and Abba Jifar II of Jimma,

2.10 Kawa *Tona, the last king of Walayta, defeated in 1894 by a force led by Emperor Menilek II*

rulers of adjoining provinces, also took part. In the face of such a formidable array of forces, Walayta resistance collapsed, and a veritable massacre followed. In the words of the eyewitness J.G. Vanderheym: 'One had the feeling of witnessing some kind of infernal hunting where human beings rather than animals served as game' (Vanderheym, 181). Tona's refusal to surrender aggravated the human tragedy. The campaign came to a merciful end when he was finally wounded, captured, and brought to Addis Ababa.

The story of the incorporation of Kafa three years later paralleled the Walayta experience in terms of the human cost. For over a decade, the ancient kingdom had defied the claims for suzerainty first of Gojjam and then of Shawa. Expeditions aimed at subjugating the kingdom had been repulsed more than once. The final reckoning came in 1897. A strong force was organized under the leadership of *Ras* Walda-Giyorgis, designated governor of Kafa in advance, and including *Dajjach* Tasamma of Gore, in Illubabor, *Dajjach* Dames of Wallaga, Abba Jifar II of Jimma, and the rulers of Kullo and Konta – the last three serving as guides to break the intricate defence system of Kafa. The decisive assault of the four-pronged attack was made by *Ras* Walda-Giyorgis from the direction of Kullo, which was not as

65

2.11   Emperor Menilek II (centre, holding sceptre) and some of his nobles, including Dajjach *Balcha Safo (fourth from left),* Ras *Tasamma Nadaw (sixth from left),* Ras *Walda-Giyorgis Abboye (seventh from left), and* Ras *Abata Bwayalaw (fourth from right).*

strongly fortified as the Kafa–Jimma boundary. The despotic rule of *Tato* Gaki Sherocho, king of Kafa, had in any case rendered mass mobilization against the invading force difficult. After Walda-Giyorgis's triumphant entry into the capital city, Andaracha, the *tato* fled. For nine months, he remained a fugitive in his own kingdom. He was finally captured, fastened with silver chains of his own supply, and taken to Addis Ababa, the eleven-year-old capital of Shawa and of the Ethiopian empire, to spend the rest of his life in miserable captivity. *Ras* Walda-Giyorgis became the governor of Kafa, in fact as well as in name.

Also in 1897, *Ras* Makonnen, accompanied by *Dajjach* Jote and *Dajjach* Gabra-Egziabher, extended the frontiers of the Ethiopian empire in the Wallaga region by incorporating the sheikhdoms of Bela Shangul (Beni Shangul), Aqoldi (Asosa) and Khomosha. The collapse of Mahdist rule in the region was a strong inducement for Menilek to expand in that direction. There is even an unsubstantiated tradition that the Mahdist ruler of Sudan, the Khalifa Abdullahi, had invited Menilek to take over the region. The efforts of Abd al-Rahman Khojale of Bela Shangul to forge a united front among the regional sheikhs were unsuccessful. In spite of his outward show of solidarity, Sheikh Khojale al-Hasan, ruler of Asosa, began establishing secret links with *Ras* Makonnen, the leader of the expeditionary force, sending a liberal supply of gold to win his favours. The intelligence that he provided for Makonnen's force was instrumental in reversing the earlier successes of Abd al-Rahman. At the Battle

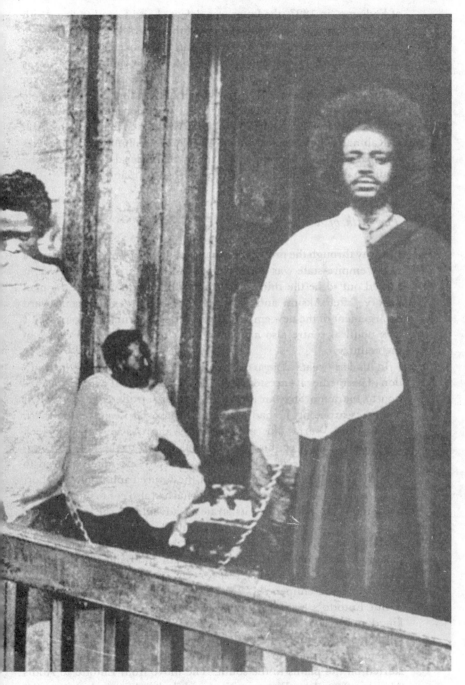

2.12 Tato *Gaki Sherocho, the last king of Kafa, in chains after his defeat in 1897 by a coalition of forces led by* Ras *Walda-Giyorgis*

of Fadogno, in 1897, the latter was defeated and forced to flee. With the defeat by Sheikh Khojale of Muhammad Wad-Mahmud of Khomosha, who had also chosen to fight, resistance in the region was broken. *Dajjach* Dames followed this up with a campaign as far as Famaka on the Sudan border. After a period of confinement in Addis Ababa, the three Muslim leaders (including Sheikh Khojale al-Hasan, who was found making what were considered dangerous contacts with the British in Sudan) were restored to their regions, Abd al-Rahman Khojale and Muhammad Wad-Mahmud with the titles of *dajjazmach* and *fitawrari* respectively; Khojale al-Hasan with the traditional title of sheikh, which he wished to maintain.

The birth of a capital

Midway through the process of expansion described above, the capital of the empire-state was born. Named Addis Ababa, New Flower, it turned out to be the third most important capital city in Ethiopian history, after Aksum and Gondar; and, because of the southward enlargement of the new empire, it was the southernmost capital. This new political centre also happened to be the geographical centre of the country.

In his early years as *negus* of Shawa, Menilek had followed the tradition of his medieval ancestors and ruled from different camps. In addition to the main Shawan town of Ankobar, on the edge of the Rift Valley escarpment, he had established camps at Leche, in northern Shawa, and Warra Illu, in southern Wallo. As he began to look southwards, however, his attention was drawn to the hills surrounding the future site of Addis Ababa. In 1881, he finally moved to Entotto (Dildila), the range north of the future capital, after a short sojourn west of the site, at Mount Wachacha (also confusingly known as Entotto). In addition to its strategic advantage, the area had for Menilek the attraction of having reputedly been the camp site of medieval kings. A sizeable settlement began to grow around the palace, with the churches of Saint Maryam and Saint Raguel on the eastern and western limits, respectively, rivalling one another for favour and pre-eminence.

But Entotto's historical importance as the centre of the Shawan kingdom was short-lived. In November 1886, four years after the first permanent structures had begun to be constructed at Entotto, a new settlement, destined to be the political centre of the empire, was started on the plains to the south. The move from Entotto to Addis Ababa, effected by Empress Taytu while her husband was on the Harar campaign, had many factors behind it. Foremost were the hot springs (Fel Weha), which had already been a regular resort of the

2.13 *Ankobar, capital of the Shawan kings until Negus Menilek moved to Entotto and then to Addis Ababa*

Entotto settlers because of their warmth and curative value. With the subjugation of the surrounding Oromo, the strategic value of Entotto had diminished. Moreover, its insufferable cold and the denudation of its forests, as well as the tiresome descents and ascents to and from Fel Weha, made the hilly settlement less and less attractive.

Although Addis Ababa came into existence in 1886, it did not become the capital of Menilek's empire until about 1892. The construction of the palace (called the *gebbi*) on an elevated site gave the growing settlement its primary nucleus. Saint George Church to the west formed not only the town's main religious centre but also its commercial centre, Arada. The nobility came to settle on the other hilltops of the emerging town, on land granted to them by the emperor as a reward for services. Round the *gebbi* of each member of the nobility clustered his dependants and followers, giving rise to the typical settlement pattern of the town, the *safar*, originally an encampment. Thus were born quarters like *Ras* Berru Safar, *Ras* Tasamma Safar and *Fitawrari* Habta-Giyorgis Safar. The settlements of the palace servants, generally located on the slopes, gave rise to such occupational areas as Saratagna Safar (the Workers' Quarters), Zabagna Safar (the Guards' Quarters) and Weha Senqu Safar (the

69

2.14   A view of Arada, the Addis Ababa market, 1935

Quarters of 'The Unprovisioned', an Imperial Army unit, said to be supplied only with water).

Many events and developments contributed to consolidating the position of Addis Ababa as capital of the Ethiopian empire-state. Of these, probably the most important was the Ethiopian victory at the Battle of Adwa in 1896. On the one hand, it marked the transition from the era of campaigning to that of settled civilian life. Most members of the nobility now began to settle in Addis Ababa and to build more or less permanent residences. On the other hand, with the growth in the prestige of Emperor Menilek, foreigners began to come and settle in Addis Ababa in increasingly large numbers. The legations had large estates carved out for them in the northern outskirts. The merchants and craftsmen settled at Arada.

The protests against moving made by the legations, who had already made some investment in buildings, and the importation of the eucalyptus tree were what saved Addis Ababa from suffering the same fate as Entotto. Beset by the perennial problem of wood, Menilek had seriously begun to consider moving his capital to Addis Alam, some 38 miles (60 km) to the west by the road built to Addis Ababa. Construction of a new palace had begun. With the abandonment of the project, the road became the first interurban road of Menilek's empire. The registration of urban land and the granting of land charters as of 1907 removed the air of impermanence and insecurity that had constantly hung over Addis Ababa. The long-awaited arrival of the railway from the French port of Djibouti, on the Gulf of Aden, in 1917, put the seal on Addis Ababa's future as the capital of Ethiopia.

Crisis in the socio-economic order: the 'Great Ethiopian Famine' 1888–1892

At a time when the geopolitical centre of the country was moving southwards, Ethiopia found herself in the grip of a famine with serious internal and external repercussions. The process of territorial expansion that has been described above was partly spurred on by this social cataclysm. Although the famine was most intense in the northern provinces, few areas in the empire escaped it. Nor was it confined to the Ethiopian region: it was evident in Sudan and East Africa as well. In the north, the social and economic dislocation that attended the famine facilitated the Italian advance to the highlands and the creation in 1890 of their colony of Eritrea. One reason for Menilek's failure to consummate the Adwa victory by pushing the Italians out of Eritrea was the acute problem of supplies that he faced. Even after

71

its immediate impact had died, the memory of the famine, known as *Kefu Qan* (Evil Days) in popular parlance, endured. It has survived to this day as a gauge to measure and compare the intensity of subsequent famines.

On the surface, the famine started as a result of the outbreak of a rinderpest epidemic triggered by Italian importation of infected cattle through Massawa. The consequent death of cattle (up to 90% in many areas, and up to 100% of personal possessions in some cases) deprived the peasant of his chief means of production. Drought and locust invasions wiped out what was left of the previous harvests. But the roots of the famine lay deeper in the social and political fabric of the country. The intermittent wars of the century had reduced the peasantry to the very edge of subsistence. Even the relatively more pacific collection of tribute left behind little surplus grain to tide over such moments of scarcity and deprivation.

The immediate consequence of the epidemic and drought was spiralling inflation in the prices of grain and cattle. This was inevitably followed by widespread starvation and death. There were some ingenious attempts to improvise. Hoes were used instead of ploughs, and donkeys, mules and horses in place of oxen. There were, too, some desperate efforts to survive. Food that was hitherto considered taboo was eaten. Some looked for grain in the excrement of cattle. Others ate the carcasses of animals, only to die painfully from the diseased meat. Still others resorted to the extreme of cannibalism. A few sought survival in enslavement. There were also those who, giving up all hope, committed suicide.

The measures taken at the official level were clearly inadequate to avert or alleviate the disaster. The first response of Menilek and Taytu was to enjoin their subjects to pray for divine intercession. When the famine refused to be daunted by this, Menilek admonished his subjects for not having prayed fervently enough. Doling out food to those who could manage to reach the royal residence was another measure. According to the chronicler Gabra-Sellase, the starving flocked to Entotto, then still the capital, from all 'the four corners'. Cattle from the newly incorporated provinces of Harar and Bale were also distributed, mostly to members of the nobility. Some hoarded grain was also confiscated for distribution to the famished population.

6. Resolution of the external challenge

Sometimes a year can make all the difference. In 1868, the Napier expeditionary force liberated the European captives of Tewodros, and withdrew from the country without even bothering to ensure the succession of a prince friendly to Britain. That was a telling, if silent, declaration of lack of interest. In 1869, the Suez Canal was opened, and suddenly the Red Sea region was invested with great strategic and commercial importance. European colonial powers rushed for possessions along the coast. Ultimately, the canal became too valuable to be left to the vagaries of internal Egyptian politics. The financial insolvency of Khedive Ismail's regime and the rise of an Egyptian nationalist movement prompted British occupation of the country in 1882.

This event had an ominous significance for Africa. It unleashed the famous scramble to partition the continent. As far as the British were concerned, their occupation of Egypt forced them to become almost paranoid about another waterway, the Nile; for Egypt was a barren desert without the Nile, a liability rather than an asset. Preventing the mortal enemy, France, from encroaching on the waters of the Nile became the primary objective of British imperialism. While the British were prepared to guard the White Nile themselves, they wanted someone to watch over the Blue Nile and its Ethiopian source and tributaries. This was the genesis of the Anglo-Italian collusion over Ethiopia: the Italians were desperate to control Ethiopia, and the British were ready to support them as long as they acted as a watchdog of British imperial interests.

Although there was to be no compromise on the vital issue of independence, Ethiopian policy at both the imperial and regional levels tended to encourage European penetration. From the time of Tewodros, Ethiopian rulers had sought European allies for a number of reasons. The first and most obvious was the need for European armaments, either imported or, as in the case of Tewodros, manufactured in Ethiopia. Encirclement by Muslim forces – Egypt – and the lack of an outlet to the sea were other prevalent themes of Ethiopian correspondence with Europe. Coupled with this was the naïve belief that, out of a sense of Christian solidarity, European powers would come to the aid of Ethiopia. Thus Tewodros concluded his fateful letter of 1862 to Queen Victoria with the words: 'You too feel my suffering, when I, a Christian, am oppressed by Muslims' (Rubenson, *King of Kings*, 48–9). The quest for an outlet to the sea, to have unrestricted access with the outside world, thus became the perennial preoccupation of Ethiopian rulers. In his circular of April 1891, Menilek expressed his hope for European support in this endeavour with characteristic diplomacy, writing that he had no plans to occupy the coast by force, but rather that he was counting on the goodwill of the European powers 'to help him to a port or two' – the last phrase marked by humour in the Amharic.

Internally, regional rulers sought external allies to subvert their imperial overlords and improve their own chances for the throne. Emperor Yohannes IV, as Kasa Mercha, collaborated with the

British against Tewodros in 1867–1868 to strengthen his bid for succession. Menilek engaged in correspondence of a dubious nature with the Egyptians, while Yohannes was poised in hostile confrontation with them. Less ambiguously and more fatefully, Menilek cultivated assiduously the friendship of the Italians, heedless of the warnings of Yohannes and undeterred by the bloody engagements in the north. The Italians reciprocated with even greater zeal. In Menilek they saw the perfect ally to subvert Emperor Yohannes from the rear. The irony of the whole situation was that, starting as the best of friends, Menilek and the Italians ended up as the worst of enemies. Although *Negus* Menilek appeared highly accommodating in their interests, the Italians found to their dismay that *Negusa Nagast* Menilek scarcely differed from *Negusa Nagast* Yohannes on the vital question of Ethiopian independence.

Menilek's contacts with the Italians can be said to have officially begun in 1876 with the coming of a geographical mission to Shawa, headed by Marquis Orazio Antinori. As the hinterland to Assab, their first coastal acquisition, Shawa represented a logical line for the extension of their interests. The mission itself was a good example of the interconnection between geographical exploration and colonial expansion which had been a characteristic feature of colonialism in Africa. In the agreement that was concluded, Menilek obtained an agent to procure arms for him from Europe, and the mission secured a station at Let Marafya, near Ankobar. In the following years, this post was to serve the Italians exceedingly well as a base for the gathering of intelligence.

It was with the coming of Count Pietro Antonelli in 1882, however, that the rather sporadic contacts assumed a deeper and more sustained character. It was to be Antonelli's fate to preside over both the climax and the nadir of Italy's relations with Menilek. His brainchild, the Treaty of Wechale (1889), was to mark the diplomatic watershed of his career, marking at the same time the high point of friendship between the two parties and the beginning of the hostilities that inexorably led to Adwa. The path to Wechale was itself marked by two treaties which could be regarded as its precursors. The first was signed on 21 May 1883. It provided for consular exchange, free movement of people, free trade and free propagation of religion. But the two most important provisions were found in Articles XII and XIII. Article XII gave Italian subjects extraterritorial rights, an anticipation of the Klobukowsky Treaty of 1908. Article XIII, envisaging the possibility of Shawan foreign contacts through the intermediary of the Italian consul at Assab, presaged the controversial Article XVII of the Wechale Treaty.

The second treaty, more exactly a convention, was signed in October 1887, in the wake of the Italian defeat at Dogali and amidst preparations for revenge. The Italians wanted at the very least Menilek's neutrality in the impending conflict with Emperor Yohannes. As a reward for this, Menilek was promised 5,000 Remington rifles. Both parties also made rather hollow-sounding pledges – Menilek not to use the arms against the Italians, the latter not to annex any Ethiopian territory.

The Treaty of Wechale, drafted by Antonelli and signed by the two parties in May 1889, in Menilek's current camp there, in Wallo, soon demonstrated how hollow indeed these pledges were destined to be. Article III granted the Italians considerable territory in the north. Not content with this, in a subsequent convention signed in Rome in October by *Dajjach* Makonnen Walda-Mikael, Menilek's cousin and now right-hand man, the Italians inserted the clause of 'effective occupation' in order to legitimize their subsequent expansion towards the Marab river. But the height of Italian colonial ambition was expressed in the Italian version of Article XVII, which bound Menilek to make all his foreign contacts through the agency of Italy, thereby reducing Ethiopia to the status of an Italian protectorate. (The Amharic version had made the use of the services of Italy optional.) In the eyes of Menilek, the role prescribed for Italy was little more than that of a glorified postman. Even as Shawan *negus* bidding for the throne, it is highly unlikely that he would have gone to the extent of seeking Italian protection. As *negusa nagast* of Ethiopia, which he had become by the time of the Treaty of Wechale, it would have been a clear case of political suicide. By virtue of this transformation of the status of Menilek, therefore, Article XVII in its Italian form could be said to have died before it was born.

For the Italians, things were much easier on the European front. With the exception of Russia, all the major powers recognized their protectorate claim on the basis of Article XVII. This was not surprising. An African chief surrendering his sovereignty to a European power was the norm rather than the exception. In the case of Victorian England, prompt recognition was dictated by self-interest as well. But the Italians knew that the issue could only be resolved in Ethiopia. To achieve their objective, they followed parallel if antithetical policies of persuasion in the south and subversion in the north. Antonelli and other emissaries tried hard but in vain to persuade Menilek to accept the Italian version of Article XVII of the Treaty of Wechale. His abrogation of the treaty in February 1893 dashed the last hope of the Italians to achieve their objective without resorting to arms.

The policy of subversion in the north, master-minded by the governor of Eritrea, Antonio Baldissera, had two facets: territorial encroachment and inciting the Tegrean princes to defect. The latter objective appeared to have been crowned with success with the Marab

2.15 Ras *Mangasha Yohannes, son of Emperor Yohannes IV, and hereditary ruler of Tegre from 1889-1898*

Convention of 6 December 1891, when the princes, headed by *Ras* Mangasha Yohannes, swore an oath of solidarity with the Italians. But the success was short-lived. In 1894, a large-scale revolt against their policy of land alienations was led by *Dajjach* Bahta Hagos of Akala Guzay, erstwhile ally of and arch-collaborator with the Italians, and sounded the death-knell of the policy of subversion. The rebellion was immediately followed by an armed clash between the Italians and *Ras* Mangasha, who had already formally submitted to Menilek. His example was to be followed by *Ras* Sebhat Aragawi and *Dajjach* Hagos Tafari, who turned against the Italians in the middle of the Adwa campaign.

The campaign of Adwa

By the end of 1895, both diplomacy and subversion had thus failed to secure for the Italians their colonial objective. Only the military option remained. The Italians took that option in October by crossing the Marab river and occupying Addigrat. In the following weeks,

Menilek mobilized a force of some 100,000 troops and, accompanied by his wife Empress Taytu, marched north to meet them. His army was remarkable not only for its size but also as an eloquent demonstration of national unity. There was scarcely any region in Ethiopia which had not sent a contingent, a state of affairs partially facilitated by the incorporation of the southern regions into Menilek's empire.

The first military engagement took place on 7 December 1895 at Amba Alage, a natural fortress near the southernmost point the Italians had reached, and already occupied by a force led by Major Toselli. The engagement was a unilateral attack by the vanguard force of the Ethiopian army. While Makonnen Walda-Mikael, now *Ras* Makonnen, was negotiating with the Italians for their peaceful evacuation, *Fitawrari* Gabayyahu, undeterred by his own illness, led his men in a literally uphill struggle against the well-entrenched Italians. The Italians were routed; their commander was among the casualties.

The second phase of the campaign was as protracted and uneventful as that at the Battle of Amba Alage was concentrated and dramatic. The Italians had built a rather formidable fort at Maqale, about 45 miles (72 km) to the north, to which some of the survivors of Amba Alage had fled. The Ethiopians laid siege to Maqale, denying the Italians access to supplies and reinforcements. The problem of water became particularly acute for the besieged. The inconclusive confrontation was also putting a strain on Menilek's supplies. Finally, a settlement was negotiated whereby the besieged were allowed to come out and rejoin their compatriots. They were even provided with mules and pack-animals. This magnanimous gesture, which was not altogether popular with the Ethiopian troops, appears to have been dictated by the hope that Menilek still entertained of a peaceful resolution of the conflict.

The gesture did not impress the Italians, who continued to put forward impossible conditions for peace. Menilek marched to Adwa, and waited for the Italians to come out of their fortifications at Addigrat and Entticho, respectively about 37 miles (60 km) and 17 miles (28 km) to the north-east of his troops, whom shortage of supplies was making it more and more difficult to hold together. In consequence, fed with false hopes of an easy victory by the Eritrean agents of Menilek, the Italian General Oreste Baratieri decided to launch a surprise attack. On the night of 29 February 1896, he made a three-column advance against the Ethiopian positions. News of his march had preceded him, and was greeted with great relief by the Ethiopians, who were waiting eagerly for a decisive engagement.

The Ethiopian troops were commanded by *Ras* Mikael of Wallo, *Ras* Makonnen Walda-Mikael, *Ras* Mangasha Yohannes and *Negus* Takla-Haymanot. Facing them were Italian columns led by Generals

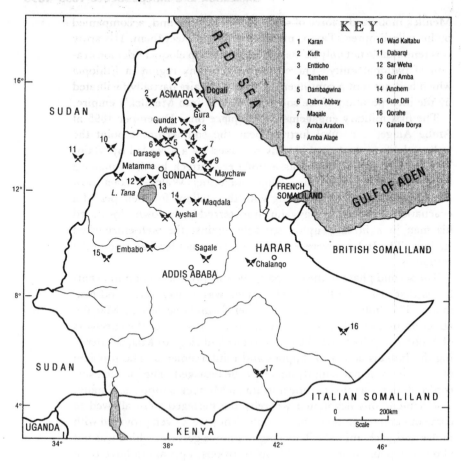

KEY

1	Karan	10	Wad Kaltabu
2	Kufit	11	Dabarqi
3	Entticho	12	Sar Weha
4	Tamben	13	Gur Amba
5	Dambagwina	14	Anchem
6	Dabra Abbay	15	Gute Dili
7	Maqale	16	Qorahe
8	Amba Aradom	17	Ganale Dorya
9	Amba Alage		

5. *Major battle sites of the nineteenth and twentieth centuries*

Vittorio Dabormida, Giuseppe Arimondi and Matteo Albertone. The root of Italian disaster lay in the failure of the three columns to co-ordinate their action. Through faulty map-reading, Albertone's brigade found itself isolated, the target of the combined fury of the Ethiopian troops. Trying to come to the rescue of Albertone, Dabormida made a fatal swerve to the right instead of to the left. The outcome was that, although Ethiopian losses were not negligible, the Italians were routed. By midday of 1 March, the Battle of Adwa was practically over. Italian colonial ambition was dead. Independent Ethiopia survived.

Sources, Chapters 1 and 2

Note. The BA and MA theses cited in the references are available in the Institute of Ethiopian Studies (IES) and/or in the Department of History, Addis Ababa University (AAU), formerly Haile Sellassie I University (HSIU).

Abbas Haji. 'The History of Arssi (1880-1935).' BA thesis (AAU, History, 1982).

Abeles, Marc. 'In Search of the Monarch: Introduction of the State among the Gamo of Ethiopia', in Donald Crummey and C.C. Stewart, eds., *Modes of Production in Africa. The Pre-Colonial Era*. London, 1981.

Ahmed Zekaria, Bahru Zewde and Taddese Beyene, eds. *Proceedings of the International Symposium on the Centenary of Addis Ababa*. IES, AAU, 1987.

Altaye Alaro. 'The Political History of Wolayita in the Eighteenth and Nineteenth Centuries.' BA thesis (AAU, History, 1982).

Asnake Ali. 'Aspects of the Political History of Wallo: 1872-1916.' MA thesis (AAU, History, 1983).

Atieb Ahmed Dafalla. 'Sheikh Khojele al Hassan and Bela-Shangul 1825-1938.' BA thesis (HSIU, History, 1973).

Bahru Zewde. 'The Aymallal Gurage in the Nineteenth Century: A Political History', *Transafrican Journal of History* II, 2 (1972).

Bates, Darrell. *The Abyssinian Difficulty. The Emperor Theodorus and the Magdala Campaign 1867-68*. Oxford, 1979.

Caulk, Richard. 'The Occupation of Harar: January 1887', *Journal of Ethiopian Studies* IX, 2 (1971).

———. 'Religion and the State in Nineteenth-Century Ethiopia', *Journal of Ethiopian Studies* X, 1 (1972).

———. 'Territorial Competition and the Battle of Embabo', *Journal of Ethiopian Studies* XIII, 1 (1975).

———. 'Yohannes IV, the Mahdists and the Colonial Partition of Northeast Africa', *Transafrican Journal of History* I, 2 (1971).

Crummey, Donald. *Priests and Politicians: Protestant and Catholic Missionaries in Orthodox Ethiopia 1830-1868*. Oxford, 1972.

———. 'Tewodros as Reformer and Modernizer', *Journal of African History* X, 3 (1969).

———. 'The Violence of Tewodros', *Journal of Ethiopian Studies* IX, 2 (1971).

Darkwah, R.H. Kofi. *Shewa, Menilek and the Ethiopian Empire 1813-1889*. London, 1975.

Dye, William M. *Moslem Egypt and Christian Abyssinia*. New York, 1880.

Erlich, Haggai. *Ethiopia and Eritrea during the Scramble for Africa: A Political Biography of Ras Alula 1875-1897*. East Lansing, 1982.

Fekadu Begna. 'A Tentative History of Wallo, 1855-1908.' BA thesis (HSIU, History, 1972).

Gabra-Sellase. *Tarika Zaman za Dagmawi Menilek Negusa Nagast za Ityopya* (A History of the Period of Menilek II, Emperor of Ethiopia). Addis Ababa, 1959 Ethiopian Calendar.

Garretson, Peter. 'A History of Addis Ababa from its Foundation in 1886 to 1910.' PhD thesis

Unification and Independence 1855-1896

(University of London, School of Oriental and African Studies, 1974).

Getachew Fule. 'The Kingdom of Janjero: A Historical Survey to 1894.' BA thesis (AAU, History, 1985).

Girma-Selassie Asfaw and David Appleyard. *The Amharic Letters of Emperor Theodore of Ethiopia to Queen Victoria and Her Special Envoy*. Oxford, 1979.

Girma-Selassie Asfaw and Richard Pankhurst. *Tax Records and Inventories of Emperor Tewodros of Ethiopia (1855-1868)*. University of London, School of Oriental and African Studies, 1979.

Guluma Gemeda. 'Gomma and Limmu: the Process of State Formation among the Oromo in the Gibe Region, *c*. 1750-1889.' MA thesis (AAU, History, 1984).

Heruy Walda-Sellase. *Ya Ityopya Tarik* (A History of Ethiopia) (incomplete bound copy of galley-proofs, *c*. 1936). IES, AAU.

Holland, T.J., and Hozier, Henry M. *Record of the Expedition to Abyssinia*. 2 vols. London, 1870. *The Journals of C.W. Isenberg and J.L. Krapf*. (New impression) London, 1968.

Lange, Werner J. *History of the Southern Gonga (Southwestern Ethiopia)*. Wiesbaden, 1982.

Legesse Gebeyehu. 'The Conquest of the Kingdom of Kaffa.' BA thesis (HSIU, History, 1971).

Mangestu Lamma. *Matshafa Tezeta za Alaqa Lamma Haylu Walda-Tarik* (A Book of Reminiscences of *Alaqa* Lamma Haylu Walda-Tarik). Addis Ababa, 1959 Ethiopian Calendar.

Marcus, Harold. *The Life and Times of Menelik II. Ethiopia 1844-1913*. Oxford, 1975.

Muhammad Hasan. 'The Relation between Harar and the Surrounding Oromo between 1800-1887.' BA thesis (HSIU, History, 1973).

Orent, Amnon. 'Refocusing on the History of Kafa Prior to 1897: A Discussion of Political Processes', *African Historical Studies* (Boston, USA) III, 2 (1970).

Pankhurst, Richard. 'The Great Ethiopian Famine of 1888-1892: A New Assessment', *Journal of the History of Medicine and Allied Sciences* XXI, 2 and 3 (1966).

Parkyns, Mansfield. *Life in Abyssinia*. (New impression) London, 1966.

Plowden, Walter. *Travels in Abyssinia and the Galla Country*. London, 1868.

Rubenson, Sven. *King of Kings Tewodros of Ethiopia*. Addis Ababa, 1966.

———. *The Survival of Ethiopian Independence*. London, 1976.

———. *Wichale XVII: The Attempt to Establish a Protectorate over Ethiopia*. Addis Ababa, 1964.

Tekalign Welde Mariam. 'Slavery and the Slave Trade in the Kingdom of Jimma (ca. 1800-1935).' MA thesis (AAU, History, 1984).

Triulzi, Alessandro. *Salt, Gold and Legitimacy: Prelude to the History of a No-Man's-Land, Bela Shangul, Wallagga, Ethiopia (ca. 1800-1898)*. Naples, 1981.

Vanderheym, J. *Une expédition avec le negous Ménélik: vingt mois en Abyssinie*. Paris, 1896.

Worku Nida. 'The Revivalist Movement of Hassan Enjamo.' BA thesis (AAU, History, 1984).

Zanab. *The Chronicle of King Theodore*, ed. Enno Littmann. Princeton, 1902.

Zergaw Asfera. 'Some Aspects of Historical Development in "Amhara, Wallo", ca. 1700-1815.' BA thesis (HSIU, History, 1973).

Zewde Gabre-Sellassie. *Yohannes IV of Ethiopia: A Political Biography*. Oxford, 1975.

3

From Adwa to Maychaw 1896–1935

1. The historical significance of Adwa

Few events in the modern period have brought Ethiopia to the attention of the world as has the victory at Adwa. As a counter-current to the sweeping tide of colonial domination in Africa, it shocked some as it encouraged others. It forced observers, politicians and businessmen to reassess their positions. George F.H. Berkeley, the pro-Italian British historian of the campaign, provides us with an example of such a reassessment:

From the broader standpoint of politics and history, it seems possible that it [the Battle of Adwa] heralds the rise of a new power in Africa – we are reminded that the natives of that continent may yet become a military factor worthy of our closest attention. The suggestion has even been made – absurd as it appears at present – that this is the first revolt of the Dark Continent against domineering Europe.

(Berkeley, viii)

The racial dimension was what lent Adwa particular significance. It was a victory of blacks over whites. Adwa thus anticipated by almost a decade the equally shattering experience to the whites of the Japanese victory over Russia in 1905.

The symbolic weight of the victory of Adwa was greater in areas where white domination of blacks was most extreme and marked by overt racism, that is, in southern Africa and the United States of America. To the blacks of these countries, victorious Ethiopia became a beacon of independence and dignity. The biblical Ethiopia, which had already inspired a widespread movement of religious separatism known as Ethiopianism, now assumed a more cogent and palpable reality. Nor was this feeling of identification with Ethiopia limited to times of glory. Forty years later, in its hour of distress, black solidarity with Ethiopia was remarkable for its breadth and depth, ranging from fund-raising to the flourishing of a number of 'Abyssinian' and 'Coptic' churches. A dramatic example of such identification was a church in the United States of America which came to be known as 'the Coptic Ethiopian Orthodox Church of Abyssinia'. Among the campaigners for Ethiopia's cause were such emerging leaders of Africa as Jomo Kenyatta of Kenya and Kwame Nkrumah of the Gold Coast (later Ghana). They represented the bridge between the early days of pan-Africanism, which was partially inspired by Adwa, and its later concretization in the Organization of African Unity (OAU), established in 1963 in the very country where the Adwa victory was scored.

Ironically, for one black country nearer home, Sudan, Adwa entailed dependence rather than independence. The Ethiopian victory was disastrous not only for the Italians but also for the British, who had counted all along on the Italians establishing themselves in Ethiopia and barring the eastern approaches of the Nile to the French. Adwa reopened the question of the Nile. With Sudan under Mahdist rule and Ethiopia independent (or, as the British assumed, open to French expansion), the British position in Egypt became perilous. That was why they came to abandon the policy of wait-and-see, which they had adopted with regard to Sudan, following their failure to stop the independence movement at its start, and launched an expedition against the Mahdists in March 1896. Some two years later, Omdurman, the Mahdist capital, fell, and Sudan became an 'Anglo-Egyptian condominium', a legalistic term which in simple language meant a British colony.

On the other hand, it was on the question of the Nile and Sudan that Emperor Menilek's diplomatic genius was most amply demonstrated. British apprehensions of French expansion towards the Upper Nile did not prove to be groundless. Soon after Adwa, the French began to execute their grandiose plan of a trans-African empire by sending two major expeditions from west and east Africa; they were scheduled to meet on the Nile. The expedition from west Africa was led by Jean-Baptiste Marchand. That from Djibouti was led by the Marquis de Bonchamps and was launched subsequent to a convention with Menilek, who had promised to give logistic support to the mission. In actual fact Menilek proved to be lukewarm in his support. He was playing an elaborate game of furthering his own territorial interests in the west without antagonizing any one of the three powers involved: Britain, France and Mahdist Sudan. To the Khalifa Abdullahi, the Mahdist ruler, Menilek sent fervent letters protesting African solidarity, but stopping short of any entangling commitments. In the treaty of friendship that he signed with the British in

May 1897, he agreed to impose an arms blockade on the Mahdist state. On the other hand, taking advantage of the Mahdist disarray, and with the possible connivance of the Khalifa, he extended his sway over the Asosa and Bela Shangul region. Accompanying the de Bonchamps mission, *Dajjach* (the future *Ras*) Tasamma Nadaw of Gore established Ethiopian authority in the Baro river region as far as Nasir, just short of the confluence of the Sobat river (as the Baro river is known in Sudan) with the White Nile. Ultimately, in 1898, the French and the British were left to sort out the question of the Nile at the White Nile village of Fashoda (now Kodok), in what turned out to be one of the most tense diplomatic confrontations before World War One: briefly, the two powers faced one another in hostility. The tension subsided when the French forces withdrew, leaving the British to establish their ascendancy over the vital waterway.

In the final analysis, Adwa left its deepest impact on the major participants in the war and above all on Ethiopia. In Italy, news of the defeat was greeted with an ambivalent mixture of jubilation and of anxiety, the former for the defeat of Italian colonialism, the latter for the prisoners. Shouts of 'Viva Menilek!' were heard in the streets of Rome and in other major Italian cities. Nearly 100,000 people signed a petition calling for Italy's total withdrawal from Africa. The defeat was a vindication of the anti-colonialist lobby in Italian politics. The architect of the disastrous Italian colonial policy, Francesco Crispi, fell, and was replaced by Antonio Starabba, Marchese di Rudini, who started his government with a renunciation of the policy of expansion. Another casualty of the débâcle was General Baratieri, commander of the Italian troops at Adwa. Only six months earlier, he had been compared to Giuseppe Garibaldi, one of the leaders of the Italian struggle for independence and unification in the 1860s, and given a standing ovation in the Italian parliament. Now Baratieri was brought to trial for his allegedly inept command.

The repatriation of the thousands of Italian prisoners captured at Adwa preoccupied the new Italian regime. To achieve this, it even managed to persuade Pope Leo XIII to write a letter to Menilek in May 1896 urging clemency. Menilek responded by making the release of the prisoners dependent on the signing of a peace treaty. 'In the circumstances,' he wrote back, 'my duty as king and father of my people dissuades me from sacrificing the sole guarantee of peace that I have with me' (Rossetti, 196). In the meantime, the prisoners, who had come to settle in what came to be known as Talian Safar (Italian Quarters) in western Addis Ababa, were treated with consideration. Some were also usefully employed in the construction of roads and bridges in the growing capital of the empire.

Addis Ababa gave its name to the treaty that was finally signed by the two parties on 26 October 1896. The main provisions of the treaty

83

were the abrogation of the Treaty of Wechale and Italian recognition of the absolute independence of Ethiopia. The question of the delimitation of the boundary between Ethiopia and the Italian colony of Eritrea was deferred for future negotiation. Until then the situation before the outbreak of hostilities (*status quo ante*) was to be accepted by both. The treaty was followed by a convention providing for the repatriation of the Italian prisoners.

Thus, eight months after the war, Menilek had been able to achieve more than Yohannes had been able to do in eight years after the Battles of Gundat and Gura. Moreover, viewed in the African context, the Ethiopians had won recognition of their independence by force of arms. They had stemmed the tide of colonialism. The future of Ethiopia became different from that of the rest of Africa. This had its impact not only on the political economy of the country, but also on the psychology of the people.

Economically, the full-scale assault of imperial capital that was seen elsewhere in Africa was lacking in Ethiopia. In the end, the balance-sheet may not have been in Ethiopia's favour. Radicals ranging from Gabra-Heywat Baykadagn in the early twentieth century to the unsuccessful coup-makers of 1960 bemoaned the backwardness of independent Ethiopia, compared with colonial Africa. In terms of national psychology, however, the Adwa victory has continued to instil in successive generations of Ethiopians a deep sense of national pride and spirited national independence. This feeling was momentarily dented by the success of Italian arms in 1936, but was quickly restored, thanks to the Ethiopian Resistance Movement and the short duration – five years – of the Italian Occupation. Ultimately, too, the fact that Ethiopia underwent what has generally been recognized as a unique process of revolutionary transformation in the 1970s has its origins in the separate destiny it came to follow as a result of Adwa.

The boundary delimitation agreement between Ethiopia and the Italian colony of Eritrea was concluded in 1900, when the Marab river became the official boundary between the two territories. What the Italians had occupied by force of arms thus obtained legal sanction. This has remained probably the most serious shortcoming of the victory at Adwa, and of Menilek's policy as far as Ethiopia is concerned. Adwa failed to resolve Ethiopia's centuries-old quest for an outlet to the sea. The quest had become particularly acute in the modern period, as evidenced by the letters and activities of Tewodros and Yohannes. Paradoxically, Menilek, architect of the largest empire ever built in the Ethiopian region, presided over a series of events which barred it completely from the sea. His successors were forced to seek in vain accommodation with the adjacent colonial powers for an outlet to the sea: the British were approached for Zeila, the Italians for Assab, and the French for a part of what is now Djibouti territory.

The problem was solved only with the liberation of Eritrea in 1941 and its federation with Ethiopia eleven years later. Moreover, throughout the early twentieth century, the Italians were to use Eritrea as a base for the subversion of Ethiopia. In 1935, it became the main launching post for their aggression. Finally, the roots of the problem of secession, which long bedevilled Ethiopia's peace and security, are to be sought rather than anywhere else in the creation of the Italian colony.

In other respects, too, Ethiopia's post-Adwa independence was not as absolute as tends to be assumed. Politically, it was circumscribed by the influence that the European powers came to exert over Ethiopia; they concluded agreements over and in spite of Ethiopia, defining and reconciling their respective interests. The Tripartite Agreement of 1906 between Britain, France and Italy, and the Anglo-Italian understanding of 1925 (signed two years after Ethiopia's admission into the League of Nations) are two examples of European high-handedness. Ethiopia's admission to the League was itself a subject of prolonged debate. Ethiopia, though independent, was deemed not yet civilized enough to join the community of free nations. On the grounds of the rampancy of slavery and the slave-trade, an arms embargo continued to be imposed on the country. The Klobukowsky Treaty (so named after the French minister who signed it with Menilek in 1908), giving foreign residents in Ethiopia extraterritorial rights and fiscal privileges, represented a serious curtailment of the sovereign rights of an independent state.

Economically, too, Ethiopia found itself under the shadow of the same imperialism that was penetrating the colonial African economy. The only difference was that the relatively more independent Ethiopian political structure limited such penetration. What evolved was a sort of semi-colonial relationship between Ethiopia and Europe, on the same lines as it evolved in such places as Turkey and Persia (now Iran). By means of concessions and trade, European capital tried to achieve the economic gains that the Adwa victory at first appeared to have denied it.

2. The socio-economic order

Mode of surplus appropriation

Two major themes dominated Ethiopian history in the nineteenth century – the process of unification and the repulse of foreign incursion. Adwa marked the consummation of both. Twentieth-century Ethiopian society was shaped by their legacy. Unification broadened

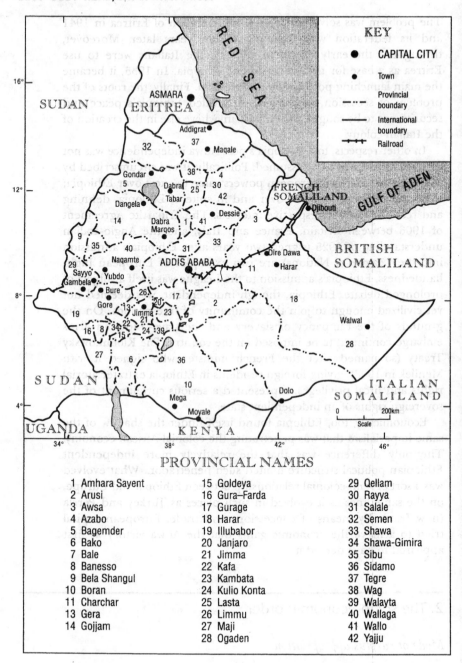

KEY

● CAPITAL CITY

● Town

–·–·– Provincial boundary

——— International boundary

+—+—+ Railroad

PROVINCIAL NAMES

1 Amhara Sayent	15 Goldeya	29 Qellam
2 Arusi	16 Gura–Farda	30 Rayya
3 Awsa	17 Gurage	31 Salale
4 Azabo	18 Harar	32 Semen
5 Bagemder	19 Illubabor	33 Shawa
6 Bako	20 Janjaro	34 Shawa-Gimira
7 Bale	21 Jimma	35 Sibu
8 Banesso	22 Kafa	36 Sidamo
9 Bela Shangul	23 Kambata	37 Tegre
10 Boran	24 Kulio Konta	38 Wag
11 Charchar	25 Lasta	39 Walayta
13 Gera	26 Limmu	40 Wallaga
14 Gojjam	27 Maji	41 Wallo
	28 Ogaden	42 Yajju

6. Ethiopia, 1935
(adapted from Margery Perham, The Government of Ethiopia, *London,*

1969, and Corrado Zoli, Etiopa d'oggi, *Rome 1935)*

the economic basis of power of the Ethiopian ruling class. Adwa determined the mode of Ethiopia's interaction with the outside world.

In the nineteenth century, as indeed also in earlier centuries of Ethiopian history, the economic basis of political power was tribute and surplus labour. Both were extracted from the peasant, who held his land (*rest*) by genealogical descent, and who was known as *gabbar* (after *geber*, tribute). The tributes were of a diverse nature. The main tribute was the land-tax or rent. Its value varied according to the degree of cultivation of the land (cultivated, *lam*; uncultivated, *taf*; semi-cultivated, *lam-taf*). Next came the tithe, *asrat*, which, as both the English and the Amharic words indicate, amounted to a tenth of the peasant's harvest. In addition to these two tributes, the *gabbar* was obliged to supply provisions, *maten* and *dergo*, for officials and visitors passing through his district. He had to provide firewood for his overlord, known as *malkagna* or *shalaqa* (representative or commander), twice or thrice a year. He made available the honey (*mar*) that was so essential to make *taj* (mead, hydromel) for the ruling class. He was also expected to express his joy by offering 'gifts' at the appointment of a new governor, his promotion or decoration, or the birth of a son to him.

The ruling class appropriated not only surplus product from the *gabbar* but also surplus labour. The chief expression of this forced labour or corvée was farming on state or governor's land (*hudad*). This generally took about a third of the *gabbar*'s labour time. The *gabbar* also ground grain for the *malkagna*. He was engaged in the construction of granaries and fences for the governor or the *malkagna*. He was custodian of any state prisoner, with liability to take his place if a prisoner escaped. He also provided transport service (*elf*), carrying personal effects of the governor or an official in times of peace and provisions in times of war.

Menilek's expansion to the south, west and east was doubly significant. On the one hand, it eased the congestion in the *rest* lands of the north by providing new areas of settlement. Secondly, it transposed the *gabbar–malkagna* relations to most of the newly incorporated regions. The areas that were spared this imposition were those that had peacefully submitted to Menilek and had thus managed to retain some degree of autonomy. A fixed annual tribute (*qurt geber*) was imposed on the province as a whole, and it was collected by the governor and delivered to the emperor in Addis Ababa with considerable pomp and ceremony. Jimma Abba Jifar, Leqa Naqamte, Leqa Qellam, Asosa and Bela Shangul, Awsa in Afar territory and Gubba in western Gojjam were provinces that fell into this category. The annual *qurt geber* of Abba Jifar II, for instance, was valued at 29,065 thalers (Mahtama-Sellase, 165).

The other provinces came under the jurisdiction of Menilek's **87**

3.1   A gabbar *and his son in north-eastern Shawa*

generals, providing them with the source for both their wealth and
their military strength. The governorship of a province was generally
given to whoever played a prominent role in its incorporation. Thus,
Ras Walda-Giyorgis Abboye got Kafa, *Dajjach* Tasamma got Illubabor, *Dajjach* Dames got Wallaga (that is, Arjo in the south-east and
Horro-Gudru in the north-east), and *Fitawrari* Habta-Giyorgis
received Borana in the extreme south, as well as Jebat and Mecha
in western Shawa. Likewise, Harar became a hereditary fief of the
family of *Ras* Makonnen Walda-Mikael. Officials and retainers of the
governor were then assigned a number of *gabbar* commensurate with
their rank. This is what came to be known as the *quter gabbar* system
(*quter*, number; not to be confused with the *qurt geber*). The number
of *gabbar* assigned to a retainer or official ranged from 5 to 100, depen-
ding on his rank and status. These *gabbar* paid tribute and rendered
labour services similar to the ones described above. The southern
farmer, who was now transformed into a *gabbar*, generally shared with
his northern counterpart a lineage system of land-ownership which
gave him usufructuary right over the land. At the outset and theore-
tically, this right was not interfered with. But, in the course of a
decade or two, forces emerged which seriously curtailed it.

One of the forces which had a profound impact on the systems of
land tenure in the south was the institution of land measurement at
the turn of the century. This was known as the *qalad*, after the rope

88

3.2   Foreign visitors receiving dergo, *the provisions peasants were compelled to supply by royal order*

used to measure land. Although land measurement had had a relatively long history in Bagemder, in north-western Ethiopia, it is in conjunction with the creation of Menilek's empire-state that it came to have wider application. While land measurement was prevalent in Shawa and its environs, many other provinces were affected as well. In Wallaga, for example, the measurement process which started in 1910 resulted in the appropriation by the state of three-quarters of the land. Peasants who had tilled the land under another lineage system of ownership known in Wallaga as *qabiye* found themselves forced to buy their own land. Failure to do so reduced them to the status of tenancy. In Walayta, some of the common lands were appropriated through the *qalad* and given out to the church for its maintenance (as *samon*) and to individuals.

A major objective that land measurement was designed to achieve was facilitating taxation. The measured land was divided into *lam*, *lam-taf* and *taf*. These terms denoted the degree of cultivation and human settlement, not, as is commonly assumed, the fertility of the soil. *Lam* land paid the highest and *taf* the lowest rate of tax. As the former category of land tended to be occupied mostly by peasants, the burden of taxation thus fell most heavily on them. In addition to taxation, registration tended to promote the twin processes of private ownership and land sale. In both northern and southern Ethiopia, traditional land tenure had had a communal character, with peasants

89

3.3   Dajjach *Dames Nasibu, later* Ras, *governor of Wallaga*

enjoying only usufructuary rights over the land. In the twentieth century, however, a steady process of privatization set in, with implications of sale and mortgage. Perhaps the most dramatic case of land
sale in the early twentieth century was that of *Dajjach* (later *Ras*) Berru
Walda-Gabr'el in Arsi. On a large tract of land given him by
Menilek, Berru forced the peasants either to buy the plots they were
farming or to become his tenants, giving him a quarter of their
harvests. Those who could afford to buy the land (at the rate of 30
Maria Theresa thalers per *gasha*, about forty hectares, of *lam* land) still
remained Berru's *gabbar*.

It was also the *qalad* system which enabled the state to appropriate
large areas of land either for its own benefit or for that of individuals
and institutions it wished to reward. The pattern of land tenure in
the twentieth century was largely determined by this policy. The local
ruler, generally referred to as the *balabbat*, retained from a sixth to
a third of the land – often erroneously characterized as *siso* (third).
The land still kept by the peasants, and subject to payment of tribute
and rendering of labour services, was known as *gabbar* land. The rest
was largely at the disposal of the state. In the old tradition of the unity
of church and state, the church was given *samon* land. Government
officials were granted *madarya*, land in lieu of salary. There were further types of land tenure which catered to the specific needs of the

3.4   Ras *Berru Walda-Gabr'el, Minister of War after the death of*
       Fitawrari *Habta-Giyorgis in 1926 and a Shawan noble noted for*
       his riches and ostentatious consumption

palace, such as *baldaras* and *warra gannu* for the upkeep of its horses
and cattle, respectively. Similarly, owners of what was known as
gendabal land rendered a host of services to the state in times both of
war and of peace. Large tracts of land also became the property, as
ganagab or *madbet* (literally, kitchen), of members of the royal family
and were administered by a representative (*meslane*). These had the
lands farmed by means of compulsory labour, and sent the harvest to
their patrons.

   The *balabbat*, mediating between the peasant and the state, played
an important role in the evolution of the tributary relationship. The
siso in effect symbolized their intermediary role in the whole exploitative system. It was the village chief, *abba qoro*, who implemented the
land measurement policy in Wallaga. The assignment of *quter gabbar*
in Harar was also effected through the agency of officials named the
damin and the *garad*, subordinate to the *damin*. On a higher level,
there was also the case of the rulers of Leqa Naqamte, who developed
their own mechanism for surplus extraction by imposing a number of
taxes, including the tithe, on the peripheral regions. Ultimately, the
Wallaga aristocracy was to prove the most successful of the southern
élite in integrating itself into the Ethiopian ruling class. It is this
reality which reinforces the point that the class basis of exploitation
and oppression was as important as the ethnic one.

In spite of the multiplicity of tenure described above, the basic mechanism of surplus extraction was the *gabbar-malkagna* or (as came to be generally the case in the south) the *gabbar-naftagna* relationship. This was also the focal point of class contradiction. *Gabbar* reaction to exactions from his overlord was varied, including flight from his plot, petitions to the central government and armed uprisings, particularly in times of crisis at the political centre. The cause of the *gabbar* was ardently championed by the progressive Ethiopian intellectuals of the early twentieth century, who began to agitate for reform. The situation even gave rise to what one may call 'colonialist revolutionaries', Europeans who resented the frustration of capitalist penetration that the debilitation of the peasantry through the *gabbar* system had entailed, and who urged a fundamental overhaul of Ethiopian society. *The Times* of London on 18 April 1931 called the *gabbar* system a far worse evil than slavery'. The first group, the Ethiopian intellectuals, aspired to what we may call national capitalist development on the Japanese model; the Europeans aimed at dependency capitalism of the colonial type.

The relatively more progressive elements of the feudal ruling class also sought to reconstitute feudalism on a new and more solid foundation. The series of measures undertaken first by *Lej* Iyyasu, Menilek's grandson and successor (r. 1913-1916, officially; in fact, 1911-1916), and then by *Ras* Tafari Makonnen in the 1920s, tended not only to buttress private property but also to release the productive potential of rural society by minimizing the wastefulness of the system. Iyyasu, for instance, forbade the confiscation of property as a penalty for embezzlement, as was hitherto the custom. He also tried to reduce the waste entailed by the prevalent system of assessment of harvest before the collection of *asrat*, with the attendant delays in harvesting when the assessors failed to come on time. Tafari reinforced the measure against confiscation, and took further steps to regularize the collection of *asrat*. Lastly, in May 1935, after he had become Emperor Hayla-Sellase in 1930, he issued a decree abolishing corvée and the tax in honey (*mar geber*). A high point in feudal reform was reached with the institution in May 1935 of fixed tax (*qurt geber*) of 30 Birr per *gasha*. But the abolition of the whole *gabbar* system had to await the post-1941 era, following the end of the Italian occupation.

Labour for the ruling class came not only from the *gabbar* but also from the slave. The difference between the two was that the former was central to the whole system of production. The latter's role was invariably limited to providing service in the household. One of the few places where slaves were involved in the process of production was in the estates of Abba Jifar II in Jimma. Ultimately, however, the significance of both *gabbar* and slave for the ruling class was in terms of consumption, rather than circulation or accumulation of goods or money.

Slavery and the slave-trade have been endemic in Ethiopian society since early times. What gave them renewed currency in the early twentieth century was the opening of new and wider possibilities for the acquisition of slaves. In the absence of effective and responsible administration, Menilek's extension of Ethiopia's frontiers and the incorporation of new areas only tended to accentuate the predatory tendencies of the ruling class and the soldiery. South-western Ethiopia became a hunting-ground for humans as well as animals. Ivory and slaves became the two precious commodities with which traders and adventurers returned from the region. Members of the upper nobility came to have thousands and sometimes tens of thousands of slaves at their disposal. Some of them, like Abba Jifar II, are reputed even to have paid their medical fees in slaves. The giving away of slaves as presents was also common. Possession of slaves, in short, became an index of social status.

The demographic and socio-economic implications of the whole activity were perhaps the most important ones. The process was attended by massive depopulation in the south-western provinces. In one slaving expedition alone – the rather notorious campaign of 1912 conducted by *Lej* Iyyasu himself – about 40,000 Dizi in south-western Ethiopia were uprooted from their homes and dragged across the country to the capital. Half of them were reported to have died on the way, from various epidemic diseases. Some of the survivors were settled to the north-west of Iyyasu's palace at Seddest Kilo in Addis Ababa, in what came to be known as Gimira Safar. Similar tales of dislocation exist about the provinces of Kafa and Maji. The chaos and insecurity that prevailed as a result of the slaving activity also disrupted agricultural production. Culturally, too, slavery and the slave-trade accentuated the differences between the central and the peripheral nationalities.

The international implications of slavery and the slave-trade were no less serious. To the neighbouring colonial powers, the frequent boundary violations that slave-raids entailed provided a convenient excuse for putting pressure on Ethiopia. Only a century or so before, they themselves had condoned and even prospered from slavery and the slave-trade. Some of them were also aware of the inherent difficulties of eradicating the problem. One British observer commented that to demolish the capitalist system in England would be a less radical measure. Yet Ethiopia was expected to perform a miracle and abolish the whole system overnight. Her admission to the League of Nations was questioned mainly because a country which still harboured slaves and slave-traders was considered not up to civilized standards. More significantly, the arms blockade that was imposed on the country for the ostensible purpose of putting a check on the

93

slave-raids eventually made Ethiopia defenceless in face of Italian aggression. That aggression itself was partly justified as a civilizing mission which would do away with such heinous customs as slavery.

International pressure as well as domestic forces succeeded in bringing about some changes in the institutions of slavery and the slave-trade. Although earlier emperors like Tewodros and Menilek had made some half-hearted gestures to check the trade in humans, it was not until the 1920s that serious measures began to be taken. In the early 1920s in particular, a vigorous campaign against Ethiopian slavery was conducted in the British press. Domestically, too, growing costs of maintaining large numbers of slaves as well as the changing life style of the ruling class had begun to render slavery both uneconomical and obsolete. As a result, a series of proclamations were issued against slavery and the slave-trade. The first, in September 1923, put a ban on the trade. Then, in March 1924, a decree was issued providing for the gradual emancipation of slaves. A bureau to implement the decree and a school for the freed slave children were established. Administration of the school was given to an ardent campaigner against slavery, *Hakim* Warqenah Eshate (known also as Dr Charles Martin). In 1932, the anti-slavery bureau was reorganized and put under a British adviser, Frank de Halpert.

Trade

Next to land, trade provided another source of income for the Ethiopian ruling class. Control of trade routes and customs duties therefore became an important factor in the political power struggle. Compared with the situation in the nineteenth century, a major reorientation of long-distance trade routes and outlets had taken place. A series of events had had the effect of giving the eastward route, terminating at Zeila or Berbera on the Somali coast, precedence over the northbound route. Shawan victory over Gojjam at the Battle of Embabo in 1882 was the first of such events. The decline of Gondar and Matamma as a result of the Ethio-Mahdist hostilities was another. The shift of the geopolitical focus to the south, signalled by the emperorship of Menilek, and the foundation and growth of Addis Ababa as the political centre of the empire, put the seal on the whole process. In terms of outlet, the Italo-Ethiopian conflict of the 1890s and then the amputation of the Marab Melash (Eritrea) had given rise to the emergence of the French port of Djibouti as Ethiopia's main outlet to the outside world. Djibouti's pre-eminence was attained at the expense not only of Massawa and Assab but also of Zeila and Berbera.

94   Another feature of twentieth-century Ethiopian trade arose directly

3.5   *A street scene in down-town Addis Ababa, 1935*

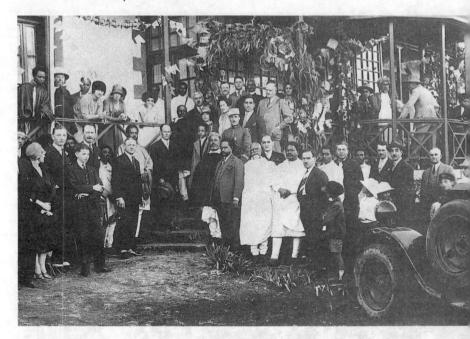

3.6   *A commemorative picture taken on the occasion of a reception in honour of a French mission, 1929. Among those present were* Ras Kasa Haylu, Blatten Geta *Heruy Walda-Sellase, and M. de Reffyé, the French minister*

from the aftermath of the Battle of Adwa. The juxtaposition of independent Ethiopia with European colonies spurred the adjacent powers to start a policy of commercial penetration of their respective 'hinterlands'. Frustration of the Italian bid for unilateral colonial domination led to multilateral competition to tap as much of the resources of Ethiopia as possible. Economic penetration of the frontier regions was sometimes thought of as ultimately conducive to political control. The establishment of consulates in these frontier regions likewise reinforced this objective. Thus the British tried to attract as much of south-western Ethiopian trade as possible to Sudan via Gambela, an inland port in south-western Ethiopia that they had leased from Menilek as a result of the Ethio-Sudan boundary delimitation treaty of 1902. Likewise, they penetrated southern Ethiopia from their colony of British East Africa, and the Harar region from British Somaliland. They established consulates at Harar, Mega in southern Ethiopia, Gore in Illubabor and Dangela in Gojjam. The Italians similarly tried to draw the northern Ethiopian regions into the economic orbit of their Eritrean colony. They too set up consulates, at Adwa in Tegray, Dessie in Wallo, and in Gondar. Control of the railway, Ethiopia's main medium of external trade, saved the French from making similar exertions. Powers with no adjoining colonies, such as the United States and Germany, were forced to concentrate all their energies on capturing the centre.

In spite of the trans-frontier challenges, Djibouti's pre-eminence as the main conduit of Ethiopia's foreign trade was beyond dispute. On the average, some 75% of the trade passed through Djibouti. The Eritrean route stood second, followed by the Sudan and British Somaliland routes. The pull from British East Africa and Italian Somaliland was not of much consequence. On the other hand, the export share of the Sudan route was much higher, rising to 20% around 1930 – a result of its attraction of much of the coffee which grew in south-west Ethiopia. As a result, the Sudan route was characterized by a favourable balance of trade for Ethiopia. Conversely, the Djibouti route showed an unfavourable balance, suggesting that the railway was more instrumental than the steamer (the means of transport used on the Gambela route) in drawing Ethiopia into a pattern of dependence.

In the items of trade, there was a significant change from the nineteenth-century pattern. Such commodities as ivory and civet musk, which had dominated the trade in the earlier century, progressively declined in importance – inevitably in view of the exhaustible nature of the animals from which they were extracted. Coffee became the principal export item, a position it has maintained to this day. Coffee's counterpart on the import side was the unbleached cotton sheeting known as *abujedid*, much valued for clothing as well as for making tents. Commercial rivalry among Ethiopia's trade partners centred on this highly marketable commodity. It was *abujedid* which brought first the Americans and then the Japanese to Ethiopia. With the completion of the railway and the relative sophistication in consumption tastes, items ranging from felt hats to Scotch whisky and French brandy also began to enter the list of imports.

The traders who controlled Ethiopia's external trade were mostly expatriates – a significant change from the pattern in the long-distance trade of the preceding century. This had largely to do with the influx of foreigners into Ethiopia subsequent to the Battle of Adwa. At the outset, benefiting from the favours that their country enjoyed during the Adwa days because of their country's policy of condoning the import of arms into Ethiopia, French traders had the upper hand. Léon Chefneux, winner of the railway concession and close confidant of Emperor Menilek, was one of them. A.C. Savouré was another. But it did not take long for the British, through their Indian surrogates, to attain prominence. The frugality and low-cost management of Indian traders gave them a sharp edge over their European rivals. One of them, Mohammedally, became the biggest name in Ethiopian import-export trade of the years before the Italo-Ethiopian war of 1935–1936. As successful as the Indians, particularly in the south-west, were the Greeks, thanks largely to the ease with which they adapted to the Ethiopian milieu, possibly, among other things, because of their Orthodox Christian faith. The Armenians, also Orthodox Christians, like the Greeks, and welcomed to Ethiopia at a time when they were suffering persecution in their homeland, were to attain the highest level of integration into Ethiopian society. They thrived mainly as craftsmen catering to the upper classes. But one of their pioneers, Sarkis Terzian, made his fortune as an arms trader and his fame by introducing the steamroller (aptly named 'Sarkis *babur*', the steam-engine of Sarkis) into the country. The Jewish merchant Benin was another successful trader, and gave his name to Benin Safar in Addis Ababa. The Syrian Hasib Ydlibi not only attained prominence and notoriety in the world of commerce and concessions but also briefly (during the reign of Iyyasu) became politically powerful. His protégé and compatriot, Majid Abud, started as a rubber trader in western Ethiopia and ended up as the most energetic agent of central government authority in the land of the intractable Anuak people. Somewhat later, the more conventional representatives of European capital, such as Seferian and Company, and A. Besse and Company, came into the picture.

Ethiopian traders were invariably relegated to internal and local trade. On the other hand, the ruling class more and more shed its martial character of the pre-Adwa days and developed business instincts. A series of profitable partnerships were struck between its members and the expatriate merchants and concessionaires. Menilek conducted a thriving business lending money to Indian traders. Empress Taytu, his consort, owned Addis Ababa's first hotel, named after her title, the Etege, and later, in the 1970s and 1980s, renamed Awraris (rhinoceros) and then Taytu. She also organized one of the most ambitious ventures of the times – an Ethiopian bank involving most of the big names in Ethiopia. The business interests of *Ras* Tafari Makonnen, heir to the throne from 1916, *negus* from 1928, and Emperor Hayla-Sellase after his coronation in 1930, ranged from a fruit plantation at Erer in Harar province to holding shares in a road-construction company (the Ethiopian Motor Transport Company, Ltd., which was engaged in the building of the Bure–Gambela road in the 1930s). *Ras* Haylu Takla-Haymanot of Gojjam was his most serious rival, economically as well as politically: he owned a cinema in Addis Ababa and ran a taxi business. *Ras* Dasta Damtaw, son-in-law of Tafari, chose to engage in selling water in Addis Ababa. But it was customs duties which aroused the rulers' greatest interest. The transformation of the *naggadras* from head merchant to financial agent of the state, begun in Gondar, was now consummated: he became one of the most important state officials. It is also of interest to note that some of the *naggadras*, like Gabra-Heywat Baykadagn and Afawarq Gabra-Iyyasus, were the luminaries of the Ethiopian intelligentsia. Menilek's interest in customs can be gleaned from the ministerial system he introduced in 1907. One of the ministries was that of commerce and customs; the ministry itself was described as 'the head of the customs and *naggadras* of Ethiopia'. Among its functions was the institution of a customs system which would increase government revenue. The ministry was further divided into five sections, two of which dealt with customs (one for Addis Ababa, the other for the rest of the country).

On this foundation, Tafari built an elaborate system of customs administration. In this he was assisted by Gabra-Egziabher François, a product of missionary education who proved to be one of Tafari's most efficient administrators, and the American financial adviser, E.A. Colson. In 1924–1925 the customs section of the Ministry of Commerce was reconstituted as a directorate-general. It had first class directors for Addis Ababa, Dire Dawa, Sayyo (later Dambi Dolo) in south-western Wallaga, and Gore, and second-class directors for Harar, Alyu Amba and Chano in Shawa. (The division itself is an illuminating commentary on the decline of the commercial centres of the nineteenth century.) The regulation also provided for the appointment of customs inspectors in the capital and at the administrative district (*awraja*) level.

The corner-stone of Tafari's fiscal policy was the centralization of customs administration. As he stated in an often-quoted speech of 1925, delivered during his visit to the Addis Ababa Customs Office: 'It is a well-known fact that customs constitute the main source for the prosperity of a state . . . Today is a great day of happiness, because I have had the good fortune to visit this customs office operating along modern lines' (*Fere Kanafer*, 15). Customs lay at the root of his conflict with some of the regional rulers. A notable example is the clash with *Ras* Gugsa Wale of Bagemder in 1930: control of Matamma customs was an important factor behind it. Another aspect of this policy was elimination of the *kella* (toll-posts) which proliferated in the provinces, and their replacement by a few recognized and centrally controlled customs posts. *Ras* Emeru Hayla-Sellase was instrumental in implementing this policy during his governorship of Gojjam in the early 1930s. *Ras* Emeru was Tafari's cousin, the son of *Ras* Makonnen Walda-Mikael's niece, and the cousins were lifelong companions.

Deemed equally important was the assertion of central government authority over the customs from external trade. The division of Gambela customs became a hot issue between the Ethiopian and **99**

Sudan governments in the 1920s. It was finally resolved along lines favourable to the former. Ethiopian rights to levy import duties had been shackled by the Klobukowsky Treaty of 1908. The treaty exempted French subjects from the laws of Ethiopia and limited the customs duty to 10% *ad valorem*; for liquor it was to be even lower – 8%. Thanks to the convenient provisions that other powers had earlier made in their treaties with Menilek for the extension of such privileges to their subjects, the treaty came to cover almost all European subjects and governments. It had profound implications for Ethiopia's relations with foreigners. The extraterritorial rights granted European subjects often became a licence for racial arrogance and irresponsible behaviour. The low import tariff encouraged the inflow of European goods into the country.

The repeal or revision of the Klobukowsky Treaty became one of the main preoccupations of Tafari, both before and after his coronation as emperor. During his tour of Europe in 1924, this was one question he broached with the French government. Lacking any positive response, he made a unilateral revision of the treaty in March 1931 by proclaiming the excise and consumption tax. This raised the import tax to up to 30% *ad valorem* on what were regarded as luxury items, such as alcoholic drinks, cigarettes, umbrellas, carpets and underwear. In spite of protests from the European legations, the government stood its ground. While it was an emphatic assertion of Ethiopian independence, the move at the same time negatively affected the Ethiopian consumer in view of the attendant rise in prices. In terms of the augmentation of central revenue, however, the new tax was not without some significance. Out of an estimated total annual revenue of about £400,000, the income from the tax was valued at £25,000, or slightly over 6% (Perham, 194).

Concessions

If trade was one medium for European penetration of the Ethiopian economy in the post-Adwa years, concessions were another. The latter were often viewed by Europeans as a sure means of making accessible to themselves the reputedly rich resources of the country that Adwa had denied them – or at least one of them, Italy. Indeed, concessions were deemed less expensive than outright colonial domination. In the words of one of the spokesmen of European imperialist penetration in Ethiopia, 'In order . . . that the great natural riches of Abyssinia may be thrown open to European trade and industry, there is no need of a war, or of a costly establishment of sovereignty over the land' (Bahru, 'Fumbling Début', 331). The quest for concessions coincided with the monopoly capitalist phase of imperialism, which was characterized by the export of finance capital.

As in trade, however, the reality did not always match the dream of a bonanza for merchants and investors. Although a large number of concessions were granted to expatriates by Ethiopian authorities, few of them achieved any practical significance. Most of them remained baits for the over-credulous European investor. Ethiopian authorities also benefited from the whole exercise through cash bribes given them for the acquisition of concessions and royalties for their duration. The whole situation gave rise to what were known as concession-hunters, who assumed the profitable role of intermediary between the European investor and the Ethiopian ruler. The most remarkable of these concession-hunters were the German Arnold Holz, the Italian Alberto Prasso and the Syrian Ydlibi.

Two concessions, however, were translated into reality of considerable import for Ethiopian history. The first was the railway concession of 1894; the second was the banking concession of 1905. They were secured by the two major rival powers in Africa – the French and the British, respectively. Although the railway concession (which initially provided for the building of a railway from Djibouti via Entotto to the Nile) was granted in 1894, it was soon overshadowed by the Adwa campaign. Construction did not begin until 1897, and the railway reached its first major terminal in 1902 – one differing from the initial plan, which involved the town of Harar. The new site was named New Harar, later renamed Dire Dawa. Thereafter, for a period of six years, construction was discontinued as a result of inter-power rivalry and Menilek's resentment at the French government's take-over of what was initially a private undertaking. The international status of the railway was regulated by the 1906 Tripartite Agreement between Britain, France and Italy. Two years later, Menilek signed with the French a new concession offering slightly better terms for Ethiopia. Work on the railway was resumed the following year, but it did not reach Addis Ababa until 1917. The idea of extending it to the Nile had already been abandoned in face of British opposition.

The completion of the railway was an event of considerable socio-economic significance for Ethiopia. It put the final seal on the centrality of Addis Ababa. It also gave birth along the railway-line to new towns: Dire Dawa, Nazareth and Mojo. It became the chief medium by which Ethiopia was drawn into the world economy. Although its service was impaired by the high tariffs imposed by the company, the railway none the less became the main means of transport for both goods and passengers to and from Ethiopia. It was also through the railway that ideas and fashions percolated to the country. Politically, it contributed to the rise of *Ras* Tafari to power, as it facilitated the speedy despatch of loyal troops from his base in Harar to the capital. **101**

3.7   A train arriving at Dire Dawa railway station

The banking concession was given to the British, more specifically to the British-controlled Bank of Egypt, in March 1905. It entitled them to exclusive banking rights in Ethiopia as well as those of the minting of coins and the issuance of notes. What came to be known as the Bank of Abyssinia was thus established with a starting capital of £100,000. Drawing from the lessons of the railway, a conscious effort was made to internationalize the venture. The founding committee was composed of three British members, three Italian members and one German member. The shares were simultaneously offered in Addis Ababa, Cairo and a number of European capitals, as well as in New York. The combined shares of the French and the Italians were fixed to be exactly equal to those of the British. Notwithstanding such precautions, however, the bank remained primarily a British concern, as evidenced in the composition of the key personnel.

Although a number of branches came to be opened in the provinces, the impact of the bank on the Ethiopian economy does not seem to have been substantial. Its high lending rate (15%) was certainly not conducive to borrowing. Nearly a decade was to pass before the bank's books showed any profits. Fundamentally, the bank faced inherent problems of a capitalist institution grafted on to a feudal structure. It was not easy to overcome the competition of the informal credit system or the ingrained habit of private hoarding. On the other hand, the monopoly it enjoyed aroused some opposition. Gabra-

3.8   Bank of Abyssinia, c. *1910*

Heywat Baykadagn, Ethiopia's leading intellectual of the period, was among its most severe critics. In 1909, Empress Taytu created a rival lending institution known as the Society for the Promotion of Agriculture and Trade, but it was unsuccessful, lasting only one year. Finally, in 1931, the bank was 'nationalized'. It came to be known as the Bank of Ethiopia, ancestor of the State Bank of Ethiopia, in the years after the Italo-Ethiopian war and Italian occupation, and the current Commercial Bank of Ethiopia, founded in 1963.

Modern education and the birth of an intelligentsia

Interest in modern education in Ethiopia goes back to the nineteenth century. The missionaries, who saw education as an effective means of proselytization, were active in establishing a number of schools and sending the more promising students abroad. As stated in Chapter Two, impressed by European technological power, and more particularly the military manifestation of that power, Emperor Tewodros II had started a school at Gafat to train young Ethiopians in the technique of arms manufacture. In the post-Adwa period, the more intensive relations with Europe created ampler opportunities for the spread of modern education. The expansion of the state apparatus (through the ministerial system and customs administration, for instance) **103**

3.9   An Ethiopian delegation to Europe, 1911. The leader, Dajjach
Kasa Haylu, later Ras, *is seated in the middle*

made the training of a cadre of officials imperative. But it was not
only as clerks and accountants that these educated Ethiopians left
their mark on Ethiopian history. Some of them were to give eloquent
expression to the problem of Ethiopia's backwardness. They constituted a passionate, if poorly organized, force for reform. Sometimes
characterized as the 'Young Ethiopians', they laid the foundation for
a radical tradition which was continued and amplified by the Ethiopian Student Movement in the 1960s and 1970s.

   The first educated Ethiopians were mostly sponsored by missionaries. The most prominent of these were Professor Tamrat
Amanuel of Gondar, one of the many Falasha who had benefited from
their close association with the missionaries; *Kantiba* (Mayor) Gabru
Dasta, also from Gondar, whose illustrious career as interpreter,
envoy, mayor, senator and Resistance fighter spanned five decades,
from the reign of Emperor Yohannes IV to the Italian Occupation;
and Onesimus Nasib, an Oromo of Illubabor, who translated the
Bible into his native tongue. There were a few others who do not
104   conform to this pattern. Mahdara-Qal Tawalda-Madhen, interpreter

3.10 Hakim *Warqenah Eshate (Dr Martin), surgeon, educator, provincial governor and Ethiopian minister to London at the outbreak of the Italo-Ethiopian war in 1935*

successively to Emperors Tewodros and Yohannes, received his education under official French patronage. Warqenah Eshate (later renowned as *Hakim* Warqenah or as Dr Charles Martin) started his career under fortuitous circumstances. Found after the Battle of Maqdala at the age of about four by one of the British officers in the Napier expedition, he was trained as a medical doctor in India and Scotland. Returning to Ethiopia in the early twentieth century, as Dr Martin, *Hakim* Warqenah recovered his family and his name, and served in various capacities: as superintendent of the Tafari Makonnen School, director of the school for freed slaves, negotiator with a United States company for the construction of a dam on Lake Tana, governor of the model province of Charchar (in Harar), and Ethiopian minister to London during the outbreak of the Italo-Ethiopian war.

Ethiopians who went abroad did not always undergo formal training. In many instances, it was through their exposure to a different environment rather than through any formal education that they came back changed. In one or two cases, in fact, Ethiopians achieved prominence abroad as teachers rather than as students. This was the case with *Alaqa* Tayya Gabra-Maryam from Gondar and Afawarq Gabra-Iyyasus from Gojjam. After spending his youth at the Swedish evangelical mission at Menkullu (near Massawa), *Alaqa* Tayya joined the high-level German diplomatic mission that visited Ethiopia in 1905, and went to Berlin, where he taught Ge'ez. Afawarq Gabra-Iyyasus, called 'professor' by the Italians, published a number of books during his sojourn in their country, including the first Amharic novel, *Tobya*. At least three Ethiopians received their scholastic foundation in Russia. Two students named Gezaw and Dagne returned with medical training and helped to set up Menilek II Hospital in 1910. Takla-Hawaryat Takla-Maryam of Shawa studied artillery in St Petersburg military school, attaining the rank of colonel. Back in Ethiopia, however, it was not as a military expert that he became famous, but rather as provincial governor, agronomist, drafter of the 1931 Constitution and treasurer (*bajerond*, his permanent title after 1931).

The most illustrious of all the pre-war intellectuals does not seem to have had any official sponsorship for his foreign visits. This was Gabra-Heywat Baykadagn from Adwa, who spent his teenage days in Germany. From there he returned with an early mastery of political economy which, when applied to the Ethiopian reality, was to be astounding in its rapid grasp of the situation and its extraordinary depth. A shorter stay in British-ruled Sudan impressed on him the disturbing contrast between the progress of colonial Sudan and the backwardness of independent Ethiopia. His ideas were to become public in his two major works: 'Atse Menilek-na Ityopya' (Emperor Menilek and Ethiopia) and *Mangest-na ya Hezb Astadadar* (Government and Public Administration), the first published in 1912, the second posthumously in 1924; the author died at the early age of thirty-three years. The most important post that he had occupied was that of *naggadras* of Harar, a title which has clung to his name.

Not all the intellectuals and prominent civil servants of the pre-war period had a missionary background or had been exposed to life outside the country. The most prolific writer of them all, Heruy Walda-Sellase, from Shawa, was a product of traditional church education. He occupied various prominent positions in the civil service, including that of foreign minister on the eve of the 1935–1936 war with Italy. In fact, the *dabtara* (the learned men of the Ethiopian Orthodox Church, of whom Heruy was one) were to constitute a significant element of the intellectual ferment and the budding modern administration of the period. The church of Saint Raguel on Entotto mountain played an important role in this regard. Among its 'graduates' who attained fame and power were Takkala Walda-Hawaryat, customs official, mayor, fiery patriot and implacable opponent of Emperor Hayla-Sellase after the war and the Italian Occupation of Ethiopia,

3.11 Naggadras *Gabra-Heywat Baykadagn, a leading intellectual of the early twentieth century*

3.12 Blatten Geta *Heruy Walda-Sellase, prolific writer, and Minister of Foreign Affairs from 1931–1936*

and Makonnen Habta-Wald, a minister of exceptional political longevity (*c.* 1930–1960) and a power-broker of the Hayla-Sellase regime.

There were also those who were influenced by the ideas of men like Gabra-Heywat Baykadagn, and who continued the reformist tradition. Of these, the most conspicuous was *Fitawrari* (later *Blatta*) Deressa Amante, member of the Wallaga aristocracy and one of the regular contributors to the *Berhanena Salam* newspaper, the voice of the progressive intellectuals. Like Gabra-Heywat, Deressa too had spent some time in Sudan.

Another adjoining colony that had an impact on the evolution of modern administration in Ethiopia was Eritrea. This happened in two ways. Firstly, a number of Eritreans, often moved by the magnetic pull of the motherland, came to Ethiopia and served in various capacities. The most outstanding of them was *Blatta* Gabra-Egziabher Gila-Maryam, passionate advocate for the restoration of Eritrea to Ethiopia, and pioneer of the Amharic press. Secondly, there were **107**

3.13 Tafari Makonnen School at about the time of its founding in 1925

Ethiopian officials who in one way or another experienced the relatively more advanced form of administration in Eritrea, and sought to imitate it. *Dajjach* Gabra-Sellase Barya-Gabr of Adwa was one such personality. The brothers Wasane and Nasibu Zamanuel, who had been successively Ethiopian consul in Asmara, were two others.

In terms of formal education, the last years of Menilek saw a significant event – the founding in 1908 of the first school set up along modern lines. This was Menilek II School. The staff, composed mainly of Egyptians of the Orthodox Coptic Christian Church, was a good example of the Emperor's concern for a happy compromise between tradition and innovation. It was felt that the Copts would filter down to their pupils a tempered version of modern ideas. The syllabus showed a distinct bias towards languages, partly an indication of the practical need for interpreters. French was the medium of instruction, and it was to remain the *lingua franca* of the Ethiopian intelligentsia until superseded by English after 1941. French cultural paramountcy was further reinforced by the opening after 1912 of Alliance française schools in Dire Dawa and Addis Ababa. Tafari Makonnen School, opened by *Ras* Tafari in 1925, was even more French-oriented than Menilek II School, with French directors and with the students sitting for French Government Certificate examinations. Ethiopian supervision was, however, provided for by the crea-

3.14   Students of an early twentieth-century school

tion of the post of superintendent. At the central administrative level, the Ministry of Education had evolved as an independent ministry by 1930; Menilek's initial arrangements had made it a mere adjunct to the office of the archbishop. The 1930s saw the founding of a number of schools in the provinces as well as in Addis Ababa.

The 1920s also witnessed the onset of a new phase of sending young Ethiopians abroad for education. The destination of most of these students was France, with the Lycée at Alexandria in Egypt serving as a transit point. A number of Ethiopians who were to occupy prominent positions after the Italian occupation belonged to this category. A smaller number found their way to Britain and the United States, with one or two going to Switzerland. All in all, a total of some 200 Ethiopians reportedly studied abroad, through government or private means, in the decade and a half before 1935.

As in many other societies, the spread of modern education in Ethiopia had two major effects: the training of skilled personnel to staff the growing bureaucracy, and the dissemination of ideas of change. In short, modern education produced functionaries and intellectuals. The functionaries were the more integrated into the state apparatus and were thus invariably too absorbed in the routine of administration to have time for strictly intellectual pursuits; Heruy Walda-Sellase was a phenomenal exception. The intellectuals were **109** generally only peripherally attached to the state apparatus. The functionaries were predominantly trained inside the country; the intellectuals tended to have lived or studied abroad. Of the functionaries, only one or two had reached ministerial level by 1935, the upper limit of their rise in the bureaucracy often being that of director-general of a department.

In their critique of the backward state of their country, the intellectuals represented a counter-current to the smug confidence that had ensued after the Adwa victory. They advocated a series of reforms in order to give socio-economic content to the political independence that Adwa had guaranteed. The reforms they recommended included the introduction of fixed tax; religious freedom; updating of the traditional code, the *Fetha Nagast* (the Law of Kings); rationalization of the Amharic alphabet, which has about 300 characters based on seven forms to which diacritical marks are added; institution of centralized and uniform customs administration; and military and currency reforms. But the two themes that received the widest attention were the elimination of the iniquities of the *gabbar* system, and the promotion of education. Many a powerful pen was employed to depict the miserable lot of the *gabbar* and to make suggestions for his liberation. And, if there was one word which could be described as the motto of the progressive intellectuals, it was 'education'. The country which they adopted as their model was Japan, dramatically transformed in a matter of decades from a feudal country like Ethiopia into an industrial power; hence the label 'Japanizers' that has come to be given to them. The 1931 constitution, which was drafted by one of these intellectuals (Takla-Hawaryat Takla-Maryam), appears to have been very strongly inspired by the Japanese Meiji Constitution of 1889.

A major handicap of the intellectuals was their amorphous and unorganized character. To implement their ideas of reform, the intellectuals had no other recourse but to seek the patronage of an enlightened prince. This quest brought some of them into temporary alliance with *Lej* Iyyasu. This was the case with both Takla-Hawaryat and Gabra-Heywat Baykadagn. Takla-Hawaryat rose to become the young ruler's most favoured confidant until, swept by the tide of opposition, he turned against Iyyasu in 1916. Gabra-Heywat's 'Atse Menilek-na Ityopya' is also addressed to Iyyasu.

After Iyyasu's downfall in 1916, *Ras* Tafari became the natural ally of the progressives. Indeed, the reforms Tafari introduced during his regency and the first five years of his emperorship have a striking affinity with the ideas of Gabra-Heywat. Takla-Hawaryat, who had had a hard time getting Iyyasu to pay attention to his explanation of an administrative manual that he had prepared, was now commissioned by Tafari to draft a constitution. But the marriage of convenience between Tafari and the intellectuals did not remain a happy one. More than they were able to use Tafari, he used them for his objective of power consolidation. The eventual quarrel between Tafari as Emperor Hayla-Sellase and Takla-Hawaryat is a clear illustration of this unhappy marriage.

3. Political developments

The decade of consolidation (1896–1906)

The decade after Adwa found Menilek at the height of his internal power and external prestige. The process of territorial expansion and the creation of the modern empire-state had been completed by 1898. The internal challenges to Menilek's power were slight, in any case not at all comparable to the problems faced by his predecessors. Externally, his victory over the Italians had earned him great fame: one foreign observer even compared him to Bismarck. Foreigners, in private or official capacity, flocked to Addis Ababa to seek favours and promote their interests. The year 1906 symbolized the end of this period of consolidation. Menilek suffered the first stroke from a disease which seven years later claimed his life. Combined with the death in the same year of his cousin *Ras* Makonnen Walda-Mikael, the man generally expected to succeed him on the throne, Menilek's incapacitation opened the question of succession. The signing in the same year of the Tripartite Agreement by Britain, France and Italy also marked the first serious challenge to the independent status of Ethiopia.

Following Adwa, recognition of Ethiopia's independence by external powers had expressed itself in two ways. The first was diplomatic representation at the court of Menilek. The second was delimitation of Ethiopia's boundaries with the adjacent colonies. In 1897, the Italians, French and British successively established their legations in Addis Ababa on large estates on the slopes of Entotto. They were each represented by ministers of considerable diplomatic skill – Federico Ciccodicola for the Italians, Léonce Lagarde for the French and John Harrington for the British. In 1903, an American mission of a decidedly commercial nature arrived, ushering in an association with the country that was to be particularly strong after 1941. Two years later, the Germans came on to the scene, generating anxiety among the tripartite powers, and precipitating the Tripartite Agreement in 1906, which was partly intended to shut off the intruders from the riches of Ethiopia.

The delimitation of the boundaries between Ethiopia and the surrounding colonies was dictated mainly by the colonial powers'

3.16   Ras *Makonnen Walda-Mikael, governor of Harar, shown with the German mission to Ethiopia in 1905*

apprehension of the expansive potentialities of post-Adwa Ethiopia. The first boundary that was to be delimited was the shortest – between Ethiopia and what came to be known as French Somaliland. This was concluded on 20 March 1897. Two and a half months later, the boundary with British Somaliland was delimited as part of a general agreement which included the promotion of trade between Ethiopia and British Somaliland and the imposition of an arms embargo on Mahdist Sudan. By a treaty with Italy, dated 10 July 1900, Eritrea was severed from Ethiopia. The largest boundary, that with the Sudan, was preceded by intense and protracted negotiations involving the strategic town of Matamma (known as Gallabat to the Sudanese), the gold-rich region of Bela Shangul, and the area where Ethiopia had made the furthest territorial expansion, the Baro river basin. The treaty signed on 15 May 1902, besides being territorially advantageous to the British, also gave them Gambela, the commercial post inside Ethiopia, and guaranteed their hydraulic interests at Lake Tana, south of Gondar. With the delimitation of the southern boundary with British East Africa (later Kenya) in 1907 and of the south-eastern boundary with Italian Somaliland in 1908, the process of **113** defining Ethiopia's modern territorial extent might be said to have been completed.

These agreements, concluded over a period of about a decade, were significant for the political history of Ethiopia. With the exception of Eritrea, which was federated with Ethiopia in 1952 and united in 1962, after Italian colonial rule (1890-1941) and British administration (1941-1952), they gave the country approximately its present shape. However, the agreements were attended by certain problems. Firstly, delimitation on the map was not always followed by demarcation on the ground. The long boundary with Sudan was only partially demarcated. The boundary with British Somaliland came to be demarcated only in the 1930s and, as we shall see, it indirectly triggered the Walwal crisis in late 1934. Secondly, the absence of effective administration in the frontier regions made the boundary delimitation little more than a cartographical exercise: the southern and southwestern boundaries were constantly violated by trans-frontier raids and incursions. In a sense, this was the frontier peoples' way of nullifying boundary agreements which were concluded without taking cognizance of their needs for seasonal movements of their flocks and for ethnic unity. But the neighbouring colonial powers did not regard the matter with indulgence. More from alarm at the possibilities of armed uprising by their subjects than out of concern for their well-being, they – particularly the British – continued to put pressure on the Ethiopian government through persistent protests and ever tighter applications of the arms blockade.

Power struggle (1908-1930)

The problem of succession

The question of what was to come after Menilek's death had begun to preoccupy the Europeans even before his first stroke in 1906. This concern was to find expression in the Tripartite Agreement of the same year: as stated in the preamble, one of the objectives of the agreement was 'to come to a mutual understanding in regard to their [the three powers'] attitude in the event of any change arising in the situation in Ethiopia'. Three articles of the agreement (1, 3 and 4) defined the legal framework for the regulation of their interests and the steps they were to take conjointly to safeguard those interests 'in the event of the status quo ... being disturbed'.

Menilek himself was not oblivious of the problem of succession. Although possibly inspired by other considerations as well, the ministerial system that he set up in 1907 appears to have been a reflection of his desire to give government an institutional basis and some degree of continuity. True, the ministers were largely old palace officials dressed in a new European cloak. A partial list of the first 'cabinet' bears out this ingenious compromise between tradition and change:

Afa Negus Nasibu Masqalo	– Minister of Justice
Fitawrari Habta-Giyorgis Dinagde	– Minister of War
Tsahafe T'ezaz Gabra-Sellase Walda-Aragay	– Minister of Pen
Bajerond Mulugeta Yeggazu	– Minister of Finance
Naggadras Hayla-Giyorgis Walda-Mikael	– Minister of Commerce and of Foreign Affairs
Azazh Matafarya Malka-Tsadeq	– Minister of the Imperial Court

The titles indicate that the incumbents were expected to perform more or less the same tasks as they had undertaken in the traditional administrative system.

As stated earlier, education was placed under the safe custody of the *abun*. With respect to foreign affairs, too, the statutes were unequivocal about Menilek's supreme prerogative in vital questions of relations with other states; the minister's powers were largely restricted to consular affairs and translation of foreign publications.

Some of the functions assigned to the various ministries were also impracticable, given the circumstances of the country at the time. The Ministry of the Interior, for instance, was expected to conduct censuses and register births, marriages and deaths. The Ministry of War was to give military training, while one of the tasks of the Ministry of Agriculture was to give prizes for good husbandry and impose fines on badly managed farms. In the statutes of the Ministry of Finance, a meticulous distinction was made between the government treasury and the private wealth of the monarch – a state of affairs which was not to be attained even by 1935. No doubt most of these provisions were designed for European consumption, to give the impression that Ethiopia had adopted a European form of government. One of the statutes of the Ministry of Agriculture underlines this point when it concludes with the phrase 'as in Europe'.

Having said all this, however, we need not overlook the enduring consequences of the introduction of the ministerial system. There is no doubt that it contributed to some measure of continuity in administration. The birth and growth of a modern bureaucracy was also associated with it. The absence for some time of a ruler of the stature and the strength of Menilek had the effect of strengthening the hands of the ministers. This became particularly evident during the reign (*de facto*, 1911–1916) of Iyyasu, who stayed outside the capital most of the time, leaving the affairs of government to the 'cabinet'. The rise of

115

3.17 Lej *Iyyasu and his father* Ras *Mikael of Wallo*

Naggadras Hayla-Giyorgis Walda-Mikael, the first *de facto* prime minister of Ethiopia, was a direct result of this state of affairs. It was the growing power – and wealth – of the ministers which was to precipitate the demonstration in 1918, calling for their removal. In essence, the appointment of ministers heralded the rise of a new nobility, of service and merit rather than of birth. Hayla-Giyorgis was the precursor of powerful ministers who were to emerge subsequently – Heruy Walda-Sellase as Minister of Foreign Affairs before the outbreak of war with Italy in 1935, Walda-Giyorgis Walda-Yohannes and the brothers Akalawarq, Aklilu and Makonnen Habta-Wald after 1941; Walda-Giyorgis and Aklilu were successively *tsahafe t'ezaz*, and Makonnen and Akalawarq held various ministerial posts.

In addition to this innovation to ensure continuity, Menilek made a provision for the future along more traditional lines. This was the designation of a successor in May 1909. In a moving document imbued with a sense of history, in which Menilek reminded his subjects of the political tribulations that had attended the deaths of Tewodros and Yohannes IV, he let it be known that Iyyasu, his grandson, the son of *Ras* Mikael of Wallo and Menilek's daughter, Shawaragga, was his chosen heir to the throne. In view of Iyyasu's minority, *Ras* Tasamma Nadaw, a scion of the Shawan nobility, was made *ras bitwaddad* and appointed as the boy's regent. In an attempt to unite the two royal houses of Shawa and Tegre, the heir had already

3.18   Empress Taytu Betul, wife of Emperor Menilek II

been united in a marriage, though ineffectual, with Romanawarq, the seven-year-old daughter of *Ras* Mangasha Yohannes of Tegre. As the little girl was a grand-niece of Menilek's wife Taytu, the arrangement appears to have been calculated to appease the empress as well, as she had begun to develop her own designs for the throne.

A woman of exceptional strength of character, Taytu had played an important role in the glorious events of her husband's reign. She was the real founder of Addis Ababa. Even more than Menilek, who was prone to compromise, she had seen from the outset through the subterfuges of Italian colonialism and was an unrelenting advocate of total rupture with the Italians. The abrogation of the Treaty of Wechale was largely inspired by her. Her active role in the Battle of Adwa, as strategist as well as a great moral force behind the Ethiopian warriors, has come to be enshrined in tradition. The incapacitation of Menilek tended to increase her powers, as she assumed the role of the invalid monarch and made *shum sher* (appointments and dismissals) to her taste. Among those who fell victim to her policy were *Dajjach* Dames of Wallaga, *Dajjach* Gabra-Sellase Barya-Gabr of Adwa, *Wag Shum* Abata Bwayalaw and *Naggadras* Hayla-Giyorgis Walda-Mikael. The last was in fact subjected to the indignity of being put in chains on charges of embezzlement.

The Shawan nobility regarded Taytu as a serious threat to their hegemony. In view of her Gondare background, her moves were

117

3.19 Dajjach *Gabra-Sellase Barya-Gabr, ruler of Adwa, and one of the leading spokesmen against Empress Taytu in 1910*

interpreted as parts of a grand plan to restore the centrality of the north in Ethiopian politics. Her policy of uniting key families by means of an intricate web of marriages lent particular force to this interpretation. Marriage alliances have been a common feature of Ethiopia's political history, but there have been few practitioners of the policy as accomplished as Empress Taytu. The masterpiece of her matrimonial politics was the union of her nephew, *Ras* Gugsa Wale, with Zawditu, Menilek's daughter. Taytu's vigorous support of Zawditu's candidature for the throne was largely motivated by considerations of promoting the political fortunes of her nephew, as well as her own political future.

In March 1910, opposition to Taytu's policy finally came to a head. Master-minding the protest against the empress were *Ras* Tasamma and *Fitawrari* Habta-Giyorgis. Serving as spokesmen of the mass agitation were men who had harboured strong grievances against Taytu: *Dajjach* Dames, *Dajjach* Gabra-Sellase and *Qagnazmach* Wasane Terfe. But the brunt of the public movement against her was formed by the somewhat specialized units of the imperial army attached to the palace, the *mahal safari*. Besides having a semi-professional military nature, their proximity to the court gave them a political character. They became a relatively well-organized pressure group that played an active role in some of the major political events of the

3.20 Abuna *Mattewos, Egyptian archbishop of Ethiopia from
1889–1926*

early twentieth century.

If the *mahal safari* were the agitators of the political struggles of the
period, the *abun* was the person to whom contenders turned for
arbitration. Opponents of Taytu thus sought to secure the blessing
of *Abuna* Mattewos, the Coptic archbishop of the Ethiopian Orthodox Church, for their enterprise. The manifesto passed at Takla-
Haymanot Church in the western part of Addis Ababa, where the
mass protest against the empress had taken place, called for Taytu's
abstention from all government affairs, and her restriction to nursing
her ailing husband. The efforts of the *abun* to transmit these demands
met with a hostile reception from Taytu. She chose to fight back by
appealing to the churches of Addis Ababa and to the foreign legations.
In her circular to the former, she complained bitterly about the per-
fidious character of the agitation directed against her at a time when
she was so preoccupied with the health of Emperor Menilek that she
could not even spare time to go to church. Her circular to the legations
was couched in diplomatic terms, asking them to ignore all past mis-
understandings and to intervene to arrange for her safe departure to
her own region, Gondar, as her political services were no longer
required in the capital.

Her appeal to the legations proved to be a piece of political miscalculation. Her opponents used it against her, accusing her of **119**

inviting foreign intervention in the internal affairs of the country. Taytu was forced to leave the palace and retire to the church of Saint Maryam at Entotto, her favoured shrine, where she stayed from 1910 until her death in 1918. It only remained to reinstate those she had disgraced and to pacify her opponents. One of the greatest beneficiaries of the removal of Taytu was *Wag Shum* Abata Bwayalaw, who was soon made *ras* and appointed governor of Arsi and Kambata. As regards opposition to the move, a revolt by *Dajjach* Ayalew Berru, a relative of Taytu's, was easily quashed. *Ras* Gugsa Wale, her nephew and governor of Bagemder, happened to be in the capital at the wrong time; he was imprisoned on conveniently filed criminal charges unconnected with the political event. *Ras* Walda-Giyorgis Abboye, governor of Kafa, now replaced him as governor of Bagemder. The most formidable opposition to the settlement was expected to come from *Ras* Wale Betul, brother of the disgraced empress, governor of Yajju, and commander of one of the best armies in Ethiopia. A period of tense confrontation followed between him and *Ras* Mikael, father of Iyyasu and hence supporter of the move that had reaffirmed his son's right of succession. The confrontation was exacerbated by the long-standing territorial dispute between the two rulers of adjoining provinces. To give Mikael the upper hand, *Ras* Tasamma thought it advisable to send a supporting force of some 10,000 troops, led by *Dajjach* Lulsaggad Atnafsaggad. Taytu was persuaded to write to each of the antagonists, reminding them of their responsibility as veterans of Menilek's empire to avert bloodshed. This was to be her last constructive act before she disappeared into comparative political oblivion. In November 1910, *Ras* Wale Betul came to Addis Ababa and surrendered. Not at all ready to indulge in the risks of magnanimity, his opponents consigned him to prison. He remained in detention in Ankobar until the Battle of Sagale (1916).

The Iyyasu interlude
The downfall of Taytu removed for the designated heir a major obstacle on the path to the throne. With the death in April 1911 of the regent, *Ras Bitwaddad* Tasamma Nadaw, the last restraining influence on the young prince Iyyasu was gone. Only the disintegrating body of Menilek remained between him and the throne. But Menilek refused to die. It was not until 1913 that the old monarch drew his last breath. The resilience of the invalid, irksome as it was, did not deter Iyyasu from exercising full powers, and his *de facto* reign thus extends from 1911 to 1916.

At the outset, however, a major challenge to Iyyasu's succession appeared in the shape of *Ras* Abata Bwayalaw, who had celebrated the downfall of his enemy, Taytu, with a triumphant entry into the capital, from which he had been banned by the empress. Soon,

rumours began to circulate that he was entertaining rather high ambitions. These were of an indeterminate nature. One version was that
he wished to establish a regency council to replace *Ras* Tasamma; no
doubt Abata would preside over the affairs of that council. Another
version had it that he was scheming to marry Zawditu and rule
Ethiopia as her viceroy or regent (*endarase*). Whatever the truth, his
attempts to enter the palace, apparently to take over the armoury,
initiated another period of tension, as the chief of the palace guards,
Fitawrari Gabra-Maryam, barred the way. A bloody clash was averted
by the intervention of the *abun* and the *echage*. Abata was persuaded
to retire to his Kambata fief. In December 1911, however, determined
to strengthen his son's precarious position, *Ras* Mikael of Wallo came
to the capital with 8,000 troops, summoned Abata and had him
imprisoned in Maqdala, where he stayed until the Battle of Sagale,
in 1916. One person to whose advantage the course of events
appeared to have worked was *Fitawrari* Habta-Giyorgis Dinagde, who
had played a rather dubious role throughout the affair. Not only did
he manage to obtain Kambata, but he also emerged as the leader of
the Shawan nobility. When Iyyasu's policies began to threaten that
establishment, Habta-Giyorgis played a pivotal role, first in engineering the coup that overthrew Iyyasu, then in organizing the defeat of
Iyyasu's father, *Ras* Mikael, when he tried to reverse the decision.

The reign of Iyyasu is one of the most enigmatic in Ethiopian
history. It was to be his misfortune that he was succeeded by a ruler
of extraordinary political longevity who found it in his interest to sup-
press any objective appreciation of the man. The charges of apostasy
levelled against Iyyasu during his overthrow in 1916 clung to him for
a long time, and his playboy manners and inordinate sexual appetites
have filled the history books. The progressive aspects of his reign,
however confused and inconsistent in practical expression they may
have been, have tended to be ignored. Popular tradition has been
fairer. His handsome features and his oratorical gifts and athletic
exploits captured the public imagination. Even his notorious dis-
soluteness was viewed with considerable indulgence. It was attributed
to his youth, and he was expected to shed it and to become more pur-
poseful with maturity.

Iyyasu's reign witnessed a series of measures which, because of the
social and economic security that they implied, may well be considered as progressive. In addition to the guaranteeing of property
and a more equitable system of *asrat* collection mentioned above, he
put an end to the *quragna* system, whereby the plaintiff was chained
to the defendant and the creditor to the debtor until justice was
delivered. He also tried to mitigate the abuses of the *leba shay*, a whim-
sical traditional mode of detection of criminals, in which a young boy
would be given a powerful drug and let loose in the neighbourhood; **121**

3.21 The quragna *system, whereby plaintiff and defendant were chained together until justice was done*

the unfortunate owner of the house where the boy finally collapsed would be declared the culprit. Through a policy of auditing of government accounts, Iyyasu facilitated the exposure of large-scale embezzlement, although, at the same time, he abused the policy by framing people he did not like. Contradiction and inconsistency were the hallmark of his character and his policies. He could be the protector of the underdog, as when in 1912 he made a punitive attack against the Afar because of their raids on the Jille Oromo in eastern Shawa. Yet, in the same year, he undertook the most nefarious campaign of his career, against the Dizi in south-western Ethiopia, which ended up with the enslavement of tens of thousands of the inhabitants. His reign saw the institution of a municipal police force, the *Terenbulle* (the Amharic version of Tripoli), so called because the recruits were returnees from the Italian campaign of annexation of Libya, which started in 1911. Yet nocturnal shoot-outs between the police and Iyyasu's escort were common, as the police tried to implement the curfew and the emperor roamed Addis Ababa in his habitual escapades.

Iyyasu also represented a challenge to the establishment, a departure from the political and diplomatic concord of post-Adwa Ethiopia. The way he went about forming his own retinue and disregarding

3.22   A leba shay, *the traditional thief-detector, as he prepares to sniff out the culprit. The* leba shay *is the young boy held on a leash, so that he will not go too far from his target, who is sometimes set up by the people following the boy*

Menilek's 'old guard', the older generation of the nobility, must have been little short of traumatic for the latter, who suddenly found themselves no longer wanted. As he set out on one of his compulsive tours of the country, Iyyasu is reported to have told them his opinion bluntly:

When I travel with my escort of young people to visit and conquer new areas, you should not follow me without my permission. You can no longer keep up with us: you have grown old and fat. In your own time you have followed my grandfather and conquered territories. Now, however, you cannot run and escape nor pursue and capture. Stay back and execute your duties here.
(Mars'e-Hazan, 'Menilek', 103)

Rendered in polite phraseology, Iyyasu's words indicated that his grandfather's advisers had done their share in the building of modern Ethiopia and that it was now the turn of his generation to take part. Much less respectfully, he is said even to have referred to them as 'my grandfather's fattened sheep' (Mars'e-Hazan, 'Iyyasu', 28).

The note of impatience in Iyyasu's dealings with the older nobility ultimately extended to include Menilek himself: the aged monarch's protracted illness, the refusal to die, left Iyyasu in a state of political limbo. His clash with the loyal palace guards in early 1913 resulted from this fact. The same guards who had barred *Ras* Abata Bwayalaw's entry into the palace in 1911 now defended their dying master when they heard rumours that Iyyasu was planning to remove

123

Menilek to Ankobar and take over the palace. Denied entry, Iyyasu laid siege to it, stopping all food supplies. Shooting broke out and lasted for about five hours; at least seventeen persons were reportedly killed. Finally, through the intervention of *Abuna* Mattewos, the palace guards surrendered. Their leader, *Fitawrari* Gabra-Maryam, was imprisoned in Bagemder; his subordinates were imprisoned in Gojjam and Ankobar. Iyyasu crowned his victory by appointing his own chief of palace guards, *Basha* (later *Dajjazmach*) Tasamma Gazmu.

Iyyasu was also a challenge to the long-established hegemony of Orthodox Christianity in Ethiopia. That fact was to provide good propaganda material for his opponents. His marriages to the daughters of the Muslim chiefs were given prominence; marriages into the ruling families of the Christian regions (for example, Wallaga, Gojjam and Yajju) were played down. His construction of mosques was highlighted; his founding of churches like Qachane Madhane Alam, in the northern outskirts of Addis Ababa, and his endowments to monasteries like the famous Dabra Libanos, in northern Shawa, were conveniently ignored. The main charge levelled against him in the coup of 1916 became apostasy. His Muslim ancestry (his father *Ras* Mikael was after all Muhammad Ali before 1878) lent credibility to the charge.

In actual fact, however, as both Ethiopian and foreign sources increasingly make clear, Iyyasu had no intention of disestablishing Orthodox Christianity in favour of Islam. Confused as it certainly was, his policy can be interpreted as one of trying to redress the injustices of the past, of making the Muslims feel at home in their own country. In this, he represented a revolutionary departure from the past. Tewodros, a man of wide vision in many respects, was bigoted when it came to Muslims, particularly the Muslims of Wallo. Yohannes, liberal and almost federal in his politics, was even more uncompromising on the question of Orthodoxy and Christianity. Menilek, builder of the largest empire Ethiopia has ever seen, did little to integrate the heterogeneous entity into one nation. Iyyasu's religious policy was the first major attempt to tackle the question of national integration, a question which has not been satisfactorily solved to this day.

Further, Iyyasu was a challenge to the political hegemony of the Shawan nobility. The religious charges brought against him actually camouflaged this political concern. His attitude towards the Shawan nobility was marked by disrespect and contempt. Many a Shawan nobleman had to swallow his pride in silent indignation as he was forced to send his wife for Iyyasu's sexual gratification. Towards the end, when Iyyasu was alerted to the plot that was brewing in the capital while he was roaming in the Ogaden, a large, mainly pastoral area in south-eastern Ethiopia, he ignored the warning, remarking contemptuously that he 'could piss on the Shawan nobility and they would not have the guts to complain' (Mars'e-Hazan, 'Iyyasu', 42).

The undermining of the Shawan nobility reached its climax with the coronation of Iyyasu's father *Ras* Mikael as *negus* of Wallo and Tegre, veritably as *negus* of the north. The fact that Iyyasu was eager to bestow such honours and favours on his father, although he himself was never crowned *negus* or *negusa nagast*, emphasized the pinnacle of power that the Wallo ruler had managed to attain. The man who had started his political career in the third quarter of the nineteenth century as a minor Muslim chieftain had thus become the most powerful figure in Ethiopia. Correspondingly, Wallo was suddenly tranformed from a buffer zone to a political centre. The coronation ceremony at Dessie appeared to have been calculated to accentuate this historic transformation in the stature of the man and the importance of the region. It was characterized by considerable pomp, with *Abuna* Petros, Emperor Yohannes's own bishop, officiating. A high-level delegation, consisting of *Ligaba* Walda-Gabr'el Bashah and the Minister of Finance, *Bajerond* Yeggazu Bahabte, was sent from the capital to represent Iyyasu, taking along the crown and imperial costume of Menilek, as well as a number of guns from the arsenal. Meanwhile, Iyyasu remained, and remains, with the more simple titles of respect, *lej* or *abeto*.

Although its general drift was towards promoting younger and more progressive persons, Iyyasu's appointment policy further contributed to alienating prominent members of the Shawan nobility. One conspicuous victim was the Minister of War, *Fitawrari* Habta-Giyorgis Dinagde, who had to relinquish his presidency of the council of ministers to *Naggadras* Hayla-Giyorgis Walda-Mikael, now promoted to the rank of *bitwaddad*. The latter's well-calculated marriage to Iyyasu's sister, Sehin Mikael, appears to have partly contributed to this particular appointment. *Dajjach* Balcha Safo, too, was removed from his fief of Sidamo, which was given to *Bitwaddad* Hayla-Giyorgis. *Dajjach* Tafari Makonnen was deprived of his financial base when Iyyasu gave the lucrative post of *naggadras* of Harar and Dire Dawa to his Syrian favourite Ydlibi. In 1916, Tafari was forced to relinquish the Harar governorship altogether, and was appointed governor of the south-western region of Kafa. The Syrian was also appointed governor of the Gambela region, thereby bringing to an end, if only temporarily, the ancestral feuds of the governors of the adjoining areas of Gore and Sayyo over control of Gambela trade. The net effect of Iyyasu's appointment policy was to create a number of disgruntled persons who were ready to come together to overthrow him. The short-lived alliance of *Fitawrari* Habta-Giyorgis Dinagde and *Dajjach* Tafari emanated from this consequence.

125

3.23 Naggadras *Hayla-Giyorgis Walda-Mikael, later* Bitwaddad,
Minister of Foreign Affairs and of Commerce after 1907 and
de facto *prime minister during the reign of Iyyasu*

Finally, Iyyasu represented a challenge to the three powers with the
highest stakes in Ethiopia: Britain, France and Italy. The independence
of Ethiopia had always contained the inherent danger of subversion
in their adjoining colonies. They had thus agreed, implicitly
and explicitly, to exert concerted pressure on Ethiopia to safeguard
their interests. The Tripartite Agreement of 1906 was a significant
step in this direction. On the part of Menilek as well, there appears
to have been an awareness of the limitations of Ethiopian independence.
Over the years a sort of diplomatic *modus vivendi* had come to
prevail between Ethiopia and the tripartite states. In this context,
Iyyasu's foreign policy had all the appearance of being bent on upsetting
the diplomatic equilibrium.

This was most dramatically illustrated in his Ogaden policy. From
the outset, Iyyasu had a kind of fixation on the south-eastern region.
He returned to that place, particularly to the outpost of Jijjiga, again
and again. His overthrow was accomplished while he was on one of
his visits to the area. Although there is need for more substantiating
data, Iyyasu's preoccupation with the region apparently arose from

his conception of a more integrative approach towards the Somali. The appointment of Abdullah Sadeq, a local personality, as governor of the Ogaden, was an administrative move presumably designed to give the inhabitants, mainly Muslim, someone with whom they could easily identify. More ominously for the colonial powers, particularly the British and the Italians, who were directly concerned, Iyyasu began to give material and moral support to *Sayyid* Muhammad Abdille Hasan, the Somali patriotic leader who had been challenging British and Italian colonial rule since the turn of the century.

Even in normal circumstances, Iyyasu's Ogaden policy would have alarmed the tripartite powers. Coinciding as it did with the outbreak of World War One in 1914, its destructive potential was all too obvious. In the eyes of the colonialists, Iyyasu assumed the shape of a demon inciting colonial subjects to uprising at a time when their masters were engaged in mortal combat with the Central Powers (Austria-Hungary, Germany and Turkey) in the European and Middle Eastern theatres of war. Conversely, Germany and Turkey, particularly the latter, tried to enlist Iyyasu to their cause. Although he did not fully respond, what he did was sufficient to convince the Allies that he was a threat that should be eliminated forthwith.

Such was the genesis of the alliance of internal and external forces which finally overthrew Iyyasu. A joint note from the Allies to the Ethiopian government in early September 1916, protesting against the inimical actions of Iyyasu, brought the simmering opposition to the boil. Allied ingenuity lent palpability to Iyyasu's apostasy (which became the main charge levelled against him) by forging pictures and documents to prove the allegation. Once again, the *mahal safari* gave a sort of popular dimension to the movement as they rallied behind the opponents of Iyyasu. As was only fitting, given the nature of the charges, *Echage* Walda-Giyorgis was the moving spirit behind the opposition. His house in fact served as the meeting-place of the plotters. The lay leader of the coup was *Fitawrari* Habta-Giyorgis, who had his own grievances against the young ruler. But it was to be Iyyasu's bad fortune that even those he had favoured and pro-moted went along with the tide and turned against him. These included officials close to him, *Ligaba* Bayyana Wandemagagnahu, *Bajerond* Yeggazu Bahabte and *Bitwaddad* Hayla-Giyorgis, and Takla-Hawaryat Takla-Maryam, Iyyasu's confidant and adviser. The dif-ference in the approaches to national integration followed by Iyyasu on the one hand and his opponents on the other was manifested in one of the accusations made against him:

He claims that he eats flesh of cattle slain by Muslims in order to extend fron-tiers and to win hearts. But these Somali and Muslims have already been brought to heel [and do not need such diplomacy]. (Mahtama-Sellase, 514) **127**

One important personality was initially reluctant to join the chorus of denunciation. This was *Abuna* Mattewos. Approached by the plotters to release them from the oath of allegiance to the ruler, he demurred, arguing that there was no cogent proof of Iyyasu's conversion to Islam. In the end, however, goaded on by the *echage*, the *abun* relented and freed the conspirators from their oath. Symbolically on the day of Masqal (27 September 1916), an Orthodox Christian holiday commemorating the finding of the True Cross, Iyyasu was deposed, and Zawditu, as Menilek's daughter by a wife previous to Taytu, was designated empress of Ethiopia. *Dajjach* Tafari Makonnen, who had played a discreet role throughout the entire proceedings, was made *ras* and designated heir to the throne. The only jarring note in an otherwise smooth arrangement of affairs was some wild shooting which went on for a few minutes in the course of the denunciation.

On hearing news of his deposition, Iyyasu hastened back to the capital. He was confronted at Miesso, about midway between Addis Ababa and Dire Dawa, by a force of over 15,000 troops. Defeated, Iyyasu fled to the Afar plains. He was to roam as a fugitive for the following five years. As expected, the major attempt to reverse the tide of events came from his father, *Negus* Mikael of Wallo and Tegre, who marched towards Shawa with an army estimated at about 80,000 men. The Shawans were able to field an army estimated to be 120,000 strong. The first encounter between the two forces took place at Tora Mask, some 80 miles (130km) north-east of Addis Ababa, on 17 October 1916. The Wallo force was victorious, the Shawan commander, *Ras* Lulsaggad Atnafsaggad, being killed in the battle. *Fitawrari* Habta-Giyorgis Dinagde, the Minister of War and military strategist in the Shawan camp, now began to buy time by sending conciliatory messages and mediators to Mikael. The Tora Mask victory as well as Habta-Giyorgis's tactics may have helped to make the Wallo leader less alert to what was coming. The final battle, the bloodiest clash since Adwa, took place at Sagale on 27 October. An encircling movement by the Shawan troops wrought disarray in the rear of Mikael's army. The Wallo forces were defeated. *Negus* Mikael was captured. The coup was now sanctioned by blood.

Creeping autocracy (1916-1930)

The political settlement reached in 1916 was in the nature of a compromise. The monarch and the heir to the throne were, respectively, the candidates of the Shawan nobility and of the foreign legations, the two forces which had united to overthrow *Lej* Iyyasu. Zawditu's sole qualification for the throne was her birth, as the daughter of Menilek. Her attraction to the nobility was her political innocuousness. While Tafari Makonnen's lineage as great-grandson of Negus Sahle-Sellase

Sellase of Shawa (r. 1813–1847) was almost as impressive, his pro-Allies stand, emanating partly from his French educational background, contributed as much, if not more, to his claim to and assumption of such an exalted post. As the years went by, Tafari's close association with foreigners was to stand him in good stead in strengthening the infrastructure of his political power. In the eyes of the traditional nobility, however, it cast him in the image of someone who was out to sell his country. Often, he was accused of having become a Catholic, with all the connotations of betrayal and apostasy that the word conjured up in the Orthodox Christian mind.

The 1916 settlement was also characterized by anomaly and permeated with ambiguity. To begin with, it was not common practice to designate the heir to the throne simultaneously with the declaration of a new monarch. Next, the Ethiopian past had indeed seen a few powerful queen-mothers who exercised considerable powers in the name of the reigning monarch: Elleni and Mentewab, both in the medieval period, were perhaps the most remarkable examples. Empress Taytu's ambition in more recent times was apparently to repeat the careers of her illustrious predecessors. But the Zawditu–Tafari relationship reversed the pattern. A woman monarch, who at the age of forty years could by no means be considered a minor, found herself in the political shadow of her junior.

The ambiguity arose from the rather indeterminate nature of the respective powers and prerogatives of the two partners. The few prophetic voices which drew attention to the dangerous implications of dual power passed unheeded. Although in his autobiography, written after he became emperor, Tafari claimed that he was made heir to the throne *and* regent, the circulars sent out to the provinces by the nobility and the *echage* immediately after the deposition of Iyyasu referred to Tafari as simply heir to the throne. The issue came to a head in 1925. *Ligaba* Bayyana Wandemagagnahu, who had been in the forefront of the agitation to overthrow Iyyasu, became resentful of the growing powers of Tafari and led a conspiracy against him. His main argument was that as Tafari had been designated heir to the throne, and not *endarase* (regent), he should wait until the death of Zawditu to assume full powers. The conspiracy was foiled; Bayyana was publicly flogged and then imprisoned in Harar.

Whatever the actual details of the arrangement, there is no doubt that Tafari, born in 1892, and younger by nearly twenty years, brought much greater political experience to government than Zawditu. By 1916, he had served consecutively as governor of Garamullata, Salale, Basso, Sidamo and Harar, even if the early appointments were only titular. Zawditu's public activity was not so impressive. She was married successively to *Ras* Araya-Sellase Yohannes, son of Emperor Yohannes IV; to *Dajjach* Webe Atnaf- **129**

3.24   Empress Zawditu Menilek, r. 1916–1930

saggad, a distinguished member of the Shawan nobility; and to *Ras* Gugsa Wale of Bagemder. With the coming to power of Iyyasu, she was shut out of public life altogether, and banished to Falle, in north-western Shawa. The turn of events in 1916 suddenly brought the unprepared princess back into the centre of the political stage. On the other hand, although the leadership role that is sometimes attributed to Tafari is exaggerated, he was certainly deeply involved in the political deliberations that finally led to Iyyasu's overthrow.

The contrast in the educational and intellectual background of the two partners of power also contributed to their divergent outlooks. Zawditu's education did not exceed the level of reading the holy books to which she was particularly attached. Tafari's education had a more modern veneer, through exposure to missionary education under the guidance of the Capuchin priest in Harar, Father André Jarosseau (known as *Abba* Endryas to the Ethiopians), and attendance at Menilek II School. From his father and his own governorship of Harar, he had also acquired both the inclination and the opportunity to meet and communicate with foreigners.

In the final analysis, however, the power struggle was not between Tafari and Zawditu, but between him and the traditional forces for whom she served as a symbol and guarantee of the continuation of the past. The acknowledged lay leader of the party of tradition was *Fitawrari* Habta-Giyorgis. For understandable reasons, the clerical establishment, spearheaded by the *abun* and the *echage*, gave spiritual support to this party. In fairly general terms, the conflict between the conservatives and Tafari could be described as one of stagnation in independence versus progress through dependence. The alliance between Tafari and the intellectuals mentioned previously in this chapter was occasioned by this conflict.

The high point of success for Tafari's open-door policy was reached in 1923 and 1924, with the entry of Ethiopia into the League of Nations and his grand tour of Europe, respectively. He himself considered the latter so important that he devoted forty pages of his autobiography to it. Although he was unable to attain his objective of an outlet to the sea, he came back with his international stature enhanced and his commitment to introducing European ways of administration strengthened. The impact also on the members of his entourage, which included some of the most important members of the nobility, was considerable.

Once Tafari had been designated heir to the throne, it was probably only a matter of time before he would become *negusa nagast* of Ethiopia. That fact in itself was sufficient to instil great political ambition in the young prince. But he did not appear to need such prompting. Thanks to his extraordinary talent for dissimulation, he slowly but steadily worked his way to the throne. The first step in the enhancement of his power was the dismissal of the ministers in 1918. This was achieved not through the customary *shum sher* or official shuffle of appointments, but following a public rally in which the *mahal safari* once again played a crucial role. Tafari's part in all this is not absolutely clear. There is no doubt that the removal of the rather well-entrenched ministers would give him the opportunity to make a clean start in affairs of state. The enthusiasm which the agitators reserved for him in their manifesto also indicates that his partisans, if not Tafari himself, were actively working behind the movement. But his response to the demands of the petitioners was somewhat ambivalent: while he expressed readiness to accede to their demands, he reiterated his alarm at the public intervention in politics. With the Russian Revolution of November 1917 fresh in his mind, he even went on to remind the petitioners of what havoc such public gatherings could bring to the country. It appears, therefore, that, while Tafari gave his implicit blessing to the agitation, he was alarmed at the dangerous possibilities inherent in it.

The resolution of the issue was significant not only because of the dismissal of previous ministers but also because of the retention of one of them. This was *Fitawrari* Habta-Giyorgis, the Minister of War, a

3.25 Fitawrari *Habta-Giyorgis Dinagde, Minister of War from 1907–1926*

post he held from 1907 until his death in 1926. His exemption from dismissal is indication either of his own complicity in the move or, if the whole thing was master-minded by Tafari, of the latter's caution not to overreach himself. Indeed, in spite of the fact that Habta-Giyorgis and Tafari were the leaders of two divergent political tendencies and groupings, there were to be few cases of open confrontation between them. Their silent struggle came to an end when Habta-Giyorgis died naturally in December 1926. Tafari promptly took over 15,000 of the *fitawrari*'s retainers as well as the lands supporting them, thereby increasing at a stroke his military power and his economic wealth.

The open challenge to Tafari came first of all from *Dajjach* Balcha Safo. More warrior than politician, Balcha was prone to give vent to his feelings rather than bide his time or try to undermine his opponent by subterfuge. He was one of those who resented Tafari's steady corrosion of Empress Zawditu's powers. Already in 1920, Balcha had become involved in a plot led by *Bajerond* Webeshat Hayle and including *Aqa* Gabru, head of the city police. The plotters had accused Tafari of selling the country, probably in reference to the many concessions he was accustomed to give to foreigners. The conspirators,

3.26 Dajjach *Balcha Safo, hero of the Battle of Adwa, and one of the conservative opponents of* Ras *Tafari Makonnen*

however, were apprehended before they were able to take any action. They were imprisoned and their property was confiscated. But Balcha managed to exculpate himself and escape their fate.

The confrontation was postponed, not totally averted. By background and temperament, Tafari and Balcha were incompatible. Tafari's winning over of some of Balcha's retainers added fuel to the latter's resentment. He reciprocated by flouting orders coming from the capital. Tafari, too, must have coveted the coffee-rich province of Sidamo, which had become Balcha's personal fief. The denouement came late in 1927. Summoned to Addis Ababa, Balcha procrastinated, on the grounds of ill health. He finally arrived with a huge army, and encamped on his estate in the southern outskirts of the capital. His subsequent conduct emphasized his displeasure with and disrespect for Tafari. The latter hit back with a stratagem, appointing *Dajjach* Berru Walda-Gabr'el, formerly governor of Sayyo, Wallaga, as governor of Sidamo in place of Balcha. On hearing the *awaj* (decree), the soldiers in Balcha's camp, most of whom were members of the *quter tor*, the imperial troops, rather than Balcha's own personal retainers, flocked to their new master. Deserted, Balcha had no option but to surrender. *Dajjach* Berru's appointment proved an interim

133

3.27 Dajjach *Abba Weqaw Berru, leader of a mutiny against* Ras *Tafari Makonnen in 1928*

measure. Three years later, the lucrative province was given to one much closer to Tafari (from 1930, Emperor Hayla-Sellase): his business-minded son-in-law, *Ras* Dasta Damtaw, married to the emperor's daughter, Tanagnawarq.

The next challenge to Tafari's growing power came from *Dajjach* Abba Weqaw Berru, head of the palace guards. A protégé of Menilek's, his rather terrifying name ('the man who thrashes people') is said to have been given to him by the old emperor, who saw him beating up boys bigger and older than himself. He remained loyal to Menilek even after the latter's death. In defending Zawditu, he was actually defending the spirit of Menilek, more or less in the tradition of his predecessor as head of the palace guards, *Fitawrari* Gabra-Maryam. When Iyyasu took action against the palace guards in 1913, he spared Abba Weqaw, with the words: 'He is a good Christian; his hallmark is physical force, not cunning.' After Iyyasu's overthrow in 1916, Abba Weqaw became chief of the palace guards. He toured the northern provinces of Wallo, Gondar and Gojjam as an apostle of change. Soon, the friction inherent in the dual power ranged him on **134** the side of Zawditu and against Tafari.

It appears that Abba Weqaw's action was provoked by yet another agitation by the *mahal safari* in the summer of 1928, this time calling for the coronation of Tafari as *negus*. The treaty of friendship that Tafari had signed with the Italians early that year must also have exacerbated the tension, for the traditionalists still viewed Italy as the old enemy. According to some reports, Empress Zawditu had expressed her dismay at Tafari's attempt to seize the full reins of power once *Fitawrari* Habta-Giyorgis had died, in 1926. But Abba Weqaw's action appears to have been unilateral rather than encouraged by the empress. Symbolically, he barricaded himself inside Menilek's mausoleum near the imperial palace, and threatened to shoot down anybody who approached. As a precautionary measure, Tafari had the first tank ever imported into Ethiopia installed in front of the building. Abba Weqaw refused all mediation, sending back with insults those sent for the purpose. Finally, Tafari prevailed upon the empress to calm down her loyal servant. A special telephone-line had to be set up between Zawditu in the *gebbi* and Abba Weqaw to confirm her messages for him to give up. He surrendered, was tried and was sentenced to death; the sentence was later commuted to imprisonment.

The crushing of Abba Weqaw's mutiny was the signal for the renewed activities of Tafari's supporters. Although the action of Abba Weqaw had been confined to the palace area, the tension had spread into the city. Now, led by such partisans as *Kantiba* Nasibu Zamanuel, Tafari's men came to the fore, openly demanding the coronation of Tafari. The empress had no choice but to acquiesce. Tafari was made *negus*. In the absence of any specific territorial circumscription of the title (as was hitherto the custom), it was assumed that he had become *nequs* of all Ethiopia, thereby giving legal sanction to his *de facto* seizure of absolute power. The coronation ceremony took place in October 1928, with a pomp and foreign attendance which was in effect a dress-rehearsal for the much more glamorous ceremony of 1930, when *Negus* Tafari became *negusa nagast*.

The final challenge to Tafari came from *Ras* Gugsa Wale, governor of Bagemder and former husband of Zawditu. By a twist of irony, he was the first to suffer personally from the 1916 settlement and the deposition of Iyyasu. Zawditu's selection then for the throne had appeared like a politically posthumous vindication of Empress Taytu, who had been trying unsuccessfully for precisely such an indirect path to political supremacy for her nephew Gugsa. For exactly the same reason, the Shawan nobility arranged for the separation of husband and wife, following Zawditu's coronation. *Ras* Gugsa, who had been living quietly with Zawditu at Falle, then returned to Bagemder. Rightly or wrongly, he regarded Tafari as the chief instigator of the separation.

3.28 Ras *Gugsa Wale, husband of Empress Zawditu and governor of Bagemder, who met his death at the Battle of Anchem in 1930*

But Gugsa's rebellion was not motivated simply by personal revenge. Other forces and factors were also at work to bring about the final clash. The tension between tradition and adaptation that marked the period 1916 to 1930 was probably at its highest in the confrontation between Gugsa and Tafari. To cite just one example: Gugsa, self-proclaimed defender of the Orthodox Christian faith, accused Tafari and the Shawans of eating dog meat; Tafari used the first aircraft in Ethiopian history to shower Gugsa's army first with propaganda leaflets, then with bombs. In characteristic fashion, Tafari also worked assiduously to undermine Gugsa in his own province, succeeding in disaffecting Gugsa's followers and Taytu's relatives such as *Dajjach* Ayalew Berru of Semen. In the final analysis, the clash between Tafari and Gugsa was inevitable, given the former's urge to spread his administrative and fiscal tentacles to the provinces and the latter's determination to retain his hereditary prerogatives. One issue of contention, for instance, was control of the customs at Matamma, the commercial post on the Ethio-Sudanese border in the north-west.

136

On Gugsa's side, he was abetted by the Italians in Eritrea and by his Ethiopian neighbours, *Ras* Haylu Takla-Haymanot of Gojjam and *Ras* Seyum Mangasha of Tegre. Endowed with greater guile than Gugsa, they urged him to a confrontation, promising to help but preferring to stay in the background when matters drew to a climax. This fact was to be rendered with some pathos in the lamentation of Gugsa's *azmari* or minstrel, Mesganaw Adugna, after the battle:

> All had conspired with us,
> But they went back without fighting.
> Tegre heard the news and submitted promptly –
> Gojjam heard the news and submitted promptly –
> Having made of my naïve lord, Gugsa Wale, a dupe.
> (Andalem, 37)

The immediate cause of the clash was a classic case of insubordination – Gugsa's refusal to respond to the summons of Tafari to meet him at Warra Illu, in Wallo. As a further test of his loyalty, Gugsa was ordered to proceed to Yajju as the leader of a campaign to reassert central government authority. Since 1928, the eastern highlands of Wallo and Tegre had been in ferment as the inhabitants, responding to the economic distress wrought by drought and locust raids, resorted to their customary raids of the Afar lowlands. The dilatory fashion in which Gugsa went about the task convinced Tafari of the need for military action. In a desperate and pathetic bid to avert the catastrophe that she saw coming, Zawditu sent letter after letter to her ex-husband, pleading with him to submit. Gugsa was unmoved. The Battle of Anchem, as it came to be known, took place on 31 March 1930. The imperial force was led by *Dajjach* (later *Ras*) Mulugeta Yeggazu, now Minister of War. Superior in numbers as well as in armament, it above all enjoyed an incalculable psychological and physical advantage because of its deployment of aircraft. Gugsa was defeated, and died on the battlefield. Two days later, the empress, still his adoring ex-wife, also died. Almost instantaneously, the last political and material obstacles in Tafari's path to the throne were removed. Tafari became Hayla-Sellase.

The emergence of absolutism (1930–1935)

The coronation ceremony of Hayla-Sellase I took place seven months after the death of Empress Zawditu and his accession to absolute power. The interval was used in preparing the most extravagant coronation ceremony in Ethiopian history. Absolutism demanded nothing less grand than that. The taste for luxury acquired through greater exposure to Europe – Tafari's tour in 1924 included a number of European countries – set new standards of pageantry. The state coach of Imperial Germany was brought to transport the royal

3.29 A traditional painting depicting the Battle of Anchem (31 March 1930). Ras Mulugeta Yeggazu, Minister of War and commander-in-chief of the imperial troops, is shown holding binoculars, at the top left-hand corner; Ras Gugsa Wale is the fallen figure, right centre

couple. Gold and velvet were evident everywhere. A vigorous campaign to beautify Addis Ababa was launched. Offensive slums were cleared. The *gebbi* was equipped with electricity, the main city roads were tarmacked and the police donned new uniforms. The capital received a lasting landmark in the equestrian statue erected in memory of Emperor Menilek II. The occasion also embraced international glamour, with the representatives of many states attending, including the Prince of Savoy for Italy and the Duke of Gloucester for Britain. Journalists, who were to become a regular feature of the Ethiopian scene in the 1930s, rushed to report the great event. Present among them was the celebrated English novelist, Evelyn Waugh, who left to posterity a well-spiced record of his impressions.

The transformation in the stature of Tafari Makonnen had begun before his coronation as *negusa nagast* of Ethiopia. The growth of the personality cult around him is discernible in the Amharic publications that came out during and after his coronation as *negus* in 1928. The date of his coronation as *negusa nagast*, 2 November 1930, marked the culmination of this trend. Having attained the height of his ambition, Hayla-Sellase stood poised to do away with the last vestiges of the *Zamana Masafent*. Tewodros had tried and failed to establish a unitary Ethiopian state. His successors, Yohannes and Menilek, had thus been forced to make varying degrees of compromise with regionalism. Iyyasu's rather heterodox approach to national integration had cost him his throne. It was to be the major historical achievement of Hayla-Sellase that he finally succeeded in realizing the unitary state of which Tewodros had dreamt. Altogether oblivious of the economic content of feudalism, the new emperor cast himself in the role of an anti-feudal crusader. In actual fact, what he was doing was to reconstruct feudalism on a new and advanced basis, enhancing the political power of the monarchy and guaranteeing the economic privilege of the nobility. That became the essence of absolutism in the Ethiopian context.

The Constitution of 1931 set up the juridical framework of emergent absolutism. The debate preceding its promulgation was illustrative of the continuing struggle between centralism and regionalism. The hereditary nobility (the *masafent*), with the exception of *Ras* Emeru Hayla-Sellase, argued for the retention of their regional prerogatives. The new élite, composed of the ministers and *makwanent*, the recently appointed nobles, true to its class origin, argued that appointments (including provincial governorships) should be by merit rather than by birth. The compromise formula that eventually emerged through the emperor's intervention was clearly weighted towards centralism, the concession to the hereditary nobility being that they would be granted hereditary rights over tributary land (*resta gult*) on the basis of their services to the state.

140

The constitution partly arose from considerations similar to those behind the ministerial system set up by Menilek in 1907. Like that system, the Constitution of 1931 was partly intended for foreign consumption, to impress on Europeans Ethiopia's political modernity, and contained quite a few provisions which were only of paper value. Again, like Menilek's ministerial system, the 1931 Constitution also attempted to grapple with the vexatious question of succession. The regulations for succession occupied an important place in the supplement attached to the 1931 Constitution. Compared with the time-honoured Ethiopian institution of imprisoning royal contenders, and even compared with Menilek's provisions, the treatment of this question in the constitution is impressive in its elaborateness and ideological sophistication. As we shall see below, the question of succession was treated with even more painstaking detail in the Revised Constitution of 1955. The irony of the whole matter appears in the fact that these elaborate provisions never came to be tested, for Hayla-Sellase proved to be Ethiopia's last monarch. Further, even more than Menilek's ministerial system, the constitution was intended as a vehicle for national integration. Parliament was to be a school of national unity. This is underlined by the speeches the emperor made to the first parliament, which assembled in November 1931.

The main issue that the constitution dealt with was the regulation of the relationship between the monarchy and the nobility. The general public seems to have been dragged into the arrangement because a modern constitution was inconceivable without some provision of rights and duties for citizens. The introductory explanation of the constitution illustrates this rather grudging concession to the people:

The constitution defines the hereditary rights, powers and honours of the *negusa nagast* on the one hand and the honours and benefits of the *masafent* and *makwanent* on the other. Further, *while we establish this law to define our relationship*, it is also fitting that provisions be made to guarantee the rights and benefits of the people due them as Ethiopians.

(Mahtama-Sellase, 763; emphasis added)

The composition of the parliament, which had two houses – a Senate and a Chamber of Deputies – emphasized the belief that the people were not yet ready for active participation in the political process. The Senate was composed of *masafent* and *makwanent* chosen by the emperor. The Chamber of Deputies was constituted through indirect elections, with the electors mostly drawn from the landed gentry. The property qualifications for a member of parliament excluded even rich merchants, let alone commoners. In the somewhat panegyrical speech that the author of the constitution, *Bajerond* Takla-Hawaryat Takla-Maryam, made on the occasion of the promulgation

141

3.30 Emperor Hayla-Sellase I, r. 1930–1974

of the constitution, he was at pains to point out how a 'constitutional monarchy', which he tried to show was being established, was the best form of government for Ethiopia. 'Democracy', he reasoned, 'has caused too much bloodshed even among the civilized nations' (Mahtama-Sellase, 804).

The constitution legalized the emperor's absolute powers in appointments and dismissals, the rendering of justice, the declaration and termination of wars, and the granting of land and honours. The traditional nobility could no longer sign treaties with foreign states, nor receive arms or decorations, without permission from the emperor. What is particularly interesting is that, in a ceremony loaded with historical drama, they were made to sign what amounted to their political death-warrant. The signing ceremony at the same time further underlined the fact that the whole constitution was a matter between monarchy and nobility. As a sort of check on them in the bodies to which they were elected, the emperor made sure that the presidency and vice-presidency of both houses were occupied by his trusted officials. Thus the president and vice-president of the Senate were, respectively, *Bitwaddad* Walda-Tsadeq Goshu and *Blatten Geta* Sahle Tsadalu, both men of humble background who made their way to the top through their loyal service to the emperor. That they presided over the deliberations of such grandees as *Ras* Kasa Haylu, Ras Haylu Takla-Haymanot of Gojjam and *Ras* Seyum Mangasha of Tegre was dramatic illustration of the transformed status of the traditional nobility: the *masafent* had become mere conduits for central government orders. Takla-Hawaryat was to confess this retrospectively in a candid and much-quoted interview that he gave in 1966:

At that time, we did not want a person who could work well in the parliament and legislate good and modern laws. We wanted people to accept those laws which were to be legislated, and these laws could only get acceptance if they were discussed by the nobility and accepted by them first . . . We wanted to speak to the people of Ethiopia through these personalities. Thus we used them as instruments for the achievement of our plans and goals.

(Markakis, 273)

Of the powerful nobles who were forced to submit to the constitution, there was one who was not prepared to give in without a fight. This was *Ras* Haylu of Gojjam, son of *Negus* Takla-Haymanot. In spite of the ignominy of defeat at the Battle of Embabo in 1882, his father had managed to retain his hereditary prerogatives. Now the constitution appeared to be threatening Gojjam with what even that defeat at Embabo had not brought about – its reduction to the status of a mere province. *Ras* Haylu Takla-Haymanot had particular reason to resent this, because, through a combination of political cunning and opportune marriages, he had managed to carve an autonomous existence for himself and his region over a period of nearly **143**

3.31 Bajerond *Takla-Hawaryat Takla-Maryam, the Russian-educated intellectual who drafted the 1931 Constitution*

three decades. His inordinate rural taxation and sharp business acumen had made him one of the wealthiest Ethiopians. If there was one *ras* who could match Tafari in cunning and foresight, it was Haylu. That is why the duel between the two had the character of a feud between foxes, altogether different from the conflicts between Tafari on the one hand and *Dajjach* Balcha Safo, *Dajjach* Abba Weqaw Berru and *Ras* Gugsa Wale on the other. But Haylu overstretched himself and played into the hands of Hayla-Sellase, for his taxation policy alienated a large section of the Gojjame population, including the clergy, and this alienation, particularly of the churchmen, was put to good propaganda use by the emperor. More disastrously for Haylu, he was implicated in a plot to arrange the escape of Iyyasu, who had been in confinement at Feche, on the Gojjam road north of Addis Ababa, since his capture in 1921. Arrested and tried on the above charge, Haylu was condemned to death. In a profitable exercise of magnanimity, Hayla-Sellase commuted the sentence to imprisonment and confiscation of Haylu's enormous wealth.

That was in 1932. A year later, Jimma was brought under central administration, thereby terminating the autonomous status sanc-

3.32 Ras *Haylu Takla-Haymanot (on horseback), hereditary ruler of Gojjam from 1901–1932*

tioned by Menilek as a reward for the peaceful submission of Abba Jifar II in 1882; in September 1934, battered and ailing, the former ruler died. The central control of the provinces might now be considered almost complete. Because of the clean start that Menilek's campaigns of incorporation had made possible, the south had not presented much difficulty in the extension of central authority. In the north, Wallo had undergone a graduated process of integration after the Battle of Sagale in 1916, culminating in the appointment of the emperor's eldest son, Asfawasan, as its governor. After the Battle of Anchem in 1930, Bagemder was put under the *ras* most loyal to Hayla-Sellase, *Ras* Kasa Haylu, who delegated his authority to his son, Bawandwasan. After the downfall of *Ras* Haylu Takla-Haymanot, Gojjam came under the enlightened rule of *Ras* Emeru Hayla-Sellase, always a close companion of the emperor.

Provincial administration of an even more integrative kind was also introduced on an experimental basis. This concerned what came to be known as the 'model provinces', the most notable example being Charchar, in western Harar province, successively administered by progressive governors such as *Ras* Emeru, *Bajerond* Takla-Hawaryat **145**

3.33 Dajjach *Seyum Mangasha, later* Ras, *hereditary ruler of Tegre, with a younger brother,* c. *1910*

Takla-Maryam and *Hakim* Warqenah Eshate. These model provinces were precursors of the centrally controlled provinces which became the norm after 1941.

A region which by 1935 still remained largely outside direct control by the central government was Tegre. It was ruled by two grandsons of Emperor Yohannes IV: *Ras* Seyum Mangesha and *Ras* Gugsa Araya. Although it had little effect on their loyalties, an attempt was made to tie them to the Shawan ruling house through the traditional mechanism of marriage alliances. *Ras* Gugsa was married to Yashashwarq Yelma, the emperor's niece; and Gugsa's son, *Dajjach* Hayla-Sellase Gugsa, was married to Zanabawarq, daughter of the emperor and Empress Manan. The emperor's son and heir, Asfawasan, was married to the daughter of *Ras* Seyum, Walatta-Israel, as his first wife.

Political and administrative control of the provinces had a direct bearing on the military resources of the state. The progressive political ascendancy of Tafari was thus paralleled by growing military strength at the centre. While the old regional basis of military

3.34   Troops of the Imperial Bodyguard, 1935

organization still prevailed, the emperor came to have stronger claims
on the provincial troops through the medium of his appointees. Yet
this should not be overemphasized, particularly in the northern provinces. The outbreak of the Italo-Ethiopian war in 1935 was to show
the fragility of the military hold exercised by the central government.
Disgruntled because he was not made successor to *Ras* Gugsa Wale
in Bagemder in spite of his services to Tafari in his confrontation with
Gugsa in the late 1920s, *Dajjach* Ayalew Berru of Semen was rather
lukewarm in the fight against the Italians, and eventually deserted to
them. The Italians reciprocated by honouring Ayalew with the title
of *ras*, and later with the governorship of their province named
Amhara. *Ras* Seyum Mangasha had a somewhat similar career.
Dajjach Hayla-Sellase Gugsa jumped to the Italian side at the first
opportunity. The Gojjame troops fought reluctantly under their
governor and relatively able commander, *Ras* Emeru.

   More significant in terms of future trends were the modern military
units which came to be trained under the direct supervision of the central government and with the assistance of foreign advisers. The war   **147**

again was to show the dedication and single-mindedness with which such units as the Imperial Bodyguard fought. They were matched perhaps only by the old imperial army imbued with the spirit of Adwa and commanded by the veteran *Ras* Mulugeta Yeggazu, the Minister of War. The Imperial Bodyguard was trained by a Belgian military mission which arrived in 1930. It had three battalions of infantry and a company armed with heavy machine-guns. It was mainly commanded by young Ethiopian graduates of Saint Cyr, the French military academy. An interesting point of continuity was that one of the battalions included 600 members of the *mahal safari*. While the main force was based in Addis Ababa, units were organized in some of the southern provinces as well. In 1934, a Swedish military mission opened the first officer-training school at Holata, west of the capital. The three-year training programme of the first batch of officers was interrupted by the Italian invasion. The cadets began to make history as impassioned patriots rather than as career officers.

Sources, Chapter 3

Note. The BA and MA theses cited in the references are available in the Institute of Ethiopian Studies (IES) and/or in the Department of History, Addis Ababa University (AAU), formerly Haile Sellassie I University (HSIU).

Abdussamed Hajj Ahmad. 'Trade and Politics in Gojjam, 1882–1935.' MA thesis (AAU, History, 1980).

Abera Paulos. 'Land Tenure System in Soddo Zuria Woreda (1894–1974).' BA thesis (AAU, History, 1987).

Aby Demissie. 'Lij Iyasu: A Perspective Study of His Short Reign.' BA thesis (HSIU, History, 1964).

Addis Hiwet. *Ethiopia: From Autocracy to Revolution*. London, 1975.

Andalem Mulaw. 'Bagemdir and Simen (1910–1930).' BA thesis (HSIU, History, 1971).

Asnake Ali. 'Aspects of the Political History of Wallo, 1872–1916.' MA thesis (AAU, History, 1983).

Bahru Demissie. 'The Role of the Progressives in Ethiopian Politics (1909–1930).' BA thesis (HSIU, History, 1970).

Bahru Zewde. 'Economic Origins of the Absolutist State in Ethiopia (1916–1935)', *Journal of Ethiopian Studies* XVII (1984).

———. 'The Fumbling Début of British Capital in Ethiopia. A Contrastive Study of the Abyssinian Corporation and the Ethiopian Motor Transport Company, Ltd.', *Proceedings of the Seventh International Conference of Ethiopian Studies*. Addis Ababa, Uppsala, East Lansing, 1984.

———. 'An Overview and Assessment of Gambella Trade (1904–1935)', *International Journal of African Historical Studies* XX, 1 (1987).

———. 'Relations between Ethiopia and the Sudan on the Western Ethiopian Frontier, 1898–1935.' PhD thesis (University of London, School of Oriental and African Studies, 1976).

Berhanou Abbébé. *Evolution de la propriété foncière au Choa (Ethiopie) du règne de Ménélik à la constitution de 1931*. Paris, 1971.

Berkeley, G.F.H. *The Campaign of Adowa and the Rise of Menelik*. London, 1902.

Caulk, Richard. 'Dependence, Gebre Heywet Baykedagn and the Birth of Ethiopian Reformism', *Proceedings of the Fifth International Conference of Ethiopian Studies, Session B*. Chicago, 1978.

148

Fere Kanafer (Collected Speeches of Emperor Hayla-Sellase 1), Volume I. Addis Ababa, 1944 Ethiopian Calendar.

Gabra-Heywat Baykadagn. 'Atse Menilek-na Ityopya' (Emperor Menilek and Ethiopia), *Berhan Yehun*. Asmara, 1912.

Girma Negash. 'The Historical Evolution of Land Tenure and Mechanization in Hetosa Warada, Arssi Region (1880–1974).' BA thesis (HSIU, History, 1972).

Gizachew Adamu. 'A Historical Survey of Taxation in Gojjam (1901–1969).' BA thesis (HSIU, History, 1971).

Gutema Imana. 'A Historical Survey of Land Tenure System in Aira-Gulisso Warada, Central Wallaga (1880 to 1935).' BA thesis (AAU, History, 1987).

Haile Sellassie I: see Qadamawi Hayla-Sellase.

Heruy Walda-Sellase. *Ya Heywat Tarik* (Biography). Addis Ababa, 1915 Ethiopian Calendar.

Kabbada Tasamma. *Ya Tarik Mastawasha* (Historical Notes). Addis Ababa, 1962 Ethiopian Calendar.

Maaza Bekele. 'A Study of Modern Education in Ethiopia: Its Foundations, Its Developments, Its Future, with Emphasis on Primary Education.' PhD thesis (Columbia, 1966)

McCann, James. *From Poverty to Famine in Northeast Ethiopia. A Rural History 1900–1935*. Philadelphia, 1987.

Mahtama-Sellase Walda-Masqal. *Zekra Nagar* (Recollection of Things Past). Addis Ababa, 1962 Ethiopian Calendar.

Mantel Niecko, Joanna. *The Role of Land Tenure in the System of Ethiopian Imperial Government in Modern Times*. Warsaw, 1980.

Marcus, Harold. 'The Foreign Policy of the Emperor Menelik, 1896–1898: A Rejoinder', *Journal of African History* IV, 1 (1963); VII, 1 (1966).

——. *The Life and Times of Menelik II: Ethiopia 1814–1913*. Oxford, 1975.

——. *Haile Sellasie I: The Formative Years, 1892–1936*. Berkeley and Los Angeles, 1987.

Markakis, John. *Ethiopia. Anatomy of a Traditional Polity*. Oxford, 1974.

Mars'e-Hazan Walda-Qirqos. 'Ba Dagmawi Menilek Zaman Kayahut-na Kasamahut' (From What I Saw and Heard in the Reign of Menilek II) (unpublished manuscript, 1935 Ethiopian Calendar). IES, AAU.

——. 'Ya Zaman Tarik Tezetaye ba Abeto Iyyasu Zamana Mangest' (My Historical Reminiscences of the Reign of *Abeto* Iyyasu) (unpublished manuscript, 1938 Ethiopian Calendar). IES, AAU.

——. 'Ya Zaman Tarik Tezetaye ba Negesta Nagastat Zawditu Zamana Mangest' (My Historical Reminiscences of the Reign of Empress Zawditu) (unpublished manuscript, 1938 Ethiopian Calendar). IES, AAU.

Pankhurst, Richard. *Economic History of Ethiopia 1800–1935*. Addis Ababa, 1968.

——. 'The Foundations of Education, Printing, Newspapers, Book Production, Libraries and Literacy in Ethiopia', *Ethiopia Observer* VI, 3 (1962).

Perham, Margery. *The Government of Ethiopia*. London, 1969.

Prouty, Chris. *Empress Taytu and Menilek II. Ethiopia 1883–1910*. London, 1986.

Qadamawi Hayla-Sellase. *Heywate-na ya Ityopya Ermejja* (My Life and Ethiopia's Progress), Volume I. Addis Ababa, 1965 Ethiopian Calendar.

Rossetti, Carlo. *Storia diplomatica dell'Etiopia durante il regno di Menelik II*. Turin, 1910.

Sanderson, G.N. 'The Foreign Policy of the Negus Menelik, 1896–1898', *Journal of African History* V, 2 (1964).

Shiferaw Bekele. 'The Railway, Trade and Politics: A Historical Survey (1896–1935).' MA thesis (AAU, History, 1982).

Tekalign Wolde Mariam. 'Slavery and the Slave Trade in the Kingdom of Jimma (*ca*. 1800–1935).' MA thesis (AAU, History, 1984).

Tekeste Negash. *No Medicine for the Bite of a White Snake: Notes on Nationalism and Resistance in Eritrea, 1890–1910*. Uppsala, 1986.

Tesemma Ta'a. 'The Oromo of Wollega: A Historical Survey to 1910.' MA thesis (AAU, History, 1980)

Teshome G. Wagaw. *Education in Ethiopia: Prospect and Retrospect*. Ann Arbor, 1979.

The Italian
Occupation
1936–1941

1. The Italo-Ethiopian war

After their defeat at Adwa in 1896, the Italians had briefly followed a policy of retrenchment with regard to their north-east Africa colonial ambitions. The newly elected prime minister, the Marchese di Rudini, had renounced the policy of expansion so energetically pursued by his predecessor, Francesco Crispi. The colonial budget had been reduced by more than half. The anti-colonialist lobby, which had been forced to lead a somewhat subdued existence before Adwa, was even emboldened to call for total withdrawal from Africa. But all this was in the heat of the moment. Italy's abiding interest in Ethiopia soon reasserted itself. In one of the most amazing twists in Ethiopian diplomatic history, Italy was fully rehabilitated in Ethiopia a year after Adwa, being the first country to be diplomatically represented at the court of Emperor Menilek II. Italy's surprisingly swift diplomatic recovery was partly due to the statesmanship of its minister in Addis Ababa, Federico Ciccodicola. In some measure, however, it was also a result of the love–hate relationship that Menilek had had with the Italians – a pattern which can indeed be said to have been the distinctive mark of Ethio-Italian relations throughout history.

As a colonial power sharing the second longest boundary with independent Ethiopia (that is, after Britain), Italy could scarcely afford to ignore Ethiopia. She soon began to synchronize her actions with the other two neighbouring colonial powers, Britain and France. The Tripartite Agreement of 1906 was the first major outcome of this **150** joint approach towards Ethiopia. The terms of the agreement implicitly sanctioned the primacy of Italian interests in Ethiopia. While the vested interests of Britain and France were defined in precise fashion (the Nile basin and the railway zone, respectively), Italy's interests were defined in a conveniently vague manner to include the hinterland of its colonies, Eritrea and Italian Somaliland – in effect, the whole of northern and south-eastern Ethiopia. It also contained the ominous phrase 'territorial connection' between her two colonies and across Ethiopia. It is in this light that one writer called the agreement 'the *magna carta* of Italian aspirations in Ethiopia' (quoted in Baer, 6).

World War One was to show the extent of these aspirations. In 1915, as the Allies deliberated on how they were going to distribute the colonial spoils of the war, Italy focused all her attention on the Horn of Africa. What she proposed was a fundamental rearrangement of territorial and economic interests in the region in her favour. This included the cession of French and British Somaliland to Italy, and the transfer of the railway and the Bank of Abyssinia to her jurisdiction. The territorial cession would have placed her in total control of Ethiopia's access to the sea. Simultaneously, Italian control of the two major viable economic concerns would have made Ethiopia a veritable neo-colony of Italy. But the two other powers were not willing to make such major renunciations of their interests in the Horn of Africa.

The advent of the Fascists to power in Italy in 1922 was a great ideological boost to Italian colonial aspirations. Dedicated to the ideal of restoring the power and glory of the ancient Roman Empire, it was only a matter of time before they turned their force against the one country which had stood as a permanent and insulting symbol of the frustration of Italian colonialism. At the outset, however, the ultimate intentions of Benito Mussolini were camouflaged, as he pursued a policy of attaining Italian objectives by diplomatic means. Thus, when the question of Ethiopia's admission to the League of Nations was raised in the early 1920s, it was Britain rather than Mussolini's Italy which led the opposition. Mussolini is said to have waived his early objection on wise advice from his subordinates that opposition was impolitic, as the likelihood of Ethiopia's admission was in any case very high. In the course of his European tour in 1924, *Ras* Tafari Makonnen was given an enthusiastic welcome in Italy, with shouts of 'Viva Etiopia! Viva Tafari!' More significantly, the Italians offered to cede the port of Assab to Ethiopia, in exchange for some economic concessions to Italy. But the draft agreement to this effect never came to be signed, as the Ethiopian delegation considered the price too high.

The peak of *rapprochement* between the two countries was reached with the signing of the Treaty of Peace and Friendship on 2 August 1928. Meant to last for twenty years, it did not survive even ten. An **151** important annexe to the treaty had provided for the construction of a road between Assab and Dessie. Had it been implemented, the project would have undercut the French railway, something that was to become a reality in more recent times. But neither Ethiopia nor Italy was prepared to push the scheme to fulfilment.

Parallel with this pacific approach, however, the Italians pursued more aggressive designs, particularly from the late 1920s onwards. The combination of strategies was somewhat akin to what had prevailed in the years before the Battle of Adwa: the policy of subversion in the north (known as the 'Tegrean policy', followed by the Italian governor of Eritrea, Antonio Baldissera) versus the policy of persuasion (the 'Shawan policy', followed by the negotiator of the Wechale Treaty, Pietro Antonelli). Now, the Eritrean colonial establishment, headed by the governor Corrado Zoli from 1928 to 1930, continued the policy of subversion, sowing disaffection in Tegre, Bagemder, Gojjam and Wallo. The Italian Legation in Addis Ababa, headed by Giuliano Cora, represented the policy of *rapprochement*. The signing of the 1928 treaty mentioned above was an index of the success of the Cora scheme. Its failure in the realm of implementation was in some measure due to sabotage by the subversionist faction. The Italian consulates opened at various times in the early twentieth century in Adwa, Gondar, Dabra Marqos and Dessie played an important role in this policy of subversion, as well as in the gathering of vital political and military intelligence.

There was another way in which the 1920s resembled the pre-Adwa days. This was in the implicit endorsement that the British appeared to give to Italian ambitions in Ethiopia. The Anglo-Italian agreement of 1925 (actually an exchange of letters of accord between Mussolini and the British ambassador in Rome, Sir Ronald Graham) was somewhat similar to the protocol agreements concluded between the two countries in 1891 and 1894. The one major difference was that, while the nineteenth-century agreements envisaged territorial partition, the agreement of 1925, true to the post-Adwa imperialist strategy, defined economic priorities. The British recognized western Ethiopia as an exclusive zone of Italian economic influence. In return, the Italians pledged to give diplomatic support to the British effort to secure a concession to build a dam on Lake Tana, with a view to regulating the flow of the waters of the Nile to Sudan and Egypt. The irony of it all was that the agreement was signed over a country which had joined the League of Nations only two years before. It made a mockery of the declared equal status of League members. It was also a foretaste of what was to come: the League's impotence to stop Italian invasion of Ethiopia.

Although it is difficult to pin-point one particular year when the decision was made by Mussolini to launch the invasion, 1932 appears to have been the crucial date. The decision became almost irreversible after Mussolini's European policy – particularly his irredentist claims in Austria – was frustrated when he had to back down from the Brenner Pass confrontation with Adolf Hitler in the summer of 1934. In humiliation and desperation, Mussolini was forced to look elsewhere for power and glory. Africa, portrayed as the geographical extension of Italy, came to be regarded as the venue of the latter's manifest destiny. The failure of Fascism on the domestic front also made it necessary to embark on colonial adventure as a diversionary tactic. War became imperative not only as a boost to the economy but also as a medium of collective psychotherapy. What was required to open aggression was only a pretext, a *casus belli*. Walwal played that historical role.

The Walwal incident (5 December 1934), so called after a frontier post on Ethiopia's border with Italian Somaliland, was a product of the ill-demarcated or undemarcated boundaries that Ethiopia had come to acquire after and as a result of Adwa. Although Walwal had fallen within the Ethiopian side of the boundary with Italian Somaliland, the Italians had profited from lax Ethiopian administrative control to take hold of the place, which was valued for its wells. Stronger Ethiopian presence in the region in the 1930s inevitably resulted in the reassertion of Ethiopian rights to the area. Italian refusal to yield and harassment of Ethiopian troops stationed nearby produced the clash that became historically notable. Although the number of Ethiopian dead was three times as high as the Italians', it was the Italians who put forward totally unreasonable demands for apologies and reparations. Ethiopia was naturally not ready to accede to these demands. Instead, she took the matter to the League. A period of futile deliberations to resolve the conflict followed. More seriously, preparations for war began on both sides – with more method and energy on the part of the Italians than on that of the Ethiopians. Diplomatically, Mussolini scored a major victory early in 1935, when France, under her premier Pierre Laval, revised her traditional hostility towards Italy and gave the latter a free hand in Ethiopia. It became increasingly clear that, in an effort to woo Mussolini away from Hitler, both Britain and France were ready to sacrifice Ethiopia. Fortified with such reassurances, Mussolini was ready to strike.

On 3 October 1935, the Italians crossed the fateful Marab river, launching a three-pronged invasion of Ethiopia. One of their targets was the town of Adwa, scene of their humiliating defeat forty years earlier. The two other thrusts were in the direction of Entticho and Addigrat. The invaders faced little opposition. For diplomatic as well as tactical reasons – to expose Italian aggression to the world and to stretch the enemy's line of supplies, respectively – Ethiopian forces had been ordered to withdraw from the lines of confrontation. Some, **153** like *Dajjach* Hayla-Sellase Gugsa of eastern Tegre, needed no such prompting. He defected to the Italians soon after the fall of Addigrat on 5 October, furnishing them with valuable intelligence. On 6 October, Adwa was occupied subsequent to intense and vengeful bombardment. On 8 November, just over a month after the opening of hostilities, the Italians established themselves in the strategic town of Maqale. Yet, for Mussolini, determined to finish the whole operation before the summer rains, the pace was too slow. The commander-in-chief, the veteran Fascist General De Bono, was blamed for this. He was replaced by the less scrupulous Marshal Pietro Badoglio, whose name is associated with the more ruthless phase of the war, including Italian resort to mustard-gas, the use of which had been banned in 1925 by the Geneva Convention of the International Committee of the Red Cross.

The Ethiopian counter-offensive, which the Italians had been expecting for some time, finally came in January 1936. The Ethiopian forces were ranged along three fronts. In the west were the forces of Gojjam and Bagemder commanded by *Ras* Emeru Hayla-Sellase. In the centre were the forces of *Ras* Seyum Mangasha and *Ras* Kasa Haylu, the latter as commander-in-chief of the northern front, to the chagrin of the Minister of War, *Ras* Mulugeta Yeggazu, who had expected to assume supreme command but was put in charge of the easternmost column. The major weakness of the Ethiopian army was lack of co-ordination between the different columns. *Ras* Emeru, for instance, could be said to have fought a war of his own in Tegre. There was little co-operation even between the relatively nearer central column and the right flank commanded by Mulugeta – a situation exacerbated by the mutual antipathies of the leaders. The major offensive launched by the Ethiopians, which aimed at isolating Maqale, foundered on this rock of poor co-ordination. In spite of the valiant efforts to dislodge the Italians from their entrenched positions, the latter won, if at considerable cost, what was known as the first Battle of Tamben (20–24 January 1936).

The repulse of the Ethiopian counter-offensive emboldened the Italians to launch a mass offensive of their own. They first turned their attention to the imperial troops commanded by *Ras* Mulugeta, who had established themselves on the nearly impregnable natural fortress of Amba Aradom, to the south of Maqale. Thanks mainly to Italian superiority in the air, the battle proved to be the reverse of the Battle of Amba Alage in 1895. To his discomfiture, the veteran of Adwa saw a replay of what had happened forty years earlier – a force which occupied a formidable stronghold losing the battle. Only, this time, it was the Ethiopians who were on the losing side. Their losses were estimated at 6,000 dead. Mulugeta himself was killed during the confused retreat. *Ras* Kasa, ordered to come to Mulugeta's aid, arrived

4.1   Amba Aradam, where Ethiopian troops commanded by Ras
*Mulugeta Yeggazu were heavily defeated by the Italians
in February 1936*

after the disaster. He himself and Seyum were soon engaged in the
second Battle of Tamben with the Italians, on 27–29 February 1936.
By now, the Ethiopians had lost the initiative. In addition to their
technical superiority, the Italians outnumbered the Ethiopians by
nearly four to one. This numerical superiority enjoyed by the Italians
was a striking anomaly of the whole war. Mussolini had clearly
resolved not to repeat what he considered to be the mistake of forty
years before: 'For the lack of a few thousand men we lost the day at
Adowa! We shall never make that mistake. I am willing to commit
a sin of excess but never of deficiency' (De Bono, 119). The battle confirmed the collapse of the central front. The leaders narrowly escaped
the encircling manoeuvre of the Italians, and rejoined the emperor
at Koram, about 110 miles (175 km) south of Maqale, with a much
depleted force.

Things were relatively better on the Shere front in western Tegre,
where *Ras* Emeru led the counter-offensive. On 15 December 1935,
in one of their most daring attacks in the course of the whole war,
the Ethiopian forces had routed a force of *askaris* (colonial soldiers)
commanded by Major Luigi Criniti at a strategic pass called Dam-
bagwina – a name that made Emeru the abomination of Italian
Fascism. But the western front was not free from problems. Particularly vitiating was the lack of enthusiasm for the war among the
Gojjame leaders and the Semen chief, *Dajjach* Ayalew Berru. Never-   **155**

4.2   Ras *Mulugeta Yeggazu, holder of various ministerial posts
and provincial governorships, one of the commanders
on the northern front in 1935–1936*

theless it is a credit to the relatively better leadership provided by *Ras*
Emeru that the reverses suffered here were not as catastrophic as on
the central and eastern fronts. About 10,000 troops were able to make
an orderly retreat across the Takkaze river. This fact partly explains
Emeru's ability to continue to create trouble for the Italians even after
they had entered Addis Ababa.

The final battle in the north, the Battle of Maychaw, which in common parlance has become the generic appellation for the whole war,
was actually in the nature of an epilogue. Emeru's army was not at
all involved. The imperial troops of Mulugeta had been virtually
nullified at Amba Aradam. The shattered and demoralized troops of
Ras Kasa and *Ras* Seyum – or what was left of them – were scarcely
in a position to make any meaningful contribution to the war effort.
The only fresh force was the Imperial Bodyguard. For the young
Ethiopians who constituted it, Maychaw was a testing-ground, as
indeed it was of modern Ethiopia. And they stood the test remarkably
well, given the fact that the outcome of the battle was almost
predetermined.

It was inconceivable that the Italians, ensconced in their impregnable fortifications and enjoying the domination of the sky which
was the hallmark of the whole war, could have been defeated by the
Ethiopians. The problem was compounded for the latter by the
156   procrastination that characterized the emperor's command. Suc-

cessive postponements of the attack squandered the only possible advantage the Ethiopians had – the element of surprise. The thirteen-hour combat which finally took place on 31 March 1936, although marked by some initial successes for the Ethiopians, ended in their rout. The disorderly retreat was to cost them more lives than the actual battle. Still smarting from a punitive campaign sent against them by Tafari's government in the late 1920s, for cattle-raiding, the Rayya and Azabo peoples found this an ideal opportunity to settle past scores. The fleeing soldiers were mercilessly mutilated and plundered. Another scene of the gruesome aftermath of the whole disaster was enacted on the shores of Lake Ashange, a short distance to the south of Maychaw, as Italian pilots sported with the harried Ethiopians, alternately showering them with bombs and mustard-gas. After that, the road was clear for the Italians, first to Dessie, which they reached on 4 April 1936, and then to Addis Ababa, which they entered on 5 May.

Although it was the most decisive, the northern front was not the only front: Ethiopians faced Italians in the south and south-east as well. The Italian forces were led by the man who was to symbolize the darkest face of Italian rule in Ethiopia, General (later Marshal) Rodolfo Graziani. He was reputed to have vowed to deliver Ethiopia to *il Duce* Mussolini 'with the Ethiopians or without them, just as he pleases' (Del Boca, 113). Through his impatience for the laurels of victory, Graziani turned a defensive assignment into a second offensive. The Ethiopian forces were commanded in the south by *Ras* Dasta Damtaw, governor of Sidamo, and in the south-east by *Dajjach* Nasibu Zamanuel, governor of Harar. Compared with the northern front, the southern front was characterized by more youthful and energetic Ethiopian leadership and slightly better armament.

Qorahe, a strategic post at the southern end of the Ogaden, proved a nodal point of the war in the southeast. In the words of its most glorious defender, *Grazmach* (posthumously *Dajjazmach*) Afawarq Walda-Samayat, 'If the Italians occupy Qorahe, it is as good as their having occupied the Ogaden!' (Graziani, 185). In spite of the valiant efforts of Afawarq and his men, however, Qorahe fell to the Italians early in November 1935. Subsequently, the Italians launched a three-pronged thrust into the Ogaden, prefacing it with the strategic bombing of such major towns as Jijiga and Harar. In spite of both numerical and technical superiority, however, the Italian advance faced stiff opposition, particularly from the forces of Illubabor, led by *Dajjach* Makonnen Endalkachaw. Italian losses were consequently much higher than on the northern front. Their advance was correspondingly slower, and Graziani had to live with the frustrating experience that his counterpart Badoglio entered Addis Ababa from the north before he himself was able to enter Harar.

4.3   An Ethiopian soldier leaving for the Ogaden front bids farewell to his relatives, November 1935

On the southern front, *Ras* Dasta had embarked on one of the most audacious campaigns of the whole war. Taking advantage of the short-lived discomfiture of the Italians at Qorahe, he led his troops in a bold thrust to the frontier post of Dolo. The exhaustingly long journey, the shortage of supplies and the outbreak of epidemic diseases made them fall easy prey to the better-prepared Italians. The Battle of Ganale Dorya (12–14 January 1936) proved to be a veritable massacre of the Ethiopians. The only sour note in Graziani's victory was struck by the desertion of over 900 Eritrean askaris to the Ethiopian side – a phenomenon which was repeated in the other theatres of war. Their presence boosted the sagging morale of Dasta's defeated troops and partly explains his continued challenge to the Italians until his capture and execution in early 1937; the Eritreans, to whom capture or surrender meant certain death, fought with great resolution.

The memory of Adwa had pervaded the war. Italians sought to erase the record of humiliation. Many Ethiopians fought in the confidence of another victory. Yet the Battle of Adwa could not be repeated. Many factors contributed to this. The most obvious was the monumental imbalance in armaments. At Adwa, the gap between the two sides, in both quantity and quality, was inconsiderable. In 1935, the Italians came benefiting from the latest in military technology; the arms blockade imposed on Ethiopia on various pretexts had deprived it of even a faint approximation to the Italian armoury. The total number of modern rifles on the Ethiopian side was estimated at between 50,000 and 60,000; the level of ammunition was perhaps twice what the Italians were to use in one battle alone. The disparity in machine-guns and artillery was no less glaring. But the fatal advantage was in the air, where an Italian air force, numbering over 300 aircraft on the northern front and about 100 aircraft on the southern front, had the sky to itself. Ethiopia had a fleet of eleven aeroplanes, of which only eight were serviceable, and they were used mainly for transport. Air superiority assumed an even more lethal dimension with Italian use of the prohibited mustard-gas.

In logistics as well, there was an all-too-evident gap. The Ethiopian army had practically no system of supplies. The wounded were able to get medical attention largely thanks to foreign voluntary organizations. The absence or inefficiency of radio communication made co-ordination of military action difficult. This was most acutely felt on the northern front. But probably the most anomalous of the disparities was the numerical one. At Adwa, in 1896, about five Ethiopians had fought against one Italian. In 1935–1936, however, the Italians enjoyed numerical superiority in many of the engagements, particularly in the Ogaden. This was a result of the Italian mobilization of their askaris from Libya, Eritrea and Italian Somaliland. The technical as well as numerical superiority of the Italians is cogently expressed in the following quotation from Angelo del Boca: 'Before they [the Ethiopians] meet the Europeans, they will endure five levels of hells. The bombs from the air. The shelling from the long-range howitzers. The deadly splutter of machine guns. The tanks. The Askaris.' Only the mustard-gas remained to complete the dismal picture.

Ultimately, however, the root of the defeat lay in Ethiopian society itself. The assertion has sometimes been made that Ethiopia was defeated because she was feudal. This is not convincing. Ethiopia was more feudal in 1896 than in 1936; yet she won a resounding victory. Paradoxical as it may seem, Ethiopia was defeated because she was less feudal. The British writer Margery Perham probably had this in mind when she characterized the Ethiopian army on the eve of the war as being in 'a dangerous moment of transition between mediaeval and modern methods' (Perham, 167). That was on the military level. Politically as well, Menilek's Ethiopia had the blessing of feudal harmony. Hayla-Sellase's Ethiopia was in the throes of nascent absolutism. Expressed in another way, Menilek led a more united Ethiopia than Hayla-Sellase's. This was partly the result of the disgruntlement **159** that the latter's centralization policy had caused. It was also partly attributable to the centrifugal influence exercised by the adjacent colonial powers.

The relative peace of the post-Adwa period – the only major battles fought in the forty-year interval being those of Sagale (1916) and Anchem (1930) – had also contributed to a decline in the martial spirit. The Ethiopian commanders at Adwa were men born in war, grown up in war and dying in war. Forty years later, they had been succeeded by men who had made their mark as civillian administrators rather than as warriors. Some of them had even become keen businessmen. The epitome of this trend was Hayla-Sellase himself. War was a burden he assumed uneasily. He entrusted his fate, and that of Ethiopia, too, to the illusion of collective security. That illusion – as well as the instinct of self-preservation – was to take him to Europe after the war was lost. Owing to the relatively higher integration into the world community that Ethiopia had attained in the twentieth century, he was the first emperor in Ethiopian history who had the option of exile. And he took that option.

---

2. Italian rule

For three days between the flight of the emperor and the entry of the Italians, Addis Ababa was caught in the grip of mass violence. There was a total breakdown of law and order. Burning, looting and random shooting became the order of the day. Arada, the commercial centre, was the focal point of the violence. It was a puzzling phenomenon, combining elements of mass psychosis and inchoate class warfare, of despair and defiance. Inasmuch as the violence had any target at all, it was the rich and the expatriate; nor was the palace, the *gebbi*, spared, arms stored in it being a major attraction. The legations became refuge for many expatriates, thus at last performing the roles for which they had prepared themselves for so long. In spite of a vaguely discernible pattern, however, the violence – like most mass violence – was blind. The casualties were mainly Ethiopians, not the foreigners whose presence had apparently aroused the rioters.

Entering against such a backdrop of anarchy, the Italians might appear as the harbingers of peace and order. Some have even interpreted the Italians' delay in entering the capital as a cynical design to give their entry the image of an act of deliverance. Indeed, there was some relief, particularly among the foreigners, when Badoglio entered Addis Ababa on 5 May 1936 at the head of the Italian army – ushering in a Fascist reincarnation of *pax Romana*. His first act was

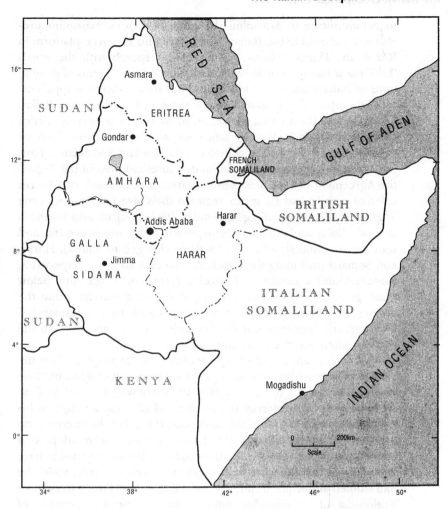

7. 'Italian East Africa', 1936–1941
(adapted from Consociazione Turistica Italiana, Guida dell' Africa
orientale Italiana, Milan, 1938)

161

to communicate to Mussolini the news of victory. Mussolini proclaimed the news to the Italian people from his favourite platform in Rome, the Piazza Venezia. He ended his speech with the words 'Ethiopia is Italian', words which encapsulated the dreams of generations of Italians but whose hollowness was soon to become apparent.

The empire the Italians formed came to be called, not Italian Ethiopia, but Italian East Africa, or, in its Italian rendering, Africa Orientale Italiana (AOI). The new entity was formed from a merger of Ethiopia with the Italian colonies of Eritrea and Somaliland. Thus the 'territorial connection' so ominously foreshadowed in the Tripartite Agreement of 1906 was consummated. The reconstituted Italian colonial empire had six major regional divisions: Eritrea (including Tegray); Amhara (including Bagemder, Wallo, Gojjam and northern Shawa); Galla and Sidama (incorporating the south-western and southern provinces); Addis Ababa (later changed to Shawa); Harar; and Somalia (including the Ogaden). The capitals were, respectively, Asmara, Gondar, Jimma, Addis Ababa, Harar and Mogadishu. Below these governorships, in descending order of hierarchy, came the district commissionerships, the residencies and the vice-residencies. Of these, the residency was the key unit of Italian control, and the resident often exercised autocratic powers.

At the very top, the chief representative of Fascist power was the viceroy. The post was first occupied by Marshal Badoglio, until he returned to Italy at the end of May 1936. He was replaced by Graziani, whose post as viceroy was terminated after the attempt on his life in February 1937. Graziani's successor, the last of the viceroys, was Amadeo Umberto d'Aosta, the Duke of Aosta, who adopted a relatively more pacific style of administration. He was reputed to have had ideas of initiating the British system of colonial rule, which he had studied and which he admired. His deputy was Enrico Cerulli, an Ethiopicist of considerable repute, and the perfect example of scholarship being put at the service of colonial administration. Incompatibility between the viceroy and the deputy viceroy, however, led to Cerulli's transfer to Harar, as governor. He was replaced as deputy viceroy by the previous governor of Harar, General Guglielmo Nasi, who conducted what appeared to be nearly successful negotiations for the surrender of the Shawan patriots led by *Ras* Abbaba Aragay.

Italian administration was characterized by a top-heavy bureaucracy and corruption. According to one writer, 'Sixty per cent of the bureaucratic machinery was working in AOI [Africa Orientale Italiana] to administer itself' (Sbacchi, 80). There was a mania for creating committees and commissions, largely so that the members might attempt to exonerate themselves from responsibility. A vast number of colonial officials were distinguished for their ineptitude and narrow-mindedness, as well as for their corruption. The Duke

4.4 Ras *Abbaba Aragay, most renowned leader*
of the Resistance in Shawa

of Aosta is reputed to have characterized 50% of his officials as inept
and 25% as thieves. There was a veritable frenzy to get rich as quickly
as possible. Badoglio himself reportedly pocketed half of the 1,700,000
Maria Theresa thalers confiscated from the Bank of Ethiopia, in the
immediate aftermath of the conquest.

Because of the Patriots' Resistance Movement during the Italian
Occupation, which is discussed below, Italian rule in Ethiopia was
largely confined to the towns; hence it was mainly in the urban centres
that the impact of the Occupation was felt. The Italians left a lasting
imprint on the architectural landscape of the capitals of the new governorships, as evidenced by the Italian-built edifices still visible in such
towns as Gondar, Jimma, Harar and Addis Ababa, not to speak of
Asmara and Mogadishu, which had longer spells of Italian rule. For
the capital of their East African empire, Addis Ababa, the Italians
drafted an ambitious master-plan whose implementation, however,
was aborted by the collapse of their rule in 1941. Yet legacies of the
enterprise remained: the birth of *Markato*, the open market in the
western part of the city, initially earmarked for the indigenous **163**

population; an acceleration of the southward growth of the city; and the creation of such areas as Kazanchis (in Italian, Case INCIS: Case istituto nazionale per case degli impiegati dello Stato, the national institution for housing the employees of the state), in the east, and Kaza Popolare (Case popolare, housing for the working classes), in the south. Addis Ababa also received its first urban supply of electricity, run by the parastatal CONIEL (Compagnia nazionale imprese elettriche, ancestor of the Ethiopian Electric Light and Power Authority, EELPA), and water, from the Gafarsa reservoir, in the north-western outskirts of the city. A number of factories were also set up, most notably the textile mills and cement factory in Dire Dawa, and the oil mills, flour mills and sawmills dotted all over the country.

In social life, despite the Fascist policy of racial segregation, there was a great deal of interaction between Ethiopians and most of the moderate Italians. The ban on marriage with Ethiopian women (nicknamed *madamismo* by Italian officialdom) remained a legal fiction. Given the enormous numerical imbalance between Italian males and females, this was inevitable; further, there was the fact that the Italians, with their open-minded Latin temperament, were largely impervious to the racist policy. The sizeable mixed population bequeathed to Ethiopia was a result of these marriages. On an informal plane, initially sponsored by the officials through the importation of European practitioners of the trade, prostitution assumed a widespread character. It has often been cited as one of the legacies of Italian rule in Ethiopia. On a slightly more positive line, the acquisition by town-dwellers of European habits and manners, already begun before the war, now became even more pronounced. These ranged from dress styles to food habits (including the eating of pasta). The cash economy, which had made a faltering start before 1935, was significantly reinforced during the Italian period.

Above all, Italian rule was distinguished for the achievement for which that people has always been famous: road engineering. This has often been somewhat overemphasized. To begin with, Italian road construction was more extensive and impressive in the northern than in the southern half of the country. This is not surprising, as Italian road-building was geared towards promoting the conquest of the country rather than its development. Moreover, the war of liberation was to take heavy toll of the road network, and the post-Liberation government was to be faced with the extremely daunting task of maintenance. All the same, the Italian network provided a skeleton for future expansion and betterment. Further, it gave an impetus to the development of motor transport. The defeated Italians left behind a number of cars, trucks and skilled personnel, all of value to such post-Liberation enterprises as the Public Transport Department, ancestor of the government-controlled Anbassa (Lion) Bus Transport Company. The *trentaquattro* (literally 'thirty-four', an Italian truck model which became the generic name for all lorries) and the *awtanti* (that is, *aiutante*, assistant to the driver) were two Italian concepts which became salient features of goods transport in the 1940s and 1950s. To this day, Italian has remained the language of automobile mechanics in Ethiopia.

In the economic sphere, Italian rule, true to the Fascist ethos that permeated it, was corporatist in character. As a prelude to complete control of the economy, a policy of weakening or destroying non-Italian expatriate firms was adopted. Among the victims of this policy were the Indian house of Mohammedally, which had been the leading import-export firm before 1935, and the French firm A. Besse; the latter, however, came back and dominated import-export trade after the Liberation. Concurrently, the Italians set up a number of parastatal organizations in industry, commerce and agriculture. Three such organizations were created to realize their most ambitious programme – the settlement of Italian farmers as colonists in selected fertile areas of Ethiopia. This was considered essential not only to ease Italy's demographic pressure, particularly in the south, but also to make the colony self-sufficient, in line with the Fascist principle of economic autarky. It was even hoped that the colony would eventually develop to a position where it would be able to feed the metropolis. Three areas which were selected for colonial settlement were Wagara in Semen, Charchar in Harar, and Jimma.

In contrast to the expectations generated by the scheme, the returns were very disappointing. Far from feeding the metropolis, the colony could not even support itself. A rare occurrence in the pre-1935 period became common practice, as grain came to be imported in mass. This was particularly the case with wheat, in high demand because of the large amount of spaghetti and other forms of pasta consumed. The main problem faced by the agrarian scheme was insecurity. The farmers lived under the constant threat of attack by the patriots' guerilla bands. Settlers who had come with wild anticipations of fast money ended up writing to their relatives back in Italy not to fall into the same trap. Thus, by the end of the period, only 10% of the projected colonization scheme had been implemented. This contrasted sharply with the much higher level of activity in the fields of commerce and industry – areas which, because of their urban location, were less subject to the pressures of the Resistance.

3. The Resistance

In spite of the lasting consequences cited above, the Occupation was denied the legitimacy of even colonial rule. Viewed in perspective, its brevity and precariousness have made it more in the nature of an interlude in the course of modern Ethiopian history. What contributed most to give it an episodic character was the nation-wide resistance it encountered. What finally sealed its fate was Mussolini's gamble in entering World War Two on the side of Hitler in 1940.

The quest for legitimization of his colonial efforts was a fairly serious preoccupation for Mussolini, both during and after the Italo-Ethiopian war. In an effort to avert the imposition of oil sanctions by the League of Nations, the British and French governments had tried to smooth matters for him. In December 1935, two months after the opening of hostilities, they came out with what were known as the Hoare-Laval plans, named after the British foreign secretary, Sir Samuel Hoare, and French prime minister Pierre Laval. These plans confirmed Italian military gains made up to that time, giving Italy parts of the Ogaden and most of Tegre (with the exception of the ancient capital, Aksum), as well as an economic protectorate over a large part of the rest of Ethiopia. In return, Ethiopia was to be given access to the sea at Assab. Hayla-Sellase rejected the proposals. The publicizing of the secret plans in Europe created a scandal, and both Hoare and Laval were forced to resign.

Secret negotiations between Ethiopia and Italy were conducted later in the course of the war through both Ethiopian and foreign intermediaries, such as the Ethiopians Afawarq Gabra-Iyyasus, Ethiopian minister in Rome at the outbreak of the war, and Heruy Walda-Sellase, the Minister of Foreign Affairs; a Palestinian, Jacir Bey; the Italian scholar, later deputy viceroy, Enrico Cerulli; and the Greek consul-general in Addis Ababa, who had been Hayla-Sellase's personal physician, Adrien Zervos. The Italian proposals amounted to an elaboration of the Hoare-Laval plans, restricting the emperor even further, to the control of Shawa only. In desperation, the emperor is said even to have toyed with the idea of a British mandate, to avert Italian occupation – in somewhat the same way as Wallaga chiefs established what was known as the Western Galla Confederation in mid-1936. The secret talks between the Italians and the emperor continued after his exile through the intermediary of an Egyptian prince, Muhammad Eknem Riza. The emperor was urged to abdicate, in return for financial compensation from the Italians. As his circumstances became more and more straitened, he is said to have been on the verge of accepting the terms. But the matter came to no conclusion, and the emperor remained in the obscurity of exile in Bath, in south-west England, until Italy's entry into World War Two brought him back to the centre of the stage. Similar attempts at negotiation with Asfawasan Hayla-Sellase, the emperor's heir, with his father in exile, came to a dead end.

Inside Ethiopia, the Italians had initially entertained the idea of ruling the country through those of the hereditary nobility, the *masafent*, who had submitted. Later, however, the idea was found unacceptable, on the grounds both of racism and the Fascist praxis of total power. The nobles were left with their titles and monthly handouts, ranging from 40,000 lire for *Ras* Haylu Takla-Haymanot, ex-governor of Gojjam, to 7,000 lire for *Ras* Getachaw Abata, son of *Ras* Abata Bwayalaw, and successively minister, ambassador and provincial governor before the Italo-Ethiopian war. But, in the wake of an attempt in early 1937 on Graziani's life, these nobles were caught in the Fascist backlash of reprisal, and many of them were deported to Italy. They were rehabilitated under the liberal and anglophile Duke of Aosta, who made some of them advisers and judges on their return to Ethiopia in 1939. On an even higher plane, and in a belated and desperate attempt to win over Ethiopians in the international conflict, some of the northern *masafent* were restored to their former positions, sometimes with exalted titles and enhanced powers. Thus, *Ras* Haylu was restored to Gojjam, and *Dajjach* Hayla-Sellase Gugsa to Tegre. *Ras* Seyum Mangasha was put in charge of the whole of northern Ethiopia, and *Dajjach* Ayalew Berru was promoted to *ras* and appointed governor-general (*taqlay endarase*) of Amhara. This last-minute revision of policy, however, did not save the Italians from the impending disaster.

Almost from the arrival in Ethiopia of their first troops, the Italians were confronted with a nation-wide war of resistance. Their efforts to divide and rule notwithstanding, the Resistance Movement embraced almost all regions and ethnic groups. The Resistance may be divided into two phases, with the reprisals that followed the abortive endeavour to kill Graziani in February 1937 forming the dividing line. The first phase was in essence a continuation of the war. It was conventional in character, and largely led by members of the upper nobility. As a result, it was characterized by vacillation and compromise. The second phase was marked by guerrilla warfare, led in most cases by members of the lower nobility. Although, as we shall see below, it had a number of fundamental weaknesses, it was uncompromising on the issue of resistance.

Ras Emeru Hayla-Sellase, *Ras* Dasta Damtaw, the emperor's son-in-law, and the brothers Abarra and Asfawasan Kasa exemplify the first phase. Given the circumstances, Emeru's performance as commander of the Shere front was commendable. But, after the collapse of the northern front and the experience of the ruthless weaponry **167**

4.5   Ras Emeru Hayla-Sellase (right), commander of the Shere front during the Italo-Ethiopian war of 1935–1936, and leader of the Black Lion Resistance operations in south-western Ethiopia, soon after his surrender to the Italians in late 1936

employed by the Italians, his will to fight was sapped. Although, as he sought exile, the emperor had designated him his viceroy, Emeru was hardly prepared to shoulder the responsibility of becoming the core of internal resistance. For himself, he is believed to have been seriously considering the idea of taking refuge in Kenya or Sudan. But, when he came to Gore, in western Ethiopia, the seat of 'the Ethiopian Government', set up as Hayla-Sellase left the country (in actual fact a device to deny the Italians legitimacy of conquest), Emeru became a symbol of authority and a rallying-point of resistance. His presence was eagerly seized upon by the members of the Black Lion organization, a Resistance group composed of military officers and civilian intellectuals, and particularly the fiery son of Heruy Walda-Sellase, Faqada-Sellase, who claimed to have come with injunctions from the emperor to continue resistance. Rather reluctantly, Emeru led the patriotic forces in a bold march towards Addis Ababa. Beset with many obstacles, foremost of which was the opposition of the local Oromo population, the march turned into a tragic odyssey in south-western Ethiopia, until Emeru and his

4.6   Ras *Dasta Damtaw (centre), commander of the southern front in the Italo-Ethiopian war of 1935–1936, being led to his execution in February 1937*

companions were forced to surrender at the Gojab river in Kafa.

In southern Ethiopia, *Ras* Dasta Damtaw, recoiling from his Dolo misadventure, continued to engage the Italians in a number of military operations, assisted in the initial phase by *Dajjach* Bayyana Mar'ed and *Dajjach* Gabra-Maryam Gari. Graziani in person led some of the operations against Dasta. But the latter vacillated between surrender and continued struggle. It has been argued that it was the presence in his ranks of the Eritrean *askaris* who had deserted the Italians that forced him to stick it out. Knowing full well what awaited them on capture, the Eritreans were more uncompromising. But Dasta's wavering had a negative effect on the morale of his followers. More or less a fugitive, he was hounded from place to place, and his dwindling force was finally beaten at Goggeti in the Gurage country, in February 1937, at the same time as the Fascists were unleashing their infernal terror in Addis Ababa, after the attempt on Graziani's life. Captured a few days later, Dasta was summarily executed.

The perfect epitome of the first phase was the ill-co-ordinated offensive of the summer of 1936. This was an audacious attempt to **169**

4.7   Moments before and after the attempt on the life of the Italian
4.8   viceroy, Marshal Rodolfo Graziani, in Addis Ababa,
        19 February 1937

attack the Italians in the capital itself. A combined attack from the
countryside was meant to coincide with insurrection in the city. The
bold venture included, among others, Abarra and Asfawasan Kasa
in the north, *Dajjach* Balcha Safo in the south, *Balambaras* (later *Ras*)
Abbaba Aragay in the north-west, and *Dajjach* Feqra-Maryam Yen-
nadu in the east. The moving spirit was reportedly *Abuna* Petros,
bishop of Wallo and unrelenting in his opposition to the Fascist
occupation. But the grand strategy fizzled out into solo adventures.
First captured and tortured, *Abuna* Petros was martyred. After
retreating to their Salale stronghold north of Addis Ababa, subsequent to the failure of their assault on the town centre, Abarra and
Asfawasan were lured out by the persuasive words of *Ras* Haylu. They
surrendered, only to be shot by the Italians without ceremony.

On 19 February 1937, Italian Fascism showed its darkest face.
Following the unsuccessful attempt on the life of Graziani by two
young Ethiopians, Abraha Daboch and Mogas Asgadom, a reign of
terror was unleashed in Addis Ababa. With official backing, the
Blackshirts, the political zealots of the Fascist order, went berserk
in the city, chopping off heads, burning down houses with their
inhabitants, disembowelling pregnant women and committing all
manner of atrocities. The educated Ethiopians were particularly

170   targeted for liquidation. These included many members of the Black

Lion organization, disbanded after Emeru's surrender, but closely watched in the capital. This elimination of the intelligentsia was to create what is often called 'the missing generation' in Ethiopia's intellectual and political history between the pre-war and the post-war generations. More immediately, the Fascist terror marked the intensification of the struggle, the transition from the first to the second phase, from conventional or semi-conventional hostilities to guerrilla warfare.

The first thing to note about the Resistance proper is its nation-wide extent. Although patriot bands were mostly concentrated in Shawa, Gojjam and Bagemder, there was scarcely any province where the Italians ruled without challenge. Availing themselves of the impregnable natural fortresses with which the country abounded, the guerrilla units kept the Italian troops under constant harassment. They shifted from offensive to defensive strategies as the situation dictated. They disrupted lines of communication, ambushed convoys and, when they deemed the odds were on their side, engaged in frontal assaults. As is the case with all guerrilla bands, their mobility and their capacity to disperse and regroup were among their greatest assets. In spite of the fact that few of them had anti-aircraft guns, they managed on the whole to deny the Italian aircraft the devastating mastery of the field that they had enjoyed during the war.

171

Shortage of supplies remained a serious problem for the patriots. Often, they had to resort to the traditional method of living off the peasant's produce, sometimes even having recourse to the billeting system. But there were attempts to find less exacting solutions to the problem. In some areas, a distinction was made between the full-time combatants, or *daraq tor*, and the peasants who engaged in food production, the *madade tor*, when the pressure subsided. Looting of collaborators was another mode of replenishing supplies. There were also cases of patriots who survived by falling back on the primordial options of hunting wild animals and gathering wild fruits. Medical supplies were practically nil, except for those secured by the *ya west arbagnoch*, the 'inner' patriots, Resistance members engaged in underground supportive work behind the enemy lines, mainly in the cities; in most cases, the patriots had to rely on traditional doctors and medicine. Arms were primarily those captured from the enemy and those brought in by deserters. At other times, patriots misdirected enemy aircraft into dropping supplies in their midst.

The guerrilla units also developed a rudimentary system for gathering intelligence. They had guards or scouts, *qafir*, to inform them about the approach of enemy troops. A prominent role was played in the field of intelligence by the *ya west arbagnoch*. From their vantagepoint inside the enemy's organizational network, they passed on crucial information about enemy strength, troop movements and planned operations. Further, they forged passes and identity papers, and provided shelter for the hunted. They furnished food and medical supplies as well as clothing. They intervened to mitigate punishment meted out to captured patriots. Sometimes they themselves engaged in sabotage operations and in urban terrorism.

Women, by reason of their capacity to arouse less suspicion, played a predominant role in this respect. The most notable example was Shawaragad Gadle, who laid the groundwork for the storming of the Italian garrison at Addis Alam. The *ya west arbagnoch* were able to attain a high level of organization, particularly in Gondar and Addis Ababa. In the capital, the leadership provided by the railway workers gave the whole affair a proletarian dimension. The *ya west arbagnoch* were a great source of exasperation to the Italians, who considered them more pernicious than the guerrilla fighters because the former were so difficult to detect, a difficulty compound by their use of code-names.

The use of diplomatic ploys to buy time was also not unknown. The most famous ruse was that employed by *Ras* Abbaba Aragay, towards the end of 1939. In negotiations he conducted with General Nasi, then deputy viceroy and governor of Shawa, Abbaba gave intimations of his readiness to surrender. Simultaneously, he wrote to other patriotic leaders explaining the actual reason for engaging in the talks: to buy

4.9   Shawaragad Gadle, an undercover patriot instrumental in the storming of the Italian stronghold at Addis Alam

time. After he had made sure that his forces had sufficiently recovered from the reverses they had suffered in the preceding months, he broke off negotiations, using as a pretext the killing by the Italians of patriots in another locality.

In general terms, therefore, the Resistance forms a glorious chapter in the history of modern Ethiopia. It is yet another demonstration of the Ethiopian's readiness to die for liberty and independence. It is all the more remarkable in that it was waged against a ruthless army of occupation which necessitated the adoption of new forms of struggle. Although the patriotic bands won few major battles, the Resistance as a whole had a corrosive influence on Italian rule, both physically and psychologically. Bewildered, battered and harassed by it, Italian troops were rendered highly vulnerable when the British launched the final campaign of Liberation in January 1941.

Having said all this, however, it is in order for us to point out the weak points of the Resistance, as they had a bearing on the kind of political order that evolved after the Liberation. To begin with, although the Resistance was indeed nation-wide in extent, it was not comprehensive. As is so often the case, where there is resistance there

173

is also bound to be collaboration. Self-interest and self-preservation induced many Ethiopians to opt for the latter. Thanks to their knowledge of the local conditions, the *banda* (the Italian word for 'band, group', used to signify Ethiopian collaborators) played far greater havoc with the Resistance than the Italian troops effected. Yet, far from being punished or disgraced, they came to occupy key positions in a post-Liberation Ethiopia which was marked by accord between the former exiles and the *banda*.

Also, among those committed to the Resistance, there was little unity. Relations between guerrilla bands were characterized by parochialism and jealousy, a situation exacerbated by their members' desertions from one band to another. Some guerrilla groups spent more time fighting one another than attacking the declared enemy. Thus, in Gojjam, *Dajjach* Mangasha Jambare was pitted against *Dajjach* Nagash Bazabeh, and *Lej* Haylu Balaw struck against *Lej* Balay Zallaqa. Neither rank nor heredity was enough to control these divisive clashes; for instance, both Nagash and Haylu were grandsons of *Negus* Takla-Haymanot of Gojjam. There was no uniting personality, let alone a common ideology or political organization. Hayla-Sellase's flight had created a serious gap in this respect. It is an indication of the weight of tradition, as well as the irrepressible magnetism of *Lej* Iyyasu, that two of his sons were resurrected from obscurity to provide a symbol of unity; such were the roles performed by Malaka-Tsahay Iyyasu in Shawa and Yohannes Iyyasu in Bagemder. At the very least, they could confer titles on patriot leaders, as, for instance, Malaka-Tsahay made Abbaba Aragay *ras*. Taking a less conventional line, *Blatta* Takkala Walda-Hawaryat, a Resistance leader of republican inclinations, scuttled from one region to another, and sometimes across the Sudanese frontier, in a futile effort to forge an organization uniting all patriots; he had little success in this. The end result of the parochial approach to the Resistance was that it lacked a clearly defined political direction. The military overshadowed the political, tactics gained precedence over strategy.

Qualifying the above weakness, however, we have to mention two developments: the Black Lion organization and the republican resistance movement in exile in Sudan. In spite of their marginal impact on the Resistance – the former was liquidated within a year of the Italian Occupation; the latter was of only academic significance by reason of its location – they represented eloquent attempts to give the struggle coherent ideological and political direction. The president of the Black Lion organization was Dr Alamawarq Bayyana, a veterinary surgeon educated in Britain. In addition to its executive committee, it had a training council headed by Lieutenant-Colonel Balay Hayla-Ab, from Holata military school, an officer of Eritrean origin. The organization had a ten-point constitution, the most interesting

4.10   Dr Alamawarq Bayyana, president of the Black Lion organization

aspect of which was its assertion of the supremacy of the political over the military command, a point which has now become one of the most fundamental canons of guerrilla warfare. The constitution also had injunctions against harassing the peasantry and mishandling prisoners of war. It forbade its members to seek exile, and urged them to prefer death to capture by the enemy. On the issue of final political authority, it remained conservative, expressing its loyalty to Hayla-Sellase and his family.

The republican movement moved one step further on that score. Its origins went back to the days before the Italo-Ethiopian war, to the activities of the French-oriented intellectuals in the railway city of Dire Dawa. In exile, the republicans issued a programme of action which, in the first place, argued for the unity of all patriots. Next, with almost prophetic foresight of the dangers of dependence, they insisted that Ethiopians should liberate themselves by their own efforts rather than by inviting foreign powers. It also called for a popularly elected government after liberation, rather than the restoration of the monarchy. Finally it advocated a federalist approach to accommodate the diversity of Ethiopia's constituent regions. It is of interest that this movement replaced the popular chant 'Ya Shawa

175

Ababa yabebal gana' ('The Flower of Shawa will continue to bloom') by 'Addis Ababa yabebal gana', arguing that invocation of the capital rather than the region was less suggestive of domination. Returning from exile, the republicans found themselves in trouble. Their republicanism and French orientation were unpalatable to Hayla-Sellase and his British allies, respectively, and they were persecuted into extinction.

The Resistance entered its last and decisive stage with the internationalization of the conflict. In early June 1940, Mussolini made the biggest miscalculation of his career: he entered World War Two on the side of Germany. With that, he recklessly brought to an end the Anglo-French connivance that had made his conquest of Ethiopia possible in the first place. In the eyes of the British, he was tranformed from a histrionic buffoon into a demon poised to attack their East African colonies. Italy's most steadfast ally from the 1890s onwards now became a mortal enemy. Correspondingly, Hayla-Sellase's political position underwent a dramatic change. As the symbol uniting all Ethiopians against the enemy, he was transported from his state of exile to the theatre of war.

The British launched their attacks from Sudan and Kenya. Forces led by Major-General Sir William Platt attacked the Italians in Eritrea. In January 1941, Colonel (later Brigadier) Daniel A. Sandford and Major Orde Charles Wingate accompanied the emperor from Sudan into Gojjam at the head of the 'Gideon Force', a small brigade of British and Ethiopian troops. Lieutenant-General Sir Alan G. Cunningham led the attack from Kenya. The Italians made some valiant attempts to save the situation, especially at Karan, in Eritrea, where they faced Platt's Army of the Sudan. Briefly, they managed even to occupy British Somaliland and to repulse the British at Matamma. But, worn down by five years of guerrilla warfare and facing a vastly superior force, they confronted inexorable defeat. On 6 April 1941, Addis Ababa was liberated. On 5 May, five years to the day from the Italian entry, Emperor Hayla-Sellase re-entered his capital, regaining the throne that he was to occupy for a further thirty-three years.

Sources, Chapter 4

Note. The BA thesis cited in the references is available in the Department of History, Addis Ababa University (AAU).

Badoglio, Pietro. *The War in Abyssinia*. London, 1937.
Baer, George W. *The Coming of the Italian–Ethiopian War*. Cambridge (Massachusetts), 1967.

The Italian Occupation 1936–1941

De Bono, Emilio. *Anno XIII: The Conquest of an Empire*. London, 1937.

Del Boca, Angelo. *The Ethiopian War 1935–1941*. Chicago, 1969.

Eshetu Tabaja. 'Tactics and Strategy of the Ethiopian Patriotic Struggle 1935–1941.' BA thesis (AAU, History, 1982).

Garima Taffara. *Gondare ba Gashaw* (The Gondare with his Shield). Addis Ababa, 1949 Ethiopian Calendar.

Graziani, Rodolfo. *Il fronte sud*. Milan, 1938.

Haile Selassie I: see Qadamawi Hayla-Sellase.

Mahtama-Sellase Walda-Masqal. *Zekra Nagar* (Recollections of Times Past). Addis Ababa, 1962 Ethiopian Calendar.

Mockler, Anthony. *Haile Selassie's War*. Oxford, 1984.

Perham, Margery. *The Government of Ethiopia*. London, 1969.

Qadamawi Hayla-Sellase. *Heywate-na ya Ityopya Ermejja* (My Life and Ethiopia's Progress), Volume I. Addis Ababa, 1965 Ethiopian Calendar.

Sbacchi, Alberto. *Ethiopia under Mussolini*. London, 1985.

Taddasa Mecha. *Tequr Anbasa ba M'erab Ityopya* (The Black Lion in Western Ethiopia). Asmara, n.d.

Taddasa Zawalde, *Qarin Garamaw: Ya Arbagnoch Tarik* (The Survivor's Reflections: A History of the Patriots). Addis Ababa, 1960 Ethiopian Calendar.

Tekeste Negash. 'Pax Italica and its Ethiopian enemies, 1936–40', in *La guerre d'Ethiopie et l'opinion mondiale 1934–1941* (Eeckaute, D., and Perret, M., collators). Paris, 1986.

5 From Liberation to Revolution 1941–1974

The period 1941 to 1974 represents a summation of modern Ethiopian history. Emperor Tewodros's efforts at centralization in the nineteenth century were consummated in the absolutism of Emperor Hayla-Sellase in the twentieth century. The perennial quest for a sea coast was finally realized with the federation and then union of Eritrea with Ethiopia. The land privatization process initiated with the institution of land-measurement (*qalad*), and unequal distribution increased. Extensive land grants by the state to its officials and supporters reduced a substantial portion of the peasantry to the status of tenancy, particularly in the southern half of the country. Peasant rebellions, rare phenomena before the Italo-Ethiopian war, became almost endemic after it. Frustrated in its bid to penetrate the Ethiopian economy in the early twentieth century, foreign capital had relatively better opportunities in post-Liberation Ethiopia. For the Ethiopian state, the pre-war policy of manoeuvring among a number of foreign powers gave way to increasing dependence on one, the United States of America, which provided the infrastructural and superstructural support for the consolidation of absolutism.

Yet, by some kind of historical paradox, the period which marked the high point of Ethiopian feudalism also witnessed its decay and eventual demise. Opposition to the regime, beginning in conspiratorial fashion, reached its climax in the Ethiopian Student Movement, harbinger of the Ethiopian Revolution of 1974, and vociferous successor to the anguished and muffled cries for reform of pre-war intellectuals like Gabra-Heywat Baykadagn.

1. The international setting

The British decade

The Liberation campaign which finally drove the Italians out of Ethiopia conditioned the nature of the country's international relations in the 1940s. The prominent role that the British played in the process, for their own global strategic reasons, gave them a position of ascendancy in Ethiopia. The tripartite competition among Britain, France and Italy for control of Ethiopia in the pre-1935 period was replaced by unilateral British domination. This fact was given legal embodiment in the agreements that Ethiopia was forced to sign with Britain in 1942 and 1944. On the basis of these agreements, and under the convenient excuse that the continuation of World War Two required making adequate provisions for Allied defence, the British came to assume extensive control over Ethiopia's finance, administration and territorial integrity.

In the first Anglo-Ethiopian Agreement of 1942, although the British nominally recognized the 'free and independent' status of Ethiopia, almost every article underlined its dependency and the preponderant role of Britain. The provision for mutual diplomatic accreditation was qualified by the stipulation that the British minister in Ethiopia would enjoy precedence over all other diplomatic representatives to the country. British subjects occupied key posts in Ethiopian administration, as advisers and judges; further, the entire police force was run by the British. Other foreign nationals could be employed by the Ethiopian government only after approval by the British.

In return for a progressively diminishing financial subsidy, the British exercised stringent fiscal control over the country. Further, they had the ultimate say in the disposal of the Italian prisoners of war, as well as that of Italian civilians. British aircraft enjoyed exclusive air traffic rights in Ethiopia. Perhaps the most dramatic illustration of the mutilated nature of Ethiopia's independence was the fact that the emperor had to seek the approval of the Commander-in-Chief of the British Forces in East Africa (the supreme British military officer in the region) to exercise the basic prerogative of a sovereign state: declaration of war. Conversely, at the request of the same British officer, the emperor would be obliged to declare a state of emergency in the country, which would give that officer extraordinary powers.

Apart from the legal provisions, the overbearing racist attitude of the British officials and officers operating in Ethiopia was calculated to emphasize their superior position in the country. Although their

179

troops passed under the curious name of the 'Ethiopian Army', they had little respect for Ethiopian sovereignty or sensitivity. They took action such as sequestration of property in defiance of the emperor's wishes. In short, the status they reserved for the country was aptly expressed by the term they chose for it, despite protests: Occupied Enemy Territory Administration.

All this was clearly not to the liking of the emperor. While grateful to the British for helping him to return from exile to the throne that he had lost five years earlier, he was not prepared to stomach for long the curtailment of his prerogatives. What he aspired to was the reconstitution of his autocratic powers on an even more solid base, in partnership with the British, but not through subservience to them. What the British sought was apparently to drag the country back to its pre-1935 level, depriving it of even the few benefits of Italian colonial rule.

The second Anglo-Ethiopian Agreement, signed in 1944, went some way to restore Ethiopia's sovereign rights. The precedence enjoyed by the British minister over all other foreign representatives was lifted. The Ethiopian government regained its freedom to appoint foreigners of any nationality as advisers or officers. The British pledge to restore a section of the Addis Ababa–Djibouti railway to Ethiopia, albeit conditionally, had both economic and military importance. Economically, it made available to the country its main conduit of external trade. Militarily, it guaranteed a line of access to arms supplies in any eventuality of conflict. Equally important, inasmuch as it meant modernizing the military organization of the nation and strengthening the coercive arm of the state, was the British undertaking to equip a military mission, to be known as the British Military Mission to Ethiopia (BMME). Answerable to the Ethiopian Ministry of War, the BMME was entrusted with the task of assisting the Ethiopian government in the 'organization, training and administration of the Ethiopian Army'.

While the Agreement of 1944 thus gave the Ethiopian state a relatively greater margin of independence, the British none the less still retained substantial control over the country's destiny. This was particularly evident with regard to Ethiopia's territorial integrity. Taking advantage of their strong military presence in the country, the British took control of both Eritrea and the Ogaden. Soon, they started to devise plans for the future: in both cases, these plans envisaged the severance of the territories from Ethiopia. The Ogaden was to be added to British Somaliland and the former Italian Somaliland, to form what was rather ominously christened Greater Somalia – the seed for Somali irredentism in subsequent decades. For Eritrea, the British had a slightly more complex arrangement. The Eritrean lowlands were to be united to Sudan, with which they shared geographical, ethnic and religious affinities. The predominantly Christian highlands, integrated with their Tegrean kin in Ethiopia, were to form a separate state. In effect, the plan envisaged a further amputation of Ethiopia in the north. It is worthy of note that the British plans for both Eritrea and the Ogaden, with the exception of the special fate reserved for the Eritrean lowlands, amounted to a perpetuation of the administrative divisions set up during the Italian Occupation.

From the time of the conclusion of the Liberation campaign, Ethiopia had put forward its claims to both the Ogaden and Eritrea. The Ogaden had been an integral part of the Ethiopian empire only five years previously; British annexation of the area was therefore hardly justifiable. In the case of Eritrea, too, Ethiopia had a strong case on the grounds of history, national defence and access to the sea. The Eritrean region, known as the Marab Melash before the institution of Italian rule in 1890, had been Ethiopia's northermost province. Twice, in 1895 and in 1935, it had served as a base for Italian aggression against Ethiopia. The region also provided the ultimate solution to Ethiopia's perennial quest for a coastline. On all these grounds, Ethiopia argued that the only proper way to dispose of the Italian ex-colony was by restoring it to the mother country.

Over a decade elapsed before the two territorial issues were resolved. While the question of the Ogaden was an affair between Britain and Ethiopia, that of Eritrea assumed a much broader international dimension. As it happened, the British proved more accommodating towards Ethiopia's claim on Eritrea than to that on the Ogaden. At one point, they even made an offer of Eritrea in return for Ethiopian renunciation of the Ogaden. During the negotiations for the 1944 Agreement, they were adamant on the retention of the Ogaden – and they had their way. For Ethiopia, failure to regain the area was a bitter disappointment. The following year, in September 1945, the London Conference of the Allied Powers rejected Ethiopia's claims to both Eritrea and the Ogaden. It was only in 1948 that the British finally agreed to withdraw from parts of the Ogaden, retaining the north-eastern part, known as the Haud, and what they called the Reserved Area, a corridor stretching from the Haud to the border of French Somaliland. It was not until 1954 that the whole region was finally restored to Ethiopia.

But the restoration of the Ogaden did not signify the end of the problem; it was merely the beginning of a new phase. The Somali nationalist party, the Somali Youth League (SYL), fanned resentment at the restoration of the Ogaden to Ethiopia. Its agitation for the eventual unity of all Somalis spread from the British and Italian colonies to the adjoining Somali-inhabited areas in Ethiopia. The independence and merger of the two former colonies in 1960 as the republic of Somalia elevated the political agitation to the level of interstate conflict. The new republic was committed to the unity of all Somalis, including those in the Ogaden, the then French territory of Djibouti, and the North Frontier District of Kenya. But it was the Ogaden which became the primary focus of Somali irredentism. The state of tension erupted in an armed clash on the Ethio-Somali border in 1963. Diplomatically, however, the cause of Somali irredentism was doomed. In the African context in particular, the Organization of African Unity, founded in 1963, for understandable reasons reaffirmed the inviolability of international boundaries, however arbitrarily they might have been drawn in the past.

The issue of Eritrea, though more complicated, was resolved some four years before the restoration of the Ogaden to Ethiopia. The Paris Peace Conference in 1946, which concluded World War Two, while it forced Italy to renounce its former colonies, had postponed the question of their disposal. That proved fertile ground for the growth of competing groups vying for attention and consideration. The demands were polarized into union with Ethiopia versus independence. The Unionists constituted the single largest political group in Eritrea. The Independence Bloc, as it was known, was a conglomeration of different groups united only by their opposition to union. It included the Muslim League, which had its stronghold in the Muslim-inhabited lowlands; the Liberal Progressive Party, which campaigned for the independence of an Eritrea united with Tegre; and a group of Italian settlers, ex-*askaris* and people of mixed race who opted for independence as a camouflage for the continuation of Italian influence.

Contrary to the general perception of the struggle to determine the fate of Eritrea, the two major divisions were not entirely along religious lines: the Christians were not necessarily for union, or the Muslims for independence. For instance, a Muslim group known as the Independent Muslim League of Massawa (a splinter of the Muslim League) was for union, provided that the interests of the Eritrean Muslims were guaranteed. The members of the pro-independence Liberal Progressive Party were predominantly Christian. What was not disputable was that the various groups had external sponsors. Thus, the unionists were understandably supported by the Ethiopian government. The Liberal Progressive Party was very much a creation of the British, who, as already cited above, had advocated a policy of partitioning Eritrea by attaching the lowlands to Sudan and uniting the Tegregna-speaking highlands. The pro-Italian faction was likewise generously subsidized by Italy, who, her bid for trusteeship rebuffed, sought to retain indirect control by supporting Eritrean independence. As a matter of fact, the Italians became chief sponsor of the Independence Bloc as a whole.

182

Unable to resolve the Eritrean question, the Four Powers (Britain, France, the Soviet Union and the United States) finally passed it on to the United Nations in 1948. The UN appointed a commission of five men, respectively from Burma, Guatemala, Norway, Pakistan and South Africa, to ascertain the wishes of the Eritrean people. Although four of the five members of the commission (Norway being the exception) came from countries with an anti-Ethiopian stand, the strongly pro-Ethiopian sentiments that they encountered in Eritrea forced at least two of them to modify their positions. Unanimity could not be achieved, however. Two members recommended granting independence (Guatemala, representing the strong pro-Italian Latin-American lobby in the United Nations, and Pakistan, championing the Muslim cause in Eritrea). Two others (South Africa and Burma) recommended federation, while the fifth member (Norway) was for union. UN Resolution 390V, adopted on 2 December 1950, endorsed the federation formula as the golden mean between two conflicting options. Designed to satisfy everybody, it ended up by pleasing no one. Partisans both of union and independence worked in their own different ways to wreck the federation.

Contributing to the adoption of the federation formula was the attitude of the powers, particularly that of Britain and the United States. In the hope of securing the Ogaden as a *quid pro quo*, Britain had modified its earlier stand on Eritrea and had come to support Ethiopia's claim for Eritrea, or at least for the highland part of Eritrea. The partition scheme had accordingly been revised to recommend attachment of the highlands to Ethiopia and of the lowlands to British-ruled Sudan. When it became clear that the Ethiopian government was not at all inclined to trade off the Ogaden for Eritrea, the British sought to withdraw their support. By then, it was too late. The federation formula had gained favour among many members of the United Nations.

Another factor for the adoption of the federation formula was the support the United States gave to it. American policy in Eritrea was mainly determined by considerations of the safety of the communications base they had inherited from the Italians – Radio Marina. They were thus inclined to embrace the federal arrangement, trusting to Ethiopia rather than to an independent Eritrea, which was an unknown quantity. Indeed, the federation, significant as it was for the country's internal history, also opened a new era in its foreign relations – the end of British domination and the beginning of a rather close partnership with the United States, a partnership which lasted until the Revolution of 1974.

The American era

Official contacts between Ethiopia and the United States of America go back to the arrival in 1903 of the Skinner Mission, named after the American envoy, Robert P. Skinner, and the subsequent signing of a treaty of friendship and commerce between Emperor Menilek and the American envoy. Yet, although American cotton goods had a fair share of the Ethiopian market, the tripartite domination of the Ethiopian diplomatic scene gave little room for the United States before 1935. It was after World War Two that the Americans emerged into the foreground. This was in large measure a local variation on the general theme of America's predominance in global politics. As in many other parts of the world, the worn-out British grudgingly relinquished the burden of empire to their more energetic ally.

The initiative for closer contacts came from the Ethiopian side, however. Distressed by the stringent control exercised by the British after the Liberation, the emperor sought the Americans as a counterweight. As already described, the British had come to exercise administrative and fiscal control over the country incommensurate with the financial or military assistance they rendered. While grateful to them for giving him asylum and restoring him to the throne, the emperor became aware that the proper reinstitution of his autocratic power could only come about through tying Ethiopia's fate to the generous ally that the United States was expected to be.

The first official contacts between the two states were made in 1943, during the visit to the United States of the then Vice-Minister of Finance, Yelma Deressa. Ethiopian requests centred on military aid and the secondment of financial and legal experts. The US response came in the form of an extension of their Lend-Lease to Ethiopia and the sending of a technical mission in May 1944. The latter, known as the Fellows Mission (after its leader, Perry Fellows), could be said to have laid the groundwork for the subsequent American involvement in Ethiopia. Its recommendations, further elaborated in 1947, laid particular emphasis on the development of infrastructure. They became eventually concretized in the Point Four Agreement of 15 May 1952. One of the most conspicuous manifestations of the American presence in Ethiopia in the 1950s and 1960s, 'Point Four', as the organization was known, was involved in agricultural and public health education, locust control, public administration training and the awarding of scholarships.

For the Ethiopian government, the value of the United States was not so much in such issues of development as in the diplomatic leverage that the USA could exercise on the British, and in the military assistance likely to be offered. In 1945, the emperor met President Franklin D. Roosevelt in Egypt, and discussed issues of

*5.1   Qagnaw, the United States base at Asmara established following the
Ethio-US Treaty of 1953*

vital concern to Ethiopia at the time – Eritrea, the Ogaden and the
railway. The granting of a concession to the American Sinclair Company to prospect for oil in the Ogaden was designed as much to
reassert Ethiopia's rights in the region as out of eagerness to exploit
a lucrative natural resource. But the Americans were not particularly
keen about giving diplomatic support to Ethiopia's territorial claims,
or about offering the military assistance that the Ethiopian government so persistently and ardently requested.

The year 1950 may be regarded as a turning-point in this respect.
The federation tied America's strategic interests in the Middle East
to Ethiopia. The withdrawal of the BMME in late 1950 lent weight
to the Ethiopian request for military assistance. The Egyptian revolution of 1952 forced on Washington a rethinking of its alignments in
the Middle East and the Red Sea. These developments formed the
background for the Ethio-US Treaty of 1953, which defined the relationship between the two countries in the following decades. In return
for continued use of the communications base in Asmara, renamed
Qagnaw to commemorate the first Ethiopian battalion which fought
as part of the United Nations forces on the American side in Korea

185

between 1950 and 1953, the United States undertook to launch a military aid programme. A unit called the Military Assistance Advisory Group (MAAG) was set up to train three divisions, each of 60,000 men, at a cost of 5 million US dollars. The US made further commitments to military assistance in subsequent years. By 1970, Ethiopia had come to absorb some 60% of US military aid to the whole of Africa.

The 1950s and 1960s might therefore justifiably be described as the American era, as far as Ethiopia's international alignment is concerned. The American impact was felt in many facets of Ethiopian life, but perhaps most conspicuously in the spheres of military organization, communications and education. In the military sphere, American influence was at the outset concentrated on the army. In time, however, other units of the armed forces, initially entrusted to non-American advisers, also came under American control. Such was the case with the air force and the navy, at first under Swedish and Norwegian direction, respectively. Even the Haile Sellassie I Military Academy of Harar, modelled after Sandhurst, the British military academy, and run by British-trained Indians, obtained American advice and assistance. The police force and the Imperial Bodyguard were perhaps the two units least affected by the American presence, the former being trained and equipped mainly by Germans and Israelis, the Bodyguard by Swedes. Yet it was the Bodyguard which supplied the men for the Qagnaw troops that fought in Korea, a situation that brought the Ethiopian soldiers into close contact with their American counterparts.

American military influence was most evident in the fields of training and equipment. US military aid in the period between 1946 and 1972 came to over $US 180 million. Over 2,500 Ethiopians underwent diverse forms of military training in the United States between 1953 and 1968. The jet aircraft, anti-tank and anti-aircraft weapons, naval craft, infantry weapons and sometimes even the uniforms were of American origin. In both equipment and training, the air force remained the most prestigious show-piece of American military aid in Ethiopia. It was also reputedly the most modern and efficient unit of the armed forces.

The Americans left their stamp on civil aviation as well as on the air force. In 1945, the Ethiopian delegation attending the founding conference of the United Nations approached the Americans for assistance in setting up a civilian airline. In the same year, an agreement was concluded between the Ethiopian government and the Transcontinental and Western Airline (TWA), setting up Ethiopian Air Lines (EAL). The agreement lasted three decades, with TWA providing the managerial and supervisory personnel for most of that period. Beginning with five C-47 aircraft (veterans of World War

5.2   *Pack animals competing for the runway with a DC-3 aircraft of Ethiopian Airlines*

Two), of which three were soon converted to the passenger version, the DC-3, EAL entered the jet age in 1962. The issue of Ethiopianization dominated the history of the airline, with the Americans trying to delay its realization for as long as possible. But the airline managed to achieve self-sufficiency in flying, technical and administrative personnel by the end of the period under study. The first Ethiopian general manager was appointed in 1971. EAL's domestic network played a vital role in facilitating national integration and the speedy transport of such lucrative commodities as coffee. Its international network was marked not only by a pioneering route to Beijing in 1973, but also the transcontinental air service, which cut the umbilical cord that had tied colony and ex-colony to the metropolis, and which, symbolically, was inaugurated in 1960, the year of African independence.

Improvement of surface transport was likewise a product of the Ethio-American connection. In 1941, the road network for which the Italians were so famous was a shambles, having been destroyed in large part, as a result of the battles of the Liberation campaign. Restoration of the network thus became one of the main issues that preoccupied the post-Liberation regime. As in many other spheres, **187** the British were not co-operative in this regard. Inevitably, therefore, the Ethiopian government turned to the Americans for support. In January 1951, the Imperial Highway Authority (IHA) was brought into existence, and entrusted with the task of maintaining and developing the country's road network, a task which was hitherto subsumed under the multifarious responsibilities of the Ministry of Public Works and Communication. The IHA was modelled after the US Bureau of Public Roads. Its managerial personnel were also seconded from the American organization until Ethiopians took over the management in 1962. Loans for its new construction undertakings also came from the American-dominated International Bank for Reconstruction and Development (IBRD), which continued to exercise a preponderant influence over the activities of the IHA.

Although telecommunications came to be a Swedish preserve, the stimulus for setting up an independent authority came from the Americans. The beginnings of telecommunications in Ethiopia go back to the days of Menilek. In addition to the domestic network, which had played a not inconsiderable role in facilitating political control, Ethiopia was linked to the outside world via two major international lines: one linked the capital with Djibouti via Harar, and the other with Massawa via Asmara. The opening of radio communication on the eve of the Italo-Ethiopian war of 1935 gave Ethiopia a measure of independence in this sphere. As in surface communications, the years immediately after 1941 confronted the Ethiopian government with almost overwhelming difficulties of maintaining its telecommunication service. Transmitters secured under the lend–lease agreement facilitated radio communication between the major towns. A contractual arrangement was also made with the American multinational International Telephone and Telegraph (ITT) organization, to repair destroyed telephone lines. Finally, in 1950, an ITT survey under the auspices of IBRD recommended the creation of the Imperial Board of Telecommunications, which was duly established in 1952. Ostensibly a share company, it was for all practical purposes a government concern, as all the shares were bought by the government. Until the appointment of the first Ethiopian general manager in 1966, the board continued to be run by Swedes.

Banking was perhaps one modern institution where the American or any other foreign presence was not so strongly felt. Post-Liberation banking had its antecedents in the British-controlled Bank of Abyssinia and the state-controlled Bank of Ethiopia. During the Italian Occupation, a number of metropolitan banks (Banco di Roma, Banco di Napoli, etc.) opened branches in Ethiopia. In 1942, the State Bank of Ethiopia was established, and continued to serve as both commercial bank and central bank of the country until 1963, when new legislation set up the Commercial Bank of Ethiopia and the

National Bank for the two respective functions. In the same year, a private bank named the Addis Ababa Bank was founded, and rose to become an energetic rival to the state-sponsored Commercial Bank in the subsequent decade. The Agricultural and Industrial Development Bank (formed in 1970 through the merger of the Development Bank and the Investment Corporation) and the Savings and Mortgage Corporation (founded in 1965) completed the pre-Revolution banking scene.

Finally, the Americans exerted a clearly preponderant influence in the field of education. The educational system of the country was conducted along more or less American lines, if we may make an exception of the few élite schools which served as the last centres of British and French educational influence. The United States became the chief destination of young Ethiopians seeking higher education. American agencies such as Point Four, USAID, the African-American Institute and the African Graduate Fellowship Program (AFGRAD) became the main source of scholarships. In the national university itself, the enrolment and evaluation system was indistinguishable – and still is, for that matter – from that of a standard American college. At the administrative level, the vice-presidential post appeared to have been regarded as a slot reserved for American nationals. In the high schools, the advent of the Peace Corps Volunteers in the 1960s presented a serious challenge to the dominant role that Indian teachers then enjoyed.

The preponderance of Americans in almost all aspects of Ethiopian life bred resentment, especially among the students, who viewed the whole situation as being within the global framework of American imperialism. Anti-Americanism grew particularly strong in the late 1960s and early 1970s. As it happened, this was also the time when the United States was pursuing a policy of disengagement from Ethiopia. Advances in satellite communication were rendering obsolete the Qagnaw station on which the Ethio-American alliance had been predicated. The pro-Western shift in Egyptian policy initiated by President Anwar Sadat must also have diminished the value of Ethiopia for American strategy in the Middle East. Thus, on the eve of its demise, the Hayla-Sellase regime began to lose its most powerful and steadfast ally.

2. The socio-economic scene

In spite of the growth and expansion of a number of towns and the establishment of a few industries in the post-1941 period, Ethiopia **189**

KEY

○ Capital city
● Town
–·–·– Provincial boundary
——— International boundary

RED SEA

ERITREA
Asmara

16°

SUDAN

BAGEMDER
&
SEMEN
Gondar

Maqale

TEGRE

12°

GOJJAM
Daga Damot   Mota
Dabra Marqos

WALLO
Dessie   Tandaho

DJIBOUTI   GULF OF ADEN

SHAWA

Harar   Jijjiga

SOMALIA

WALLAGA
Naqamte

Addis Ababa   Matahara
Wanji

ARUSI
Asalla

HARARGE

8°

Mattu
ILLUBABOR   Jimma

KAFA

Awasa   Gobba

BALE   El Kere

SUDAN

Arba Mench
GAMU
GOFA   Adola

SIDAMO

SOMALIA

4°

KENYA

UGANDA

0   200km
Scale

34°   38°   42°   46°

remained a predominantly rural society. Agriculture engaged more than 80% of the population, and accounted for about 60% of the gross domestic product in the 1960s. Over 90% of the value of exports was derived from agricultural commodities, of which perhaps 60% came from coffee. Internally, however, grain constituted the most important agricultural product, followed by pulses and oil-seeds. The country's livestock population was reputedly one of the largest in Africa, and the per capita consumption of meat was among the highest in the continent. The dominant role that agriculture played in the national economy necessarily gave a pivotal place to land and its ownership.

Agriculture and land tenure

The underlying theme in this period in the area of land tenure was an acceleration of the process of privatization of land, which had already started before 1935. Only in the northern provinces did the old communal kinship system of land tenure continue to wage a defensive struggle against the pervasive influence of privatization. In the south, private tenure increasingly became the norm. The process had three facets. Firstly, northern settlers who had acquired tributary rights over southern peasants, the *gabbar*, ended up by owning the land altogether, through purchase from the distressed *gabbar* or through forcible seizure. Secondly, *madarya* land given to those in government service in lieu of salary was made convertible to freehold. Thirdly, and this appears to have been the most prevalent pattern, the government made extensive land grants from its large reserve, which came under the conveniently vague rubric of government land (*ya mangest maret*).

The ultimate objective of these government grants was evidently to broaden its basis of support. Begun soon after the Liberation, the policy reached its peak during the last decade of Hayla-Sellase's life, as the regime became more and more desperate for political support in face of mounting opposition. The main beneficiaries of these grants were patriots, exiles, soldiers and civil servants. Subsequently, the policy was given an egalitarian and developmental façade by extending it to include 'landless and unemployed Ethiopians'. But the overall pattern of land allotment left no doubt as to the target group of the government policy, that is, those who served it in war and in peace. Of the nearly 5 million hectares allocated after 1941, only a few thousands reached the landless or the unemployed.

The privatization process had a number of consequences. At the conceptual level, it was attended with changes in the connotation of some important terms. *Rest*, in origin signifying the usufructuary rights enjoyed under the kinship system, now denoted absolute **191** private property. Likewise, the term *gabbar* lost its exploitative associations and assumed the more respectable connotation of taxpayer. Absolute private ownership rights to land above all entailed unrestricted freedom to dispose of it, most significantly through sale. The post-Liberation period thus witnessed a remarkable growth in land sales, particularly in the last decade and a half before the Revolution of 1974. Correspondingly, the price of land continued to rise in most areas. In eastern Shawa, for example, the average price of land increased threefold between the 1950s and the 1960s. An inevitable result of the increase in land sales was the growing concentration of land in the hands of the few. Large holdings were prevalent in the south, where the privatization process was most advanced. Holdings as big as 200,000 hectares were recorded for some areas. Conversely, in the north, where the kinship system of tenure still predominated, the main problems were litigation over land-use rights and fragmentation of holdings, as the initial plot was subdivided *ad infinitum*.

But undoubtedly the most important consequence of the growth of private tenure was the concomitant spread of tenancy. Some 50%–65% of all holdings were estimated to fall under this category. Understandably, tenancy was most widespread in the southern provinces (for example, 75% in Hararge, 67% in Shawa and 62% in Kafa), and less so in the northern provinces (15% in Bagemder, 20% in Gojjam and 25% in Tegre). Absentee landlordism, estimated at about 25% in the 1960s, constituted the other side of the coin. Most tenancy agreements were verbal, involving sharecropping arrangements known as *erbo* (a quarter), *siso* (one-third), or *ekul arash* (half). As the value of land rose with commercial farming and mechanization, the arrangement tended to be weighted increasingly against the tenant, often culminating in his eviction. In addition to the agreed-upon share that he paid to the landlord, the tenant often had to bear the burden of the tithe (*asrat*), and sometimes even that of the land-tax.

Parallel with the privatization process went the efforts of the central government to increase the revenue it obtained from land. In broad terms, this involved the elimination of the intermediary tiers of revenue appropriation, and gave the government direct access to the source of revenue. Concretely, it meant the conversion of tribute to tax. Like many other developments, the process had begun before 1935, but it was after 1941 that it speeded up. Aware of the precarious nature of its hold, the government proceeded rather cautiously at first. Thus, the first land-tax decree (1942), 'taking into account the sufferings of Our people and Our country in the past five years', fixed the tax rate on both measured and unmeasured land at half that in force in 1935. For measured areas, the rate for forty hectares (*gasha*) was

$Eth.15 for cultivated land (*lam*), $Eth. 10 for semi-cultivated land (*lam-taf*), and $Eth. 5 for uncultivated land (*taf*).

The reprieve granted the tax-paying population was terminated some two and a half years later. In late 1944, a new decree was issued which raised the tax on measured land to a total of $Eth. 50, 40 and 15 per *gasha* of *lam*, *lam-taf* and *taf* respectively. The increase was represented by the tax in lieu of *asrat*, now commuted from kind to cash in all the three categories. The measured lands subject to this rate were located in Shawa, Harar, Arusi, Wallo, Wallaga, Sidamo, Illubabor, Gamu Gofa and Kafa. A lower rate was fixed for Shawa *rest* land, but Gojjam, Tegre and Bagemder were to pay the land-tax at the 1935 rate plus the *asrat* on assessment.

In theory, the decree of 1944 represented the first step in the rationalization of land revenue. The abolition of the numerous fees and labour services traditionally imposed on the tiller is a case in point. In practice, however, such labour services continued to be exacted. A proclamation in 1947 further emphasized that the church was exempted from the abolition order. With regard to the land-tax as well, a great deal of revenue that was due to the state was absorbed by holders of hereditary tribute right (*resta gult*), tribute levied by the landlord or *balabbat* (*siso gult*), and by church lands (*samon*). No land-tax was exacted from *madarya* holders unless they had become *gabbar* by converting their holdings into freehold. The introduction of education and health taxes on land in 1947 and 1959, respectively, could thus be said to have provided much needed additional sources of revenue to the state.

The third decree on land-tax, issued in 1966, was apparently designed to terminate the intermediary role of the *gult*-holder in the surplus-appropriation process. All owners of land under *resta gult* and *siso gult* were to pay the land-tax directly to the state, instead of to the *gult*-holder as was hitherto the case. In effect, this was tantamount to the abolition of both *resta gult* and *siso gult*. In practice, the holders of such rights, particularly of the *resta gult*, were too well entrenched and too close to the centre of power to allow the full implementation of the decree. Measures to terminate the church's *gult* were not even considered.

Despite persistent efforts to augment the revenue accruing from land, therefore, the state was unable to obtain the maximum it could possibly get. By the mid-1960s, revenue from the agricultural sector, undoubtedly the most important sector of the economy, amounted to only 7 % of the total. Such was the background of the initiation of the government's last measure to augment agrarian revenue: the agricultural income tax of 1967, which was part of a general revision of the country's income-tax regulations.

On the surface, the new tax schedule represented a more rational **193** basis for the collection of agricultural tax. The disparity between measured and unmeasured land was removed, as tax was levied on agricultural produce irrespective of the status or nature of the land. The progressive nature of the tax also promised greater social equity and more revenue yield to the government. In practice, however, the implementation depended on assessment committees which, subject as they were to various influences, could not be expected to be completely honest in their determination of income. Moreover, the new tax met stiff opposition in the *rest*-holding regions of northern Ethiopia, as it was viewed as a veiled attempt to introduce the *qalad* in the north. The Gojjam peasant uprising of 1968 was triggered by government attempts to implement the new tax law.

When we come to consideration of the government's strategy for agricultural development, the result is disappointing. Budgetary allocation for agriculture was 2% in 1967. This was attended by a correspondingly low growth rate of the agricultural sector. When the government did turn its attention to agriculture, in the third of its Five-Year Plans, 1968–1973, priority was given to commercial rather than to peasant agriculture. This probably reflected the government's eagerness for higher revenue as well as its own class interests, since it was the big landlords who stood to gain from commercial farming. The last decade of the regime thus saw extensive commercialization and mechanization of agriculture. Some observers even began to speak of the birth of an agrarian bourgeoisie. This agrarian transformation had three agents: private Ethiopians, expatriate concessionaires and the government. The first, landlords turned entrepreneurs or enterprising professionals leasing out land, were particularly active in southern Shawa and in Satit Humara in north-western Bagemder. Of the foreign-owned plantations, the Italian Elaberet farm in Eritrea and the Tandaho cotton plantation in the Awash river valley, run by the British Mitchell Cotts Company, deserve particular mention. Finally, a government agency, the Awash Valley Authority, was set up in 1962, to act as an umbrella organization, sponsoring a host of agricultural, agroindustrial and hydroelectric enterprises.

Rather belatedly, a not so successful attempt to promote peasant agriculture was made. A 'package' approach to agricultural development was introduced, mainly in the central provinces, to provide high quality seeds and fertilizers to poor peasants. The government set up a unit known as the Extension Project Implementation Department (EPID) to co-ordinate what were termed 'minimum package programmes'. The Swedish International Development Agency (SIDA) ran similar extension programmes, of which the most notable was the Chilalo Agricultural Development Unit (CADU). Ostensibly designed to benefit the poor peasants, CADU ended up by enriching the rich landlords, who contrived ways of circumventing the prerequisites of eligibility for the extension facilities. Further, the programme accelerated the process of mechanization of agriculture and the eviction of tenants, as landlords found it more profitable to work the land themselves or to lease it out to commercial farmers. The Wallamo Agricultural Development Unit (WADU), financed by the United Nations World Bank, was relatively more successful in easing land congestion through its settlement scheme.

The cumulative effect of the process and policies described above was to polarize rural society into landlords and tenants, particularly in the southern half of the country. The problem of tenancy became too acute to ignore. Largely pushed by its external sponsors, the government was forced to consider what came to be known rather loosely as 'land reform'. A committee on land reform was first set up in 1961. In 1965, this concern crystallized into the Land Reform and Development Authority, which was reconstituted as the Ministry of Land Reform and Administration a year later.

But all efforts to introduce any meaningful changes in the conditions of tenancy foundered on the inescapable reality that they impinged on the vested interests of the landlord class which dominated the state apparatus. It is also of some interest that the Amharic name for the new ministry had no element of 'reform' in it: a more strict English translation would be Ministry of Land *Tenure* (*yezota*) and Administration. It was Parliament, the declared spokesman of the people, which thwarted government initiatives in this regard. Given the high representation of landlords in that institution, the outcome is not surprising. A tenancy bill was first presented to Parliament in 1964. The obstruction it faced in Parliament formed the background for the student demonstration of 1965, under the banner of 'Land to the Tiller' – a political act that augured the radical phase of the Ethiopian Student Movement.

A much more comprehensive bill to regulate the terms of tenancy was presented to Parliament in the twilight of the Hayla-Sellase regime. There was nothing radical about the bill. It did not insist on written leases. It envisaged a rent going as high as half the tenant's produce. It did not promise security to the tenant, as the contract could be terminated unilaterally, and as mechanization was deemed sufficient ground for eviction of a tenant by the landlord. Perhaps the only progressive aspect of the bill was its provision for the taxation of unutilized land. All the same, the bill had scarcely any supporters. A few opposed it because it did not go far enough. Many opposed it because they felt it went too far. The net effect of the bill was to accelerate the process of eviction of tenants, as landlords rushed to pre-empt the legislation.

The increasing pressures on the peasantry, combined with natural disasters such as droughts and locust raids, made it easy prey to **195** famine. This is seen in the high incidence of famines in this period, particularly in the northern parts of the country. An outbreak of famine in Tegre in 1958 claimed the lives of about 100,000 peasants. In 1966, Wallo was the scene of famine affecting a number of districts. Government response to famines was characterized by bureaucratic inertia and deliberate efforts to cover up the disaster. This became particularly evident in the course of the most devastating famine of the period, the Wallo Famine of 1973. When the human catastrophe was finally unveiled by university staff and students and the foreign media, it exposed the bankruptcy and irresponsibility of the old regime, and became one of the immediate causes for its demise.

Trade and industry

The striking thing about trade and industry as aspects of economic activity is their insignificant role in the national economy. In the 1960s, trade constituted a mere 7% of the gross domestic product; industry's part was even less than that. This implies a rather low rate of circulation of goods, as well as revealing the infant stage of industrialization in Ethiopia. The trade pattern, too, reflected the predominantly agricultural character of the country. Agricultural products constituted the bulk of the country's exports. Coffee, as indicated earlier, was valued at from 50% to 65% of the total exports, followed by hides and skins; next came pulses and oil-seeds.

While the pre-eminence of coffee as an export item continued unchallenged, a significant shift was taking place on the import scene. Textiles were giving way to machinery and chemicals. This was in large measure a result of the policy of import substitution that underpinned the country's industrialization, as local production of textiles became the most notable achievement of that policy. With regard to the nature of the country's trade partnership, it reflected its international alignment. Forty per cent of the country's trade was with the United States, which absorbed about 70% of the total coffee export. On the import side, however, the United States came third after Italy and Japan. The balance of trade was generally unfavourable to Ethiopia, a situation aggravated by the steadily declining price of exports and the rising price of imports.

With respect to internal trade, the commercial centrality of Addis Ababa, begun in the late nineteenth century, was further consolidated. The competition it faced from trans-frontier trading posts dwindled until it died altogether with the end of colonial rule. Inside Addis Ababa itself, the Italians left behind an enduring legacy as far as the commercial topography of the city was concerned: the pre-war market of Arada, renamed the Piazza by the Italians, was eclipsed by the Mercato. Correspondingly, the expatriate domination of trade met a serious challenge from a class of national traders – a process partly facilitated by the Italian policy of destroying the expatriate mercantile class in favour of state monopoly of trade. The Mercato became the stronghold of these national traders, most notably the Gurage traders. Their displacement of the Yemenite Arabs, who had earlier dominated retail trade, remains a remarkable example of national enterprise.

This is far from saying that a national commercial bourgeoisie had come into existence, however. Only a handful of Ethiopians were involved in the export–import trade. Apparently taking their cue from the Italians, Ethiopia's rulers set up a series of parastatal organizations which controlled the country's foreign trade. The first of such organizations was the Ethiopian National Corporation (ENC). Created soon after 1941 by the Minister of Commerce and of Agriculture, Makonnen Habta-Wald, the ENC made substantial profits from the sale of cereals to war-torn Europe in the years between the liberation of Ethiopia and the end of World War Two. In 1944, its profits were estimated at over £1,200,000 sterling. A parallel organization, the Ethiopian Society for Commerce and Transport (popularly known as the *Mahbar Bet* or Self-Help Association), enjoyed a virtual monopoly of the import of cotton goods. The latter-day National Coffee Board, Livestock and Meat Board and the Grain Corporation could be viewed as successor organizations to the ENC, designed to control the three most important export commodities: coffee, hides and skins, and grain.

The government, propelled by the perennial desire to augment its revenue, also gave particular attention to the collection of customs. This was a continuation and elaboration of the pre-war policy of the government's assertion of its rights to levy import and export duties at rates it deemed appropriate, as symbolized by the 1931 Excise and Consumption Tax Proclamation. But the pre-war efforts had the appearance of tentative steps in customs legislation as compared with the elaborate provisions of the post-1941 laws. The standard was set in the Customs and Export Duties Proclamation of 1943, a lengthy document which fixed the rates for almost all conceivable imports. The bias was clearly towards import rather than export duties. Only four commodities were singled out in the latter category: hides and skins, civet musk, wax and coffee. As a result of this, import duties constituted an important source of government revenue, rising to a quarter of the total, as opposed to the insignificant share contributed by export duties. An idea of the importance of customs duties for government revenue, particularly in the early years, can be obtained from the fact that in 1944, out of a total revenue of £2,843,600, £650,000 was from customs, while £590,000 was from land-tax.

In the industrial sphere, although negligible when viewed in absolute terms, there was some progress when compared with the situation before 1935. This was partly due to the foundation laid down by the Italians; partly, too, it was the result of post-Liberation policies and efforts. In the former category, we have already cited Dire Dawa's textile mills and cement factory, and oilmills, flour mills and sawmills throughout the countryside. In Addis Ababa, there were fibre mills and four flour mills and the capital's electricity supply from the hydroelectric plant set up south of Addis Ababa during the Occupation by the Italians. We may note here that the major hydroelectric plant at Qoqa, in south-eastern Shawa, which later became the main source of power for a large part of the country, was built with money paid by the Italians as war reparations.

The man who presided over the administration of these plants inherited from the Italians was Makonnen Walda-Yohannes, brother of the famous power-broker of the post-1941 order, *Tsahafe T'ezaz* Walda-Giyorgis Walda-Yohannes, the Minister of Pen. As Custodian of Enemy Property, Makonnen amassed a considerable fortune for himself and the emperor, until the disgrace of the brothers in 1955.

The thrust of the government's industrial policy, more particularly in manufacturing, was towards import substitution. Textiles, the major import commodity, thus became the main focus of attention. Many textile mills were opened, of which the two most important were the Indo-Ethiopian Textile Mills at Aqaqi, on the southern outskirts of Addis Ababa, and the Bahr Dar Textile Mills in northern Gojjam. Beverages constituted a second area of import substitution. The Saint George Brewery, a pre-1935 enterprise which became one of the most lucrative businesses for the emperor, was supplemented by the Metta Abbo Brewery. Soft drinks factories began to operate under patent, including the famous American brands Coca Cola and Pepsi Cola.

But the big success story of post-1941 industrialization was the sugar-manufacturing industry monopolized by the Dutch firm, Handelsvereeninging Amsterdam (HVA). Expelled from Indonesia by President Achmed Sukarno, HVA found a propitious investment climate in Ethiopia. In 1954, it set up two major centres of sugar-manufacturing, the first at Wanji, the second at Matahara, both along the Awash river. Like many other industrial undertakings of the post-Liberation era, the Wanji sugar-plant had Italian antecedents: it was established on the site of a sugar-cane plantation run by an Italian firm during the Occupation. In 1958–1959, the Dutch company was reorganized to ensure greater Ethiopian participation, and at the same time it was renamed HVA-Ethiopia, but the Ethiopian share in its capital rarely exceeded 20%. Assisted by the liberal investment policy of the government, and through ruthless industrial exploita-

5.3   Tsahafe T'ezaz *Walda-Giyorgis Walda-Yohannes, the most powerful figure under Hayla-Sellase in the period 1941–1955*

tion, HVA made huge profits from its sugar-manufacturing enterprise. In 1966–1967, for example, profits exceeded $Eth. 10 million. Conversely, the high price the company charged for sugar cast doubt on the benefits of the whole government policy of import substitution.

As indicated above, an important factor for the success of HVA was the government's liberal investment policy. An income-tax proclamation of 1949 had ruled that no profit tax would be levied for a period of five years on an initial capital of $Eth. 200,000 invested in mining, industry and transport. Further, tax on business enterprises was not to exceed 15% of the net profit. The Third Five-Year Plan (1968–1973) also provided for duty-free import of tractors and chemicals. Additional inducements for foreign capital investment in Ethiopia were a generous remittance policy, high tariffs on competitive imports, and ready co-operation in fixing high prices for commodities produced locally.

Mining, the big bait of foreign capital before 1935, had relatively greater success in an area which hitherto had not attracted the prospector's attention. In the early decades of the twentieth century, many an adventurer had come to Ethiopia in search of gold.   **199**

Numerous mining concessions had been granted, and much heat and excitement had been generated in the centres of European finance. Ultimately, however, the record was one of futility, if we may except the Yubdo platinum mine in Wallaga, run by the Italian Alberto Prasso. After 1941, a gold-mine at Adola in Sidamo became a steady booster of the royal coffers. In 1944, for instance, the official revenue figure from Adola came to nearly a fifth of total government revenue. Appropriately enough, the name Adola was changed to Kebra Mangest (Glory of the State). In the public vocabulary, however, 'Adola' remained, signifying terror both in the forcible recruitment of labour and in the conditions of penal servitude that prevailed in the labour camp.

A notable feature of industrialization in Ethiopia was its concentration in three cities of the Empire: Addis Ababa, Asmara and Dire Dawa. About half of the industrial establishments were in the capital. This was a reflection of the unintegrated nature of the country's development. Concentration of industry, however, meant concentration of the labour force as well, with the obvious implications for industrial and political struggle. In 1970, the labour force employed by the various industrial establishments was estimated at only 50,000 personnel. But the small overall number of personnel was compensated for by its concentration. Labour agitation for better pay and working conditions became a regular feature of the industrial scene. In Wanji, the first strike took place in 1954, the very year of the factory's establishment. Starting as mutual aid and savings associations (*eder* and *equb*, respectively), the workers' organizations matured into full-fledged trade unions in the 1960s. Unable to resist the pressure from labour any longer, the government issued the first labour legislation in the country's history in August 1962. A year later, the Confederation of Ethiopian Labour Unions (CELU) was formed. The banner of industrial agitation, since the 1920s carried by the railway workers alone, now came to be shared by those of the Addis Ababa Fibre Mills, Indo-Ethiopian Textiles, Wanji Sugar Estate, Ethiopian Air Lines, and General Ethiopian Transport (Anbassa Bus Company) – to mention only the more prominent unions.

In conclusion, the post-1941 Ethiopian economy, although not totally stagnant, was only growing at a sluggish rate. Backwardness and underdevelopment were the hallmarks of the socio-economic order. The per capita income, estimated at just over $Eth. 150 ($US 72.50) in 1967, was among the lowest in the world. Illiteracy affected more than 90% of the population. The doctor–patient ratio was in the region of one per 70,000 of the population. In spite of the injection of some degree of industrialism, the economy remained overwhelmingly agrarian. Even then, more than 90% of the agrarian sector was of a subsistence character. The industrial sector itself, negligible as it was, was dominated by foreign capital. This dependency was compounded by the government's increasing resort to foreign loans to narrow the growing gap between revenue and expenditure. The country's indebtedness rose from $Eth. 30,310,000 in 1966 to $Eth. 445,189,000 by 1969. The fact that some 75% of this loan directly or indirectly originated from the United States underlined Ethiopia's dependence on that country, a dependence duplicated in the military and educational spheres.

---

3. Consolidation of absolutism

The period after 1941 witnessed the apogee of absolutism in Ethiopia. The tentative beginnings in this direction of the pre-1935 years matured into untrammelled autocracy. The power of the state reached a limit unprecedented in Ethiopian history. This was clearly manifested in such spheres as provincial administration, military organization and fiscal control. A ruling class based on landed property, but with interests in trade and industry as well, exercised this power. The architect and physical embodiment of the absolutist order was Emperor Hayla-Sellase.

The emperor

For over half a century, Ethiopian life was dominated by the personality of Hayla-Sellase. Not only the state but also the country came to be identified with him. This fact invested him with a special and almost supernatural aura. He came to be regarded as a permanent factor, as immutable as the mountains and the rivers of the country. To ask what would come after him, let alone provide for it, became almost taboo. Foreigners were as mesmerized as nationals by his awesome personality – the more so because the Ethiopian monarchy took them on a nostalgic trip to the exotic past.

As he struggled to seize power before 1930, the career of Tafari Makonnen, as he was then known, had purpose and progressive content. This continued to be the case during the first five years after his coronation, and in the initial years after 1941. With an almost forgivable exaggeration, and oblivious of the economic essence of feudalism, he characterized his struggle against the hereditary nobility as anti-feudal. Once that struggle was over, however, Hayla-Sellase's activities were bereft of social purpose. His political vision more or less ended with the subjugation of the nobility and the creation of a centralized state. Thereafter, power became an end in itself.

201

This obsession with power bordered on megalomania. At the same time, it was marked by complete absorption with the present and total disregard for the future. It was as if the emperor mistook political longevity for immortality. He did scarcely anything to prepare the country for the future, whether along monarchical or republican lines; this fault remains his greatest indictment in history. All his energy was geared to the preservation of power and the elimination of actual and potential threats to it. Security became a matter of top priority. An elaborate intelligence network spied on the nation and fed him with information. The mania for security became institutionalized in the Private Cabinet. Set up in 1959 as a high-level advisory body to the emperor, it developed into an agency spying even on the spies, and furnishing carefully filtered intelligence.

An assiduously fostered cult of personality stripped Hayla-Sellase of all human attributes, and elevated him to superhuman heights. The media played a crucial role in this regard. In the early stages, the educational system served the same purpose. Pupils grew up chanting songs praising the emperor and wishing him a life as long as that of Abraham and Methuselah. In an exercise of paternal munificence, he showered them with gifts of cakes, oranges and sweaters on Ethiopian Christmas Day, 7 January. The more privileged students were visited on an almost weekly basis. Almost all significant urban landmarks bore his name: two schools, a hospital, a theatre, the stadium, what was then the main avenue, and a square in Addis Ababa, as well as many institutions in rural towns. His birthday and coronation day became national holidays. The silver jubilee of his coronation (1955) was the occasion for an international jamboree of unprecedented proportions. His eightieth birthday (1972) was celebrated with extraordinary pomp, a climactic, if unwitting, farewell to a reign that could not brook political liberalization.

The ultimate effect of this exercise was to abstract him from mundane issues. The most vigorous champion of the landlords became supra-class; the most astute politician became supra-politics. The good was invariably attributed to him, whereas the bad was blamed on his subordinates. The humblest of his subjects could appeal to him, incriminating the highest. Although ultimate author of the system, the emperor could pose as impartial arbiter between the wrongdoer and the wronged.

As the years progressed, the emperor tended to detach himself from domestic issues altogether, and to devote his attention to foreign affairs. Partly this arose from frustration with the intractable issues on the home front; partly it emanated from the magnetic pull of the glamour of international diplomacy. Throughout his reign, foreigners were more unstinting in their admiration of Hayla-Sellase than were his own subjects. He reciprocated in equal measure. He was possibly the most widely travelled head of state in the world. His globe-trotting knew no ideological or geographical boundaries. He carved for himself a place as a venerated father figure in international diplomacy. The so-called Non-Aligned Movement of nations which claimed to be politically independent of both East and West provided a good forum for exercising this diplomacy. The Organization of African Unity (OAU), over whose creation in 1963 Hayla-Sellase presided, proved even better.

As he pursued international fame and prestige, the emperor became oblivious to the signs of trouble at home. It never occurred to him that the smouldering fire of dissent would flare up into a conflagration that would consume him. The Revolution of 1974 caught him unawares. His senility made matters even worse for him. For a moment he seems to have toyed with the illusion that he was actually at the head of the Revolution. It was as if he viewed the '*Darg*', the co-ordinating committee of the Ethiopian armed forces that toppled him on 12 September 1974, as just another of the *mahal safari* movements which he had manipulated on his way to the throne in the early twentieth century.

The governing élite

As Hayla-Sellase devoted more and more of his time to foreign affairs, the domestic chores were increasingly left to his ministers. The almost obsessive concern for detail which was reputedly a notable feature of the emperor's character became less evident as time passed. Yet this did not necessarily mean that the ministers enjoyed full powers. Few major policy decisions were made without the approval of the emperor. The class background of the ministers was such that they posed no challenge to him. He continued his pre-war policy of recruiting men of low and humble background to ensure their loyalty to him as well as to use them as a counterweight to the hereditary nobility. The friction between the emperor's men and the aristocracy of birth was to form an undercurrent of Ethiopian politics through much of the post-1941 period.

The reinstitution of ministerial government was one of the first things to which the emperor turned his attention after the Liberation. In 1943, two imperial orders set up eleven ministries and the office of the prime minister. Although the ministries were empowered to draft their own laws and to appoint junior officials, their subservience to the imperial prerogative was spelt out in no uncertain terms. The council of ministers that was set up was not a council in the strict sense of the word, implying corporate identity. It was merely a generic phrase to embrace all the ministers. An order of 1966 changed little **203**

5.4 Ras Bitwaddad *Makonnen Endalkachaw,*
prime minister from 1943–1957

5.5 Tsahafe T'ezaz *Aklilu Habta-Wald,*
prime minister from 1961–1974

as far as the power equation was concerned: although the prime
minister was empowered to select his team, and the council of
ministers came slightly nearer towards a cabinet, final decisions on
policy matters, as well as the appointment of all ministers (including
the prime minister), vice-ministers and assistant ministers remained
the emperor's preserve. The post of prime minister was little more
than a glorified conduit for the flow of appointments and decisions.

Until 1957, the post of prime minister was occupied by *Bitwaddad*
Makonnen Endalkachaw. One of the commanders of the Ethiopian
forces on the Ogaden front in 1935–1936, and one who went into exile
after the Italian victory, his towering physique contrasted with his
political impotence. He was a mere ceremonial figure, given more to
intellectual pursuits than to political machinations. The *de facto* prime
minister was *Tsahafe T'ezaz* Walda-Giyorgis Walda-Yohannes; a man
of humble origins, he won the emperor's trust and confidence during
the years they spent together in exile. The unique position occupied
by the Ministry of Pen as the institution closest to the palace, as well
as his own knack for political intrigue, made Walda-Giyorgis the most
powerful man next to the emperor. For a decade and a half, he dominated Ethiopian politics. In addition to being *tsahafe t'ezaz* for the

whole of that period (1941–1955), he also held the portfolios of the Ministries of the Interior and of Justice on various occasions.

The person who played an important role in Walda-Giyorgis's demise was Makonnen Habta-Wald. The son of a priest, his career goes back to the pre-1935 days, when he was director in charge of commercial affairs. He lived in exile in France during the Italian Occupation. He then returned to assume the posts of Minister of Commerce and of Agriculture, until he took the portfolio of the Ministry of Finance, with which his name was closely associated, and through which he left a long-lasting impression on Ethiopian public administration. He was Minister of Finance from 1949 to 1958, two years before his death at the hands of the instigators of the abortive coup of 1960. His great assets were his system of patronage and the control of an elaborate personal intelligence network. The latter particularly endeared him to the emperor, and may have tipped the balance in his favour in his struggle with Walda-Giyorgis.

It was under Makonnen's protection that his younger brother Aklilu Habta-Wald emerged into the forefront of Ethiopian politics. He made his début in the field of foreign affairs: he attained prominence representing Ethiopia's case in the UN debates on Eritrea. After assuming *Bitwaddad* Makonnen Endalkachaw's post as deputy prime minister in 1957, he became prime minister in 1961, and remained in that post until 1974. Combining the offices of *tsahafe t'ezaz* and prime minister, he symbolized the merger of the two sources of authority – the traditional and the modern. But, whereas the former's importance was gradually being eclipsed, the latter was in the ascendant. Yet Aklilu's impact on Ethiopian politics is not so readily identifiable. He lacked the capacity for political manipulation shown by his predecessor as *tsahafe t'ezaz*, Walda-Giyorgis, and his own brother, Makonnen. Aklilu was more of a leading functionary than a power-broker.

In contrast with the leading lights of the Hayla-Sellase regime cited above, the aristocracy tended to be somewhat peripherally attached to the government. The career of the most prominent figure of the group, Asrata Kasa, son of *Ras* Kasa Haylu, epitomizes this detachment. He was governor of various provinces until he ended his career as crown councillor. Endalkachaw Makonnen, son of *Bitwaddad* Makonnen Endalkachaw, and Mikael Emeru, son of *Ras* Emeru Hayla-Sellase, tended to be preferred for ambassadorial posts. Abiy Abbaba, son-in-law of the emperor, provides one exception to the rule of peripheral government connection. He was Minister of War in the 1940s and 1950s, and later served as Minister of Justice and of the Interior. Even he was subsequently shunted to the honorific post of the presidency of the Senate. A second exception, Yelma Deressa, was a scion of a minority aristocracy, that of Wallaga. Next to Makonnen

Habta-Wald, he left the strongest mark on the Ministry of Finance. The above analysis should not suggest, however, that the hereditary aristocracy had been consigned to complete political oblivion. Institutionally, the crown council, which served as an advisory body to the emperor, provided it with a forum to exercise some degree of political influence. Such leading figures of the nobility as *Ras* Kasa Haylu, *Ras* Seyum Mangasha, *Ras* Masfen Selashi, *Ras* Haylu Balaw and *Ras* Emeru Hayla-Sellase, as well as the *abun*, were members of the council at various times; nor should we ignore the considerable leverage enjoyed by some members of the imperial family, notably the emperor's eldest daughter, Tanagnawarq. It might not be too farfetched to argue that the emperor, seasoned manipulator of men that he was, thought it politic to play off the nobility of birth against the nobility of service.

The Revised Constitution of 1955

In 1955, on the occasion of the silver jubilee of his coronation, Hayla-Sellase promulgated a new constitution, revising the first constitution issued in 1931. It was designed to give Ethiopian government an even more impressive façade of modernity as well as to rectify the anomaly created after the federation of Eritrea with Ethiopia in 1941 by the juxtaposition of the Constitution of 1931 with the more advanced Eritrean constitution. The drafting committee included three American advisers and the two leading figures of the post-1941 order, Walda-Giyorgis Walda-Yohannes and Aklilu Habta-Wald. The crown council closely supervised the deliberations of the drafting committee, underlining wherever possible the prerogatives of the crown. It is thus not surprising that the constitution opens with affairs of the crown, devoting more than a quarter of its provisions to the question of imperial succession and the powers of the emperor.

Even more than its 1931 predecessor, the Revised Constitution of 1955 was a legal charter for the consolidation of absolutism. In the words of one of the American members of the drafting committee, John Spencer, it was 'a screen behind which conservative positions could be entrenched' (Spencer, 260). The absolute powers of the emperor were spelt out in unmistakable terms: 'By virtue of His Imperial Blood, as well as by the anointing which he has received, the person of the Emperor is sacred, His dignity is inviolable and His power indisputable' (Article 4). Provisions for human rights, such as freedom of speech and of the press, were inserted largely for the sake of form. In most cases they were accompanied by such nullifying phrases as 'in accordance with the law' or 'within the limits of the law'.

In two important respects, the Revised Constitution represented a departure from the past. These were the introduction of universal adult suffrage, and the provisions for an elected Chamber of Deputies. In reality, however, their practical significance was slight. Popular participation in elections remained consistently low, and the elected deputies did not turn out to be dedicated champions of the popular cause. The property qualification for election predetermined the class bias of the deputies. The non-existence of parties deprived campaigning of national breadth, and reduced it to the level of individual competition. Given the attractive salary of deputies as well as the social status enjoyed by them, that competition was understandably keen. Parliament thus became a vehicle for self-promotion rather than a forum of popular representation.

The apparatus of coercion

If the Revised Constitution of 1955 was essentially an exercise in public relations, the emperor was very serious about strengthening the coercive arm of the state. One of the first tasks to which he addressed himself after his restoration to the throne in 1941 was to resume the work of military reorganization so rudely interrupted by the Italian invasion. As we have already seen, the Imperial Bodyguard was reconstituted, with Swedish assistance. It remained the élite force of the empire until discredited in the wake of the attempted coup of 1960. Designed to serve as a controlling agency over the other units, it turned out to be the most bitter enemy of the regime that had fostered it. For a decade and a half it was commanded by one of the most popular officers in the armed forces, Major-General Mulugeta Buli, a pre-war cadet and instructor at the Holata military school. By his colleagues, he was more than half-expected to emulate the Egyptian colonel, Gamal Abdel Nasser, who staged a coup in 1952 that overthrew the dynasty, a century and a half old, of Muhammad Ali. But Mulugeta met a different fate. He was killed by his fellow cadet and successor, Brigadier-General Mangestu Neway, leader of the abortive coup.

In February 1942, the modern Ethiopian police force was organized, largely along British lines, with such characteristic titles as 'constable', 'superintendent' and 'commissioner'. Later, the Germans and the Israelis became its mainstay. Allied to it in the task of maintaining internal security was the Department of Public Security, under the Ministry of the Interior. The denial of democratic rights in the country made that department an indispensable arm of the state in the suppression of political dissidence. Finally, the army first trained by the British, then taken over by the Americans, proved

*5.6   Major-General Mulugeta Buli, commander-in-chief
of the Imperial Bodyguard from 1941–1955*

the most important bulwark of state power. Although primarily set
up for external defence, it was deployed in extreme cases for the suppression of internal dissidence as well. Worthy of mention are also
the territorials, established soon after the Liberation to defuse the
disruptive potential of the irregular band of warriors and *shefta* who
had fought against the Italians, and later formalized into a territorial
army.

The priority accorded to the apparatus of coercion can be gleaned
from the budgetary allocations of the government. The Ministries of
the Interior and of Defence consistently attracted the two highest
allocations. In 1944–1945 for instance, out of a total of some $Eth. 38
million, nearly $Eth. 11 million was earmarked for the Ministry of
the Interior, of which security absorbed almost $Eth. 5 million; about
$Eth. 8 million was allocated for war. In 1967, the figures were over
$Eth. 80 million for the Ministry of Defence, and nearly $Eth. 60
million for the Ministry of the Interior, out of a total of about
$Eth. 400 million (US $1.00: Eth. Birr 2.07).

Yet it was these same armed forces, fostered and nurtured by the regime, that gave it the final decisive blow in 1974. The instruments of coercion were turned against the very state that had brought them into being. This had been foreshadowed in 1960. It was the inevitable fate of an order which gave no room for organized expression of political views. As the tide of opposition swelled, the armed forces, as part of the social order, were inexorably drawn into it. It is to the growth of this opposition that we shall now turn our attention.

4. Opposition

The Revised Constitution of 1955 contained the most elaborate provisions for Hayla-Sellase's succession that any Ethiopian emperor had ever made. The Revolution of 1974 terminated not only one of the longest reigns in Ethiopian history, however, but also the so-called Solomonic dynasty, which counted its lifespan in terms of millennia rather than centuries. We may feel that Hayla-Sellase's handicap was that he ruled for too long. A man who started his career battling against conservatives ended as a bastion of reaction. Phrased in fundamental terms, the end of Hayla-Sellase reflected the ultimate crisis of feudalism in Ethiopia. The advanced feudal order which he helped to create could no longer absorb the forces of change generated within it. Hence the Revolution.

The Revolution was preceded by decades of opposition, both covert and overt. As Addis Hiwet has correctly observed, the attempted *coup d'état* of 1960 marks a watershed in the political opposition in post-Liberation Ethiopia. Before the coup, opposition tended to be conspiratorial and élitist; after it, opposition was more open and mass-based. Opposition to the regime also had many facets. Peasants rebelled against increasing demands on their produce. Nationalities rose in arms for self-determination. Intellectuals struggled for their vision of a just and equitable order. Even some members of the ruling class thought the removal of Hayla-Sellase necessary to avert the total collapse of the socio-economic order.

Plots and conspiracies

Opposition to the emperor first arose as a sequel to the Resistance, and such opposition lends itself to various interpretations. It might be seen as a delayed reaction to the emperor's desertion of the country in 1936. More immediately, it expressed resentment at his restoration to power after spending five years in the safety of exile, while the **209** patriots led a precarious existence fighting for liberty. The feeling of resentment was exacerbated by the honours and privileges accorded not only to other exiles but to known *banda*, to those who had served the Italians. Three ex-patriots who were to find themselves pitted against Hayla-Sellase were *Dajjach* Balay Zallaqa, *Bitwaddad* Nagash Bazabeh and *Blatta* Takkala Walda-Hawaryat.

Balay Zallaqa had risen to become perhaps the most charismatic of the leaders of the Resistance. His base was Bechana in eastern Gojjam. His popularity automatically made him suspect in the eyes of the restored emperor. With a view to removing him from his base of power, the emperor offered Balay governorship of one of the southern provinces, with the title of *ras*. Seeing through the ploy, Balay refused. For his part, he was disgruntled at the exalted position given to the other patriot leaders in Gojjam. Haylu Balaw had been made *ras* and governor-general of Gojjam, while Mangasha Jambare had been promoted to *bitwaddad* and made deputy governor-general; Balay's reward had been the title of *dajjazmach* and the governorship of Bechana district. The loss of Motta and parts of Dabra Marqos district, which had been under his control, added to his discontent. He expressed his displeasure by flouting orders coming from both the governor-general and the central government. In February 1943, a combined force from Gojjam and Addis Ababa invaded his district. After three months of fighting, he surrendered and was brought to the capital, where he was kept in detention. A few months later, he broke out of prison, but was caught on his way to Gojjam. Brought back to Addis Ababa, Balay was publicly hanged.

Bitwaddad Nagash Bazabeh, grandson of *Negus* Takla-Haymanot of Gojjam, was another leader of the Resistance in that province. After the Liberation, he occupied a post as vice-minister, and had then been appointed president of the Senate. In 1951, he led a conspiracy against the emperor which reportedly planned to assassinate Hayla-Sellase and proclaim a republic. Some military officers were attracted to the plot, including a certain Baqqala Anasimos, who is credited with most of the planning.

The plotters were betrayed by another patriot leader, *Dajjach* Garasu Duki, whom they had approached to enlist to their cause. Ironically, the man who was entrusted with the task of apprehending the conspirators was none other than Mangestu Neway (then Colonel), the future leader of the failed coup in 1960. Arrested during one of their clandestine meetings, the conspirators were tried and sentenced to various terms of imprisonment.

But no single individual was as implacable and as persevering in his opposition to the emperor as *Blatta* Takkala Walda-Hawaryat. For over three decades he battled against the emperor with a bitterness that had all the marks of a personal feud. It all started with the emperor's flight in 1936. Before that time, Takkala had been one of Hayla-Sellase's loyal servants, both during the regency and in the first five years of the emperorship. Takkala was one of those who had strongly opposed the idea of the emperor's seeking exile. Once the emperor took that option, Takkala did all he could to prevent him from regaining his throne. When British arms supported the return, Takkala dedicated the rest of his life to trying to dethrone Hayla-Sellase.

His first plot to that end occurred soon after the Liberation. It was an immediate reaction to the axis of exiles and *banda* then emerging. It was couched in constitutionalist terms and used one of the sons of Iyyasu, Yohannes, as front. At the same time, Takkala had managed to win over to his side some contingents of the army. But the plot was uncovered and its instigator detained. Released in 1945 and appointed as deputy *afa negus* in one of the many attempts to buy him over to the regime, he became involved in another plot the following year. This time his detention lasted until 1954. On his release, Takkala was once again given high government posts, becoming successively Vice-Minister of the Interior and *afa negus*. For some time, it appeared that the old warrior was finally mollified. But he was only biding his time. In November 1969, the final act of his opposition, three decades long, was played in dramatic circumstances. A new plot to assassinate the emperor having been uncovered, Takkala barricaded himself in his house and engaged in a shoot-out with the police, in which he was killed.

The attempted coup d'état *of 1960*

The nearest the emperor came to losing his throne was in 1960. Despite its failure, the coup represented the most serious challenge to his power between 1941 and 1974. As already indicated, it also marked a watershed in the history of political opposition. The two brothers who organized it, Mangestu and Garmame Neway, epitomized the military and intellectual components of that opposition before as well as after 1960.

Brigadier-General Mangestu Neway belonged to that unique generation of Ethiopians, the pre-war cadets who channelled their fervent patriotism into the Black Lion organization. But not all those cadets turned out to be opponents of the regime. If anything, Mangestu stands out as a significant exception to the rule. Ranged against him during the coup were his former fellow cadets, now generals, Abiy Abbaba, Assafa Ayyana, Isayyas Gabra-Sellase and Kabbada Gabre. It might be said that the latter officers remained

5.7   *The leaders of the abortive* coup d'état *of 1960, Brigadier-General Mangestu Neway (left) and his brother Garmame Neway*

faithful to one of the tenets of the Black Lion organization: allegiance to Hayla-Sellase and his family.

Garmame Neway's radical credentials were less ambiguous. In more senses than one he represented a bridge – a rather solitary bridge, we should add – between the pre-war intellectuals and the student radicals of the 1960s and 1970s. His educational development started in Addis Ababa at Haile Sellassie I Secondary School. He then proceeded to the United States, where he obtained a BA from the University of Wisconsin, and an MA from Columbia. His formal education contrasted with the often somewhat delayed and informal exposure to foreign cultures of the earlier intellectuals, and anticipated the future pattern. He also had a keener sense of organization than his predecessors. During his stay in America, he was president of the Ethiopian Students Association. On his return, he was elected president of the clandestine alumni association of his former school. Ultimately, however, just as the pre-war intellectuals had sought the support of an enlightened prince, Garmame resorted to the armed force of his brother Mangestu to bring about change.

212

There is no doubt that Garmame was the moving spirit behind the attempted coup. His record as a civil servant was one of a high sense of civic responsibility and concern for the underprivileged. This made him suspect in the eyes of the regime, and he was exiled to distant administrative posts, first Walayta, then Jijjiga. He converted these exile posts into stations experimenting in equitable administration. In Walayta, he made efforts to ease the burden of the tenants by introducing a settlement programme, as well as written tenancy contracts. In Jijjiga, too, he endeared himself to the Somali by taking measures to improve their lot. The obstruction he encountered even in these remote posts convinced him of the need for change, and he began to work on his brother to that end.

Notwithstanding its chief author's dedication to change, however, the embryo coup was characterized by confused articulation and inept organization. The latter factor in particular condemned the coup to failure beforehand.

A strong theme in the coup-makers' pronouncements was Ethiopia's backwardness, in contrast with the forward strides taken by several newly independent African states. Restoration of Ethiopia to its former glory was thus one of their pledges. In an apparent effort to allay fears of such allies as the United States, they promised to honour all international commitments and to continue the friendly relations entered into by the regime they were trying to overthrow. A populist element is also discernible in their declared concern for the masses, and the promise to found new factories and schools. But the fundamental issue affecting the masses, land, was not raised, except in the form of a general commitment to increase agricultural production. The emperor's heir, Asfawasan, who was to be the future salaried constitutional monarch of Ethiopia, was made the mouthpiece of the rebels. On 14 December 1960, a new government was declared. It was to be headed by the liberal aristocrat *Ras* Emeru Hayla-Sellase, and the popular general Mulugeta Buli was designated chief of staff of the armed forces. A salary rise for soldiers was also promised.

A fatal mistake of the rebels was their neglect of the other units of the armed forces, particularly the army and the air force. They made no serious effort either to win them over to their side or to neutralize them. Instead they tried to achieve their objectives by camouflaging their intentions. As they rounded up the ministers and other stalwarts of the regime, they declared they were doing it for their own protection, because the army had rebelled. This was at best a delaying tactic. Soon the rebels found themselves confronting the united might of the army and the air force. Brigadier-General Abiy Abbaba, representative of the crown in Asmara, was selected as liaison between the loyalists and the emperor, who was in South America at the outbreak

213

of the coup, but came hurrying home to save his imperilled throne. The patriarch brought in the weight of tradition, supporting the loyalists by anathematizing the rebels. The Americans, after a preliminary assessment of the situation, threw in their lot with the loyalists. The Imperial Bodyguard was clearly no match for the forces arrayed against it. Brigadier-General Tsegge Dibu, commander of the police, appears only to have joined in the coup attempt under duress and lacked the backing of his force.

Probably intimidated by this, the rebels asked for a cease-fire and talks soon after the initial exchanges of fire. But the loyalists, confident of victory, spurned the rebel overtures for peace, and won their victory after a battle that lasted barely two days. In a final desperate act, the Neway brothers shot the hostages held in the Gannata L'ul Palace (now the University Administration building at Seddest Kilo), and fled to the outskirts of Addis Ababa. As they made their exit, the emperor made his triumphal entry into the capital, to the ululations of a populace which evidently preferred 'the devil it knew'. Hounded by soldiers and volunteers keen to get the reward money put on their heads, the brothers had little chance of escape. Garmame died fighting. Mangestu was wounded and captured. He was subsequently tried and hanged.

This piece of retributive justice accomplished, the emperor sat back to rule in the old way. As far as he was concerned, the failed coup was the work of a couple of ungrateful miscreants. His subsequent moves focused on rewarding those who had defended his throne, not in trying to solve the problems indicated by the rebels, albeit in a nebulous manner. But the clock of time could not simply be wound back to its former place. For one thing, the army had to be pacified. In a bid to rival the rebels, the loyalists had also promised a salary increase. And, soon after the restoration of the old order, the soldiers reminded the government of its promise, and it was forced to introduce increases in the salaries of both men and officers – the first increase in decades. But it certainly did not prove to be the last. For the army, the increase, aside from its monetary significance, was a gauge of its own political muscle.

The torch of change that the rebels had kindled was not extinguished with their physical elimination. On the contrary, it sparked a more outspoken and radical opposition to the regime. This can be seen in some of the underground leaflets that began to circulate soon after the end of the coup. They had such uncompromising motifs as 'Better be a lion for a day and die than live the life of a lamb for a thousand days', 'There is no solution without blood', and 'What is sinful is to be ruled by despots, not to rise against them'. Above all, the students became the true heirs of the rebels. They had come out on the streets in support of the rebels in 1960. Thereafter, they gave breadth and coherence to the opposition that the rebels had conceived and executed in such a confused manner. As for the regime, unprepared to concede reform, it condemned itself to being swept away by revolution.

Peasant rebellions

Opposition to the regime was not confined to the élite. It assumed a broader dimension with the outbreak of peasant rebellions in a number of provinces. Their incidence as well as their intensity was much greater than in earlier periods, and attests to the increasingly heavy pressures being exerted on the peasantry. These rebellions differed in their duration (from a few days to several years), their ideological articulation, the external factors in their outbreak or suppression, and the manner in which the government reacted to them.

The first of the rebellions belongs to the immediate aftermath of the Liberation. It occurred in Tegre province, and has come down in history as the *wayane* rebellion. Many elements contributed to its outbreak. The general insecurity that prevailed in the immediate post-Liberation years and the numerous arms left behind by the Italians were conducive to brigandage. What converted this brigandage into rebellion were administrative inefficiency and corruption, and the rapacity of the territorial army units stationed in the province. At the same time, the rebellion was a continuation of the pre-Italo-Ethiopian war confrontation between the Rayya–Azabo peoples and the government. As in the late 1920s, the government's campaign of retribution against their raids on the lowland Afar ignited the general rebellion. Finally, a section of the nobility tried to take advantage of the situation to try to reassert their hereditary privileges and their region's former political centrality.

The rebels scored their first major victory at Addi Abun in Tamben, on 22 May 1943. They followed this up with the capture of Qwiha and Enda Iyyasus, small towns near Maqale, the capital of Tegre, and finally Maqale itself. A major factor for their success was the remarkable leadership provided by *Blatta* Hayla-Maryam Radda, who couched the popular grievances in millenarian phraseology. Alarmed by the steady growth of rebellion, the government entrusted the command of its forces to the redoubtable patriot leader, *Ras* Abbaba Aragay, and resorted to the British for assistance. British aircraft played a decisive role in the final phase of the fighting, which took place in late September and early October. The *wayane* rebellion was crushed in a barrage of artillery fire and air bombardment.

Exactly two decades elapsed before the next major peasant eruption. This was the rebellion in the south-eastern province of Bale, and **215** it lasted from 1963 to 1970. Here the connection between peasant exploitation and rebellion was much more direct than in the case of Tegre. The institution of the *qalad* in 1951 had had the effect of reducing many peasants to the status of tenants. The peasants' inability to pay the increased taxes accompanying new land measurements in 1963 had led to large-scale alienation. The conditions of the peasants were worsened by the multiplicity and venality of government officials. The imposition of Christian settlers over a predominantly Muslim population also engendered religious antagonism. Settler arrogance, as well as political and economic domination, reached its peak under the administration of *Fitawrari* Warqu Enqwa-Sellase, whose appointment as provincial governor in 1963 might be said to have triggered the rebellion. Islam indeed became the ideology that rallied the Somali and Oromo rebels. Further, what ignited the growing disgruntlement and lent it both magnitude and longevity was Somali expansionism, which considered Bale a part of its *terra irredenta*, land of which the Somalis felt they had been deprived. It was the Somalis who, to suit their own designs, named the movement the Liberation Front of Western Somalia.

The rebellion began in the Somali-inhabited frontier district of El Kere. It was initially led by Kahin Abdi, who had opted for the life of a bandit or *shefta* on the imprisonment of his son for failure to pay land-tax. The rebellion soon spread to other districts: Wabe, Dallo and Ganale. New leaders also emerged, of whom the most important was Waqo Gutu, the self-styled 'General of Western Somalia'. He visited Somalia and was in steady contact with the Somalis, who provided the rebels with arms and military training.

The government at first adopted a fairly pacific approach, promising the return of confiscated land in cases where it had not already been granted to other individuals. In a bid to co-opt the local élite to its side, it also granted *siso* land to the *balabbat*. As the rebellion spread unchecked and claimed the lives of two district governors in 1965 and 1966, the government resorted to extreme measures. In December 1966, it placed the province under the martial rule of the commander of the army's Fourth Division. The following year, it launched massive operations involving the army, the police, the territorials, the settler militia (*nach labash*) and volunteers (*waddo zamach*). Reeling back under the weight of this government offensive, the rebels found themselves without the external support that had sustained them, as the Somalis became absorbed in their own political changes in 1969. The rebellion collapsed. Waqo surrendered on 28 March 1970.

While the government was absorbed in crushing the Bale uprising, another broke out in the north, in Gojjam. That was a province which had successfully resisted pressures from the political centre. The government had scarcely been able to collect taxes there in the post-Liberation period: the amount collected was so low that it could not even cover the salaries of local officials. In 1950, the new governor, *Dajjach* Kabbada Tasamma, tried to change the situation. He raised the tax rate from the low pre-war level that had been in force (as in Bagemder and Tegre) and initiated a policy of assessment and classification of land to determine taxation. Besides resenting the higher taxes that this policy entailed, the Gojjame suspected that the land classification policy was the prelude to the introduction of the dreaded *qalad*. Rebellion broke out in Mota, Qolla Daga Damot and Mecha districts. The emperor was forced to reduce the new tax rate by a third, remove Kabbada, and reinstall the hereditary governor, Haylu Balaw.

Part of the animosity the Gojjame felt for Kabbada probably emanated from his being of Shawan origin. It was under another Shawan successor to Haylu, Tsahayu Enqwa-Sellase, that things came to a head between Gojjam and the central government. Like his brother Warqu in Bale, Tsahayu initiated an administration marked by iniquity and insensitivity. The population was forced to make contributions for such self-ingratiating projects as erecting an imposing statue of the emperor. In an effort to eradicate banditry, Tsahayu subjected the peasantry to the rapacity of the *nach labash*. Reversing the conciliatory approach of the emperor, he also ordered the payment of tax arrears and the registration (with fees) of firearms.

What finally set off the Gojjam uprising of 1968 was the attempt to introduce the new agricultural income tax. More than any other measure thus far taken by the government, this was seen as the final assault on the *rest* system of land-ownership. The population resisted the tax assessors, sent the customary petitions to the emperor to reverse the order and, when no response was forthcoming, rose in rebellion. The uprising was centred in the districts of Mota and Daga Damot, and was led by veterans of the Resistance, who were quick to bestow upon themselves titles such as that of *l'ul* and *fitawrari*. Thus, by a twist of irony, Tsahayu, himself a renowned patriot, found himself pitted against his fellow patriots.

But matters soon went out of his control. In clear contrast to the way it was handling the Bale rebellion (probably because of the Somali implications in Bale), the government was far more accommodating over the Gojjame demands. Committees were successively set up to try and placate the rebels, and, on the recommendation of one of the committees, Tsahayu was transferred to Kafa province, and a general amnesty was proclaimed. When the revolt continued in spite of these concessions, the government launched a military campaign involving the army, police and *nach labash*. By the end of 1968, the rebellion was suppressed. But the peasants had not lost their cause: not only was

217

the new tax abandoned, but also tax arrears from 1950 to 1968 were waived. Many government officials who had not been over-popular were transferred.

Two other areas which witnessed significant peasant uprisings in this period were Yajju in Wallo, in the north-east, and Gedeo (Darasa) in the southern province of Sidamo. In Yajju, rebellions erupted twice. In 1948, peasants rose after appeals against alienation of their land were ignored. Led by a *Qagnazmach* Malaku Tayye and a certain Unda Muhammad, they attacked the prison in the district capital, Waldya, and liberated the prisoners. The rebellion was finally suppressed with the help of the *nach labash*, and the leaders were publicly flogged on a market-day. Another uprising in 1970 was provoked by the encroachments of mechanized farming on pasture-land. The peasants managed to kill the leading beneficiary of that process, a member of the Yajju nobility named *Qagnazmach* Abata Haylu, before their uprising was quelled.

The Gedeo uprising of 1960 also had its genesis in land alienation. The coffee-rich lands of the district had invited a veritable land-grabbing rush among the northern nobility and gentry. Amongst those involved was the emperor's daughter, Princess Tanagnawarq. In the process, many Gedeo had been reduced to tenancy. The economic exploitation of the Gedeo was coupled with the degradation of their culture. As in many other instances of peasant rebellion in Ethiopia, the Gedeo uprising was preceded by futile appeals and petitions to higher authorities. The peasants then challenged the oppressive system by refusing to pay the *erbo*, the quarter of his produce that a tenant was expected to pay to the landlord. The clash with the authorities began when the peasants went on to collect the coffee without waiting for the assessors who could customarily determine the amount of *erbo* to be paid.

It was an unequal struggle. Armed mostly with spears and swords, the peasants confronted a well-equipped enemy composed of landlords and government troops. In the first of the clashes, eighty-eight peasants were killed as against three on the other side. In the final engagement at Michille, the peasants were lulled into discontinuing fighting by conciliatory gestures from the government envoy, *Afa Negus* Eshate Gada. Taking advantage of this, the government troops stepped up their offensive, killing over a hundred peasants and destroying much peasant property. An 'arbitration' commission presided over by the same *afa negus* restored the previous status, and fined the elders (*hayicha*) who had provided an organizational base for the rebellion. The defeat of the peasants was total.

Eritrea: federation, union and separatism

No other rural insurrection sapped the power of the government and pinned down its forces as much as the armed struggle in Eritrea which began in 1961. In terms of organization, external support and longevity, it was the most serious provincial challenge to the old regime. The insurrection was rural only in its location. Its leadership, as well as a considerable proportion of its rank and file, came from urban petty-bourgeois elements. Both in its own right and in the radicalizing influence it exerted on the Ethiopian opposition in general, it played a significant role in the regime's collapse in 1974. It was in turn nurtured by the support and manpower it got from the radical opposition in the rest of Ethiopia.

As indicated above, the formulas for federation had few friends. Both Unionists and the partisans of independence were unhappy with it. It could be argued that neither group was ready to give the federal scheme a chance. In spite of some expansion of facilities in Eritrea during the federation, its opponents alleged that the Ethiopian economy was expanding at the expense of Eritrea, and continued to portray the federal association in the darkest of colours. Nor was the Ethiopian government particularly keen to honour the federal arrangement. An autonomous Eritrea, enjoying a relatively higher degree of democratic and civic liberties, was a dangerous anomaly in the oppressive political climate prevalent elsewhere in Ethiopia.

The chief executives, including the first of them, Tadla Bayru, who was himself to seek exile later, aggravated the situation through high-handed measures stifling political opposition and plurality of views. A series of steps were taken which eroded the autonomous status of Eritrea. Finally, on 14 November 1962, the Eritrean Assembly, the legislative body created by the Federal Act in 1952, voted itself out of existence, by terminating the federal arrangement and deciding to unite Eritrea with the rest of Ethiopia.

The separatist movement in Eritrea first expressed itself in 1958 with the founding of the Eritrean Liberation Movement (ELM). The ELM was a movement which sought to achieve its objective by political and diplomatic means, including intervention from the United Nations. It was soon eclipsed by the Muslim-dominated Eritrean Liberation Front (ELF). Formed in 1961 by Eritrean exiles in the Middle East, the ELF launched armed attacks in September of that year, under the leadership of a veteran *shefta*, Idris Awate. The ELF cast its struggle for Eritrean independence within a pan-Arab mould. This factor attracted much sympathy and support for it in the Arab world. Syria and Iraq, who regarded Eritrea as an integral part of the Arab homeland, became the ELF's mainstay.

But the ELF's sectarian conception of the struggle soon engendered **219** tensions and divisions within it. It could not accommodate the people with divergent backgrounds and aspirations who had joined it because it was the only organized body at the time. Strife developed between guerrillas of the Barka lowlands in western Eritrea, ELF's base, and those of the Red Sea plains, between Christians and Muslims, and between different zonal commands. Many Christian guerrillas were persecuted and harassed into surrendering to the government. Splinter groups emerged: the Eritrean Liberation Forces in the Barka area (also known as the Obelites), the People's Liberation Forces in the Red Sea area, led by Osman Saleh Sabby, and the *Salfi Nasenet Eritrea* (Front for Eritrean Independence) in the Akala Guzay region, led by Isayyas Afawarqi. These three groups merged in 1972 to form the Eritrean Liberation Front and Popular Liberation Forces (ELF-PLF), reconstituted as the Eritrean People's Liberation Forces (EPLF) the following year.

The last years of the old regime in Ethiopia thus saw two organizations vying for recognition as leaders of the Eritrean separatist movement: the ELF and the EPLF, or, in their more popular Arabic designations, *Jabha* (Front) and *Sha'abiya* (Popular). A veritable civil war was waged during the period 1972 to 1974, as the two organizations fought for supremacy. Contrary to common assumptions, the divisions did not follow any clear-cut ideological or religious lines. The ELF had some important Christian elements, just as the EPLF's widely advertised Marxist–Leninist credentials were not as impeccable as its partisans made them out to be. The issue, as is so often the case in such circumstances, was one of struggle for power.

The Ethiopian Student Movement

The most implacable opposition to the regime came from the students. Their resilience as well as their strategic location – in the towns, particularly in the capital – had a most unsettling effect on the regime. Rural protest, however sustained and well organized, had a natural tendency to be peripheral, and could scarcely capture as much attention as urban movements, more particularly as it often failed to gain reportage. For something like a decade from 1965 on, the students came out into the streets in almost ritual annual demonstrations, daring to defy a political order that had managed to secure the cowed submission of a large part of the population. As impassioned advocates of change, more than any other sector of the society, they proved to be the grave-diggers of the old regime and the generators of the Ethiopian Revolution.

220   Ethiopia after 1941 saw a considerable expansion of educational facilities. Although still inadequate when viewed in the context of the needs of the country, these facilities none the less represent a significant improvement over the pre-war situation. By the end of the 1960s, the student population numbered some 700,000 young people. Not all the schools were the result of government initiative. In addition to those opened by the government, a number of schools were sponsored and run by missionaries and private individuals. In the 1960s and 1970s, the public came to assume more and more the financial burden of constructing schools. International organizations such as the Swedish International Development Agency (SIDA) also played an important role in the building of schools, particularly elementary schools.

But the expansion of education was at the same time marked by some significant drawbacks. The male–female student ratio was overly biased towards the former. There was a clear concentration of educational facilities in a few favoured areas, with the capital being the most privileged, followed by Eritrea and Shawa. The attrition rate was very high, rising to about 70% at the primary level in the 1960s. There was a short-sighted concentration on academic education, to the neglect of vocational education. An attempt to rectify this imbalance, the educational sector review of 1971–1972, came to grief over allegations of its tendency to perpetuate the class divisions of the society.

The post-1941 period was also significant because of the opening of secondary schools and institutions of higher education. Of the secondary schools, two were to attain national importance, not only because they were exclusively secondary schools which had boarding facilities for boys from all over Ethiopia, but also because they became the main producers of the country's political élite, in power as well as in opposition. These were Haile Sellassie I Secondary School (Kotabe) and General Wingate Secondary School, both then on the outskirts of Addis Ababa. The former was opened in 1943 on the premises of what was formerly an Italian agricultural research centre. It enjoyed very close association with the palace, which even provided food for the students until the school's kitchen facilities were completed. Although modelled on the British school system, the school's direction was for most of the period in Canadian hands. Even closer to the British school model was General Wingate School, founded in 1946 and co-sponsored by the British Council and the Ethiopian Ministry of Education.

Higher education in Ethiopia began with the founding of the University College of Addis Ababa (UCAA) in 1950, consisting of the Faculties of Arts and Science. By the middle of the decade, the Engineering College and the Building College in Addis Ababa, the Agricultural College in Alamaya, near Harar, and the Public Health

College in Gondar had also been opened. In 1961, the various colleges and faculties were integrated in Haile Sellassie I University, which later included the School of Social Work, the College of Business Administration and the Faculties of Education, Law and Medicine. The student population rose from 71 in 1950 to about 10,000 by 1973 (including extension or night-school students). For higher degrees, however, students continued to go abroad. The largest concentration, estimated at 700 in 1970, was in the United States.

The Ethiopian Student Movement went through various phases of evolution, starting as a cultural and intellectual forum of an élite and growing into a mass revolutionary movement in the late 1960s and early 1970s. It had two distinct components: the external and the internal. The story of the movement was one of steady radicalization. Both objective and subjective factors contributed to this end. The country's worsening situation, more specifically the deteriorating condition of the peasantry and the urban masses, provided the objective basis of the radical motivation. The escalation of government repression only succeeded in inciting students to ever bolder challenges to authority. Repression and opposition both grew in an ascending spiral, until they had their final resolution in the crescendo of the Revolution of 1974.

On the subjective level, various influences worked on the students to give them a sharper perception of their society and a more radical formulation of their ideas of changing it. Beginning in 1958, the advent of scholarship students from other countries in Africa had a clearly invigorating effect on Ethiopian university students: the impact was immediate and cogent. The unsuccessful coup in 1960 had a similar eye-opening effect. Although the students had greeted it with a mixture of expectancy and caution, its contribution in exploding the imperial mystique was considerable. Following in the footsteps of the rebels, the students amplified and deepened the latter's challenge to imperial authority. Finally, the Ethiopian University Service (EUS), initiated in 1964, whereby students spent a year in the countryside, mainly teaching in secondary schools there, served as a bridge between campus and society, bringing students into direct contact with the people whose life they wanted to change. The EUS also provided a medium for closer rapport between university and high school students.

The early years of the student movement were characterized by the struggle for a free press and free union. In the 1950s, student views had found forums in *The UC Calls*, a University College paper with a decidedly didactic and apolitical stamp. *News and Views*, initiated in 1959, represented a step towards radicalization, although the heavy hand of authority ensured that it would not assume a more radical line. The earliest form of student organization was the student council, which goes back to the establishment of the University College. Being under the aegis of the Dean of Students, it could hardly claim to be an independent body. The struggle for a free union and a free press was essentially an on-campus affair, as students were pitted against the authoritarian rule of the French-Canadian Jesuit fathers who administered and taught at the college in its early years.

As was the case with the opposition in general, 1960 was a turning-point in the students' expression of views and ideas. Before that time, student activities tended to be geared more towards their own intellectual growth and the enrichment of campus life. After that, we notice greater efforts being made to reach out to society. The Debating Society is a good example of the first phase. Started in 1961, the poetry contests, which were held on College days, typify the second. The poems were characterized, above everything else, by political critique and social satire. In 1962, the entries so offended the authorities that the poets were suspended and the members of the executive council of the student union, the University College Union (UCU), were expelled.

The really militant phase of the student movement started in the mid-1960s. The emergence in 1964 of a radical core known as the 'Crocodiles' was crucial in this respect. The Crocodiles proved true to their name, often staying under cover, rarely occupying posts in the union leadership, but instead preferring to advance their ideas and programmes through front figures. The students' uncompromising opposition to the regime, as well as the beginning of acceptance of Marxist ideas, is traceable to this period. Both the brave achievements and the fatal blunders of the Ethiopian Student Movement are ultimately attributable to this group.

The first manifestation of radical opposition came in February 1965. While parliamentarians debated the regulation of tenancy, students came out on to the streets chanting the revolutionary slogan of 'Land to the Tiller'. That event inaugurated a decade of student radicalism, punctuated by annual demonstrations exposing the inequities of what came to be characterized as the feudo-bourgeois regime in Ethiopia, and expressing solidarity with the anti-imperialist and anti-colonialist struggles elsewhere in the world.

The issues highlighted and the causes championed varied from year to year. In 1966, it was in protest against the 'Shola Concentration Camp', a so-called relief centre on the outskirts of the capital where destitute men and women were kept under inhumane conditions. In 1967, students came out in defence of civic liberties as a parliamentary bill threatened to make demonstrations virtually impossible. In 1968, rallies and demonstrations were held in solidarity with the people of Vietnam, and in protest against the minority regime in Rhodesia. In the same year, a fashion show held in one of the halls on the Seddest

5.8   *A student demonstration against the Hayla-Sellase régime. Among
the slogans the demonstrators are carrying is the popular one: 'Land
to the Tiller'*

Kilo campus of the university provoked violent clashes as students tried to stop a function which they regarded as a manifestation of cultural imperialism. In 1969, the cause of educational reform brought students all over the country into the streets. The beginning of the academic year 1969-1970 saw university students addressing themselves to perhaps the most sensitive issue, the question of nationalities. Student support of the right of nationalities to self-determination alarmed the government into launching its most determined offensive to date. An orchestrated press campaign against the students was followed by the assassination of the student union president and the killing of a number of students as they gathered to honour their slain leader.

Parallel with their growing radicalization, the students attained ever higher forms of organization. The University College Union (UCU) had been the main student organization in the early 1960s. The transfer in 1965 of the Faculties of Arts and Education from their original location at Arat Kilo to the new premises at Seddest Kilo shifted the centre of political activities. It also necessitated the formation of a new union, known as the Main Campus Student Union (MCSU). Before a year passed, the radical wing of the student body began to agitate for a city-wide union. A national student organization, the National Union of Ethiopian University Students (NUEUS), had been in existence since 1963, but it was too nebulous and ceremonial to play an effective role in channelling student opposition. An organization uniting all the students of the capital was deemed the best mode of giving that opposition maximum effect. After an intense debate, the University Students Union of Addis Ababa (USUAA) was formed. USUAA and its paper, *Struggle*, marked the organizational and ideological ascendancy of the left in Ethiopian student politics.

The Ethiopian Student Movement also had an important external component. Student activity abroad was centred in North America and Europe, and was conducted by two organizations: the Ethiopian Students Union in North America (ESUNA), successor of the Ethiopian Students Association in North America (ESANA), and the Ethiopian Students Union in Europe (ESUE). Distance, and better access to revolutionary literature, uncensored, lent Ethiopian student activity abroad a theoretical advantage. As students on the home front were absorbed in the day-to-day reality of their country, ESUNA's *Challenge* and ESUE's *Tataq* ('Gird yourself') evolved as the theoretical organs of the student movement. But there was hardly any meaningful symbiosis between the practical struggle at home and the theoretical discussions abroad. The last years of the old regime also saw the Ethiopian student body abroad rent in bitter and acrimonious divisions – divisions which were to be transposed to the Ethiopian scene in the course of the Revolution, with disastrous consequences. For its idealism and its commitment to change, the Ethiopian Student Movement has few parallels. In a social order which banned overt political dissent, Ethiopian students assumed the burden of opposition with heroism and dignity. It was a task for which the Ethiopian past had hardly prepared them. The absence of a democratic and critical tradition left its mark on the character of the movement. Dissenting opinions were treated with intolerance. Ideological disputes were vaguely reminiscent of the doctrinal controversies of the *Zamana Masafent*. Marxism–Leninism was embraced as a creed rather than as a system of thought to help interpret the Ethiopian reality. Slogans came to be mistaken for theory. The assumption of a radical posture became a self-justifying pursuit: in other words, the further to the left, the better.

Government repression left no option other than the increasingly radical movement. Beginning with the detention of student leaders in police stations in Addis Ababa, the regime had escalated its repression to mass deportations to the torrid Gibe river valley by 1972. Students meanwhile had elevated their opposition from rallies and demonstrations to the armed hijacking of a DC-3 passenger aircraft. The particularly repressive atmosphere of the early 1970s forced many activists to flee the country, swelling the student opposition abroad, particularly in North America. Yet, despite the growing intensity of the confrontation, the outbreak of the Ethiopian Revolution in 1974 caught both the regime and the students unawares. The regime had scarcely thought the end was so near. The students, their years of opposition notwithstanding, had not yet formulated a clear and viable alternative.

Sources, Chapter 5

Note. The BA and MA theses cited in the references are available in the Institute of Ethiopian Studies (IES) and/or in the Department of History, Addis Ababa University (AAU), formerly Haile Selassie I University (HSIU).

Addis Hiwet. *Ethiopia: From Autocracy to Revolution.* London, 1975.

Ahmed Hassan Omer. 'Aspects of the History of Efrata-Jille Wareda (Shoa Region), with Particular Reference to the Twentieth Century.' BA thesis (AAU, History, 1987).

Assefa Bequele and Eshetu Chole. *A Profile of the Ethiopian Economy.* Nairobi, 1969.

Assefa Tewodros. 'History of Telecommunications in Ethiopia up to 1974.' BA thesis (AAU, History, 1985).

Ayele Tarekegn. 'The History of the Imperial Highway Authority (IHA): 1951–1980.' BA thesis (AAU, History, 1987).

Bahru Zewde. 'Environment and Capital: Notes for the History of the Wonji-Shoa Sugar Estate, 1951–1974.' Paper presented at the Sixth Eastern Africa History Conference. Ambo, 1984 (AAU, IES).

———. 'Some Aspects of Post-Liberation Ethiopia 1941–1950', *Proceedings of the Eighth International Conference of Ethiopian Studies* (Taddese Beyene, ed.), Volume I. Addis Ababa and Frankfurt-on-Main, 1988.

Balsvik, R.R. *Haile Selassie's Students: The Intellectual and Social Background to Revolution, 1952–1977.* East Lansing, 1985.

Clapham, Christopher. *Haile Selassie's Government.* New York, 1969.

Cohen, J.M., and Weintraub, D. *Land and Peasants in Imperial Ethiopia: The Social Background to a Revolution.* Assen, 1975.

Eshetu Chole. 'The Mode of Production in Ethiopia and the Realities Thereof', *Challenge* XII, 1 (1971).

———. 'Towards a History of the Fiscal Policy of the Pre-Revolutionary Ethiopian State: 1941–1974', *Journal of Ethiopian Studies* XVII (1984).

Gebru Tareke. 'Rural Protest in Ethiopia, 1941–1970: A Study of Three Rebellions', PhD thesis (Syracuse, New York, 1977).

Getnet Bekele. 'The Peasant Rising of 1960 in Gedeo.' BA thesis (AAU, History, 1983).

Gilkes, Patrick. *The Dying Lion. Feudalism and Modernization in Ethiopia.* London, 1975.

Gizachew Adamu. 'A Historical Survey of Taxation in Gojjam (1901–1969).' BA thesis (HSIU, History, 1971).

Lefever, Ernest W. *Spear and Scepter. Army, Police and Politics in Tropical Africa.* Washington, DC, 1970.

Marcus, Harold. *Ethiopia, Great Britain, and the United States, 1941–1974. The Politics of Empire.* Berkeley, California, 1983.

Markakis, John. *Ethiopia. Anatomy of a Traditional Polity.* Oxford, 1974.

Mesfin Wolde Mariam. *Rural Vulnerability to Famine in Ethiopia: 1958-1977.* New Delhi, 1984.

Molla Tikuye. 'System of Land Tenure and Peasant Protests in GubalaftoWorada *c.* 1875-1974.' BA thesis (AAU, History, 1984).

Nega Ayele. 'Centralization versus Regionalism in Ethiopia: The Case of Gojjam.' BA thesis (HSIU, Political Science, 1970).

Negarit Gazetta. [Several numbers.] Addis Ababa.

Perham, Margery. *The Government of Ethiopia.* London, 1969.

Shumet Sishagn. 'Power Struggle in the Eritrean Secessionist Movement.' MA thesis (AAU, History, 1984).

Spencer, John H. *Ethiopia at Bay: A Personal Account of the Haile Sellassie Years.* Algonac, Michigan, 1984.

Stahl, Michael. *Ethiopia: Political Contradictions in Agricultural Development.* Stockholm, 1974.

Tafarra Degeffe. 'Credit Institutions in Ethiopia: An Historical Outline', *Ethiopia Observer* VIII, 4 (1965).

Taye Gulilat. 'The Tax in Lieu of Tithe and the New Agricultural Income Tax: A Preliminary Evaluation', *Dialogue* II, 1 (1968).

Tesfatsion Medhanie. *Eritrea: Dynamics of a National Question.* Amsterdam, 1986.

Zawde Ratta. *Ya Erta Guday* ('The Eritrean Question'). Addis Ababa Ethiopian Calendar.

Zelalem Assefa. 'Dajazmach Balay Zalaqa (1912-1945): A Tentative Biography.' BA thesis (AAU, History, 1983).

6 Revolution and Its Sequel

1. Typology

The Ethiopian Revolution of 1974 caught almost everybody by
surprise. Although they had been calling and fighting for it for
almost a decade, even the most radical of the students were unprepared. As for the ruling class, while it might have had a premonition
that something might go wrong, it took quite some time for it to
gauge the magnitude of the crisis. Indeed, the equivalent term for
'revolution' (*abyot*) was a relatively recent one in the Amharic lexicon;
many came to learn of it only after its eruption. Hence the highly
expressive characterization of the very process of that eruption: *abyot
fanada* ('revolution exploded/erupted'). It certainly did explode in
the faces of both the regime and its opponents. How to handle, let
alone direct, that explosion became one long process of adjustment
and improvisation that ultimately delivered the country into the
clutches of a totalitarian dictatorship.

In the suddenness of its occurrence, the Ethiopian revolution was
not unique. As the American historian Crane Brinton has concluded
after his survey of the classical revolutions, 'The actual revolution is
always a surprise'. But it is more than the element of surprise that the
Ethiopian revolution shared with its predecessors. It fitted very well
into the standard pattern of 'a form of massive, violent and rapid
social change' (Dunn, 12), of 'a world turned upside down'. It conformed also to Lenin's famous characterization of a revolutionary
situation – the people refusing to be ruled in the old way and the
ruling élite failing to exercise its customary political control. There
was also, in Ethiopia as in earlier revolutions, a revolutionary élite

228

with a formula for a better future, just as there was to be a fatal gap between initiating a revolution (the ideal) and controlling it (the reality).

Like the Chinese revolution, the Ethiopian one ushered in a radical land reform that changed the rural landscape in a decisive manner. But it is with the French and Russian revolutions that the Ethiopian experience has the closest parallels. Like its French and Russian predecessors, it did away with a dynasty (even if the French one was restored for some decades in the nineteenth century). Like both of them, too, the revolutionary spring was followed by the heavy and dark winter of terror. Popular exercise of power soon gave way to personal dictatorship. In the immortal phraseology of George Orwell, some animals fast became more equal than others. The malignancy of the dictatorship that emerged was admittedly graduated. The French revolution produced the relatively benign imperial autocracy of Napoleon. The Russian equivalent gave birth to the fearsome reign of Stalin. And the Ethiopian edition delivered the country to the murderous regime of Mangestu Hayla-Maryam.

And it is the personality of Mangestu, and the deep impression that he stamped on the Ethiopian revolution, that have continued to colour its legacy. For much of the West, the years 1974–1991 marked one long period of unqualified disaster. For many Ethiopians, too, the blood and tears born of the terror and the civil war that attended it have overshadowed any positive achievements the revolution might have registered. Even on sober reflection, one is hard put to single out with confidence any unequivocal benefits that could have ensued after nearly two decades of social mobilization and economic remodelling. Only the land reform – in as much as it eradicated centuries of social inequality – appears to have had enduring positive content, and even this, as we shall see below, was not an unqualified success. But all this should not detract from the popular character of the revolution when it first erupted. And it is this aspect we will now consider.

2. The popular upsurge

The popular upsurge of 1974, which attained its peak in the last days of February, was essentially an urban phenomenon. Although later there was some agitation among the peasantry, the countryside remained relatively quiescent. But in the cities and towns, different sectors of the population rose in various acts of defiance – the students, the teachers, the unemployed youth, the civil servants, the taxi drivers, and the soldiers. It was a mutiny by soldiers of a brigade of the army's Fourth Division stationed in the southern frontier post of Nagalle Borana, in the first half of January, that marked the prelude to the universal declaration of dissent.

As was generally the case at this early stage in the unfolding of the revolutionary process, economic rather than political issues moved the Nagalle soldiers to mutiny. Their complaints centred around the shortage of water (apparently caused by the prevalent drought) and a food shortage resulting from the fact that the rations kept in the store had gone bad. An additional factor was frequent delay in the payment of salaries. Underneath these obvious hardships was resentment at the customary master–servant relationship between officers and soldiers of subordinate ranks. And, as the mutiny gained momentum, the soldiers broadened their demands to include the provision of a hardship and pension allowance, better uniforms and the opening of a secondary school in the town. In an effort to win over the solidarity of fellow soldiers, they sent radio messages to other army divisions. When attempts by their battalion and division commanders to cool them down failed, the commander of the Ground Forces, General Derase Dubala, appeared in person in a vain attempt to persuade the mutinous soldiers. Instead, he ended up joining the brigade commander and other officers who had already been detained. So that he could have a first-hand experience of their lot, he was forced to eat the spoilt food and drink the water that had been the fare of the disgruntled soldiers. In the end, it was another general, Abarra Walda-Maryam, who succeeded in pacifying the mutineers and securing the release of his fellow general.

What impact the Nagalle mutiny had in the rest of the country is difficult to tell. But the radio messages the mutineers sent could not have failed to send a ripple through the army ranks. The demands for a pay increase and improved conditions put forward by other army units (notably the Fourth Division in the capital and the Air Force in Dabra Zayt, some fifty kilometres to the south) echoed those of the Nagalle unit. Interestingly, too, it was another frontier division, more strategically located and with bigger muscle, that took matters a stage further. This was the Second Division, based in the troubled province of Eritrea, which called on other units not to be placated by the granting of their economic demands. Seizing the radio station in Asmara, the Eritrean capital, it called for a change of regime and thus proved instrumental in the resignation of the Aklilu cabinet in late February.

But, at this early stage, the more visible manifestation of opposition came from civilian elements rather than from the military. On 18 February, the nation's teachers came out on a general strike. Their principal target was an educational reform programme known as the Education Sector Review. The teachers, supported by many secondary school students and some parents, perceived the review as detrimental to the interests of the poor and protested against its imminent implementation. Things assumed a much more confrontational character when, on the same day, taxi drivers came out on strike demanding an increase in fares commensurate to the 50% rise in the petrol price. The latter was the result of the global energy crisis following the 1973 Arab–Israeli war. The strikers had a helping hand from students and the unemployed youth who, apparently in an effort to stop all traffic and thereby enhance the effect of the strike, attacked all moving vehicles. Buses and luxury cars were especially targeted, the former because they were government-owned and the latter in a fit of class resentment.

Under this massive if uncoordinated popular pressure, the regime buckled. On 28 February, the cabinet of Prime Minister Aklilu Habtawald was forced to resign. One of the two survivors, the incumbent Minister of Communications, *Lej* Endalkachaw Makonnen, was instructed by the emperor to form a new cabinet. Endalkachaw formed a fresh team, including from the former cabinet only the Minister of Foreign Affairs, Dr Menase Hayle. Although the profile of the new team was impressive both in its relative youth and its educational formation (including as it did three Oxford-educated ministers), it made little impression on the popular tide of protest, which continued to expand and to assume ever more radical form and orientation.

The general tenor of the popular movement was one of the low rising against the high and mighty – the soldiers and junior ranks against the high officers, the poor against the rich, employee against employer and labour against management. The coercive arm of the state, which traditionally had stifled such opposition, was unable or unwilling to exercise its customary function. The police either joined in the popular agitation or shepherded it sympathetically. Early in March, the Confederation of Ethiopian Labour Unions (CELU), which until then had been notable for its lethargy rather than its militancy, waged a four-day general strike. The workers' demands included wage increases, the passing of new labour legislation, and freedom of association. On 20 April, in an emphatic call for social redress, over 100,000 Muslims and their Christian symphathizers came out in a mammoth demonstration chanting slogans for religious equality, separation of church and state, and the national observance of Muslim holidays. Calls for the dismissal of high officials in government ministries and departments were common; some officials were even temporarily detained in their offices. The agitation spilled over to the provinces. In Jimma, capital of a coffee-rich south-western province, a popularly elected committee assumed power and dismissed the governor, the highly unpopular *Dajjazmach* Tsahayu

231

Enqwa-Sellase. Radicals were quick to liken this dramatic exercise of popular power to the establishment of soviets during the Russian revolution.

The Endalkachaw cabinet was unable to stem the tide. Its plea for patience (the celebrated Amharic word for this was *fata*) fell on deaf ears. The unsympathetic response of the radicals was that 'changing the stove does not make the stew any better', alluding to Endalkachaw's close association with the fallen government. Its promises of reform failed to placate the popular movement. Thus, in early March, on instructions from the emperor, an agenda for constitutional reform was unveiled. Later in the month, a commission of enquiry was set up to look into the misappropriation of funds by government officials. It was mandated to examine the record of former officials and bring them to justice. Early the following month, the new cabinet issued a fairly comprehensive declaration of its economic and social policy.

Although he tried to cut a relatively fresh and more progressive image, Endalkachaw was a prisoner of his past. He was stigmatized for his aristocratic origin and deeply implicated in almost all the sins of the previous regime. The students greeted his appointment with a hostile demonstration on 1 March. The University Teachers' Association came out with an uncompromising critique three days later. Then followed the general strike mentioned above, which was as much a political as an industrial act. The armed forces, notably members of the Air Force, were likewise far from quiescent.

Anxious to put an end to this apparently interminable wave of protest, the harried cabinet tried to combine diplomacy and intimidation. On 30 April, the government announced the setting up of the National Security Commission in order to put an end to what it characterized as continuing lawlessness. At the same time, the prime minister desperately sought to woo the rebellious soldiers to his side. In late February a committee had been set up to coordinate the soldiers' demands and moves. In due course, Colonel Alamzawd Tasamma, the commander of the Airborne Brigade and reputedly a relative of Endalkachaw, had assumed a leadership position within that committee. An opportunity thus appeared to present itself to the prime minister to steer the soldiers' movement gently onto the side of the new cabinet. It was Alamzawd, apparently on the request of Endalkachaw and with the consent of the emperor, who presided over the detention of a number of former cabinet ministers and other high government officials towards the end of April. By this move, the emperor and prime minister probably sought to use their former loyal servants/colleagues as sacrificial lambs. Little did they suspect that they would join their ranks in a few months' time.

6.1   The building in the Fourth Division headquarters where the Darg was born

3. The 'creeping coup'

The committee of soldiers that administered the *coup de grâce* to the tottering *ancien regime* in September 1974 went through various phases of development. And the history of that evolution is far from clear. It appears to have first emerged in late February in an effort to coordinate the pursuit by various military units of demands ranging from the improvement of their conditions of service to general political and social reform. The second phase of activity came in April, when Colonel Alamzawd emerged as its leader and steered the committee towards support of the Endalkachaw cabinet. A third chapter then began which was to lead to the formation of the Darg and its formal launching on 28 June. The officer who appears to have played a central role in the formation of this third – and ultimately most significant – committee was Major Tafara Takla-Ab of the Engineers Corps. His colleagues eventually found him to be too radical and had him detained. The constant factor in all three phases was Major Atnafu Abata, a representative of the Fourth Division. He was in fact elected chairman of the Coordinating Committee of the Armed Forces, the Police and the Territorial Army, as the Darg was officially known, but was soon replaced by another major from the Third Division, Mangestu Hayla-Maryam. When the chairmanship was given to the more senior Lt General Aman Mikael Andom, Mangestu became first vice-chairman and Atnafu second vice-chairman.

The term *darg*, like *abyot* (revolution), was a new addition to the Amharic political lexicon. It was a little known Ethiopic equivalent for 'committee'. What was not new was the intervention of the military in Ethiopian politics. Historically, palace regiments had made decisive interventions in political affairs, making and unmaking kings and, as in the case of the Yajju princes, establishing their own dynasties. In the early twentieth century, the Mahal Safari, as we have seen, had provided the mass movement for major political changes – in 1910, 1916 and 1918. Then, in 1960, there was the abortive *coup d'état* led by the commander of the Imperial Bodyguard, Brigadier General Mangestu Neway. And it appears that it was the 1960 experience that weighed most heavily on the soldiers who found themselves stationed between the popular movement that goaded them on towards fundamental change and the forces of law and order. They were determined not to fail like their precursors of 1960. For this reason, they proceeded with caution and method. Their ever-tightening grip on the reins of state power was punctuated by declarations of loyalty to the emperor and fervent disclaimers of any ambition to seize power. The expression 'creeping coup' characterizes accurately the slow but systematic erosion of imperial power culminating in the deposition of the emperor.

The Darg, which first started as a movement within the capital, was subsequently broadened with the inclusion of representatives of various units from all over the country. Each of the forty military units was expected to send three representatives, bringing the total to the celebrated figure of 120. In actual fact, their number was less than 110. The Darg was thus a sort of military parliament, with the vital difference, however, that the units, once they had elected and sent their representatives, lost all power over them. By design, members of the Darg were privates, NCOs and junior officers up to the rank of major; senior officers were deemed to be too compromised by close association with the regime. They had not gone far, however, before they realized that they needed a senior military officer to give them some measure of respectability. For this task they chose the charismatic commander of the Third Division, Lt General Aman Mikael Andom, who became successively chief of staff of the armed forces, defence minister and chairman – or, more accurately, spokesman – of the Darg.

The Darg's first act was a request to the emperor to declare a general amnesty for all political prisoners and exiles, the speedy completion and implementation of the new constitution, and the postponement of the parliamentary summer recess. They accompanied their request with profuse expressions of their loyalty to the emperor and admiration for his wise leadership. Perhaps partly because of that, the emperor readily granted their request. The soldiers' next move was to detain a number of high government officials and members of the aristocracy whom they considered a threat to the continuation of the political change. Except for one or two incidents, this was accomplished with surprising ease. To rally popular support, the Darg enunciated the crisp if somewhat ambiguous slogan of *Ityopya Teqdam* ('Ethiopia First') and started haranguing the populace with statements distinguished more by bombast than substance. Expressions of support and suggestions for what moves to take next poured in; the Darg had facilitated this by positioning suggestion boxes at various sites. In a dramatic show of force and confidence, units of the army came out in late August on a motorized parade in the capital, mounting their slogan on the vehicles.

As far as the affairs of government were concerned, dual power prevailed for something like a month – that of the Endalkachaw cabinet and the Darg. A committee of four members had been chosen to liaise and maintain a good relationship between the two bodies. But this proved far from being a practical proposition; power continued to slip progressively out of the hands of the former and into those of the latter. Finally, Endalkachaw was dismissed on 22 July and subsequently joined his former colleagues in detention, much to their gratification and his chagrin. He was replaced as prime minister by his former colleague Mika'el Emeru, son of the emperor's relatively progressive cousin, *Leul Ras* Emeru Hayla-Sellase.

As his entire world was collapsing in front of him, the emperor bore everything with a nonchalance that bordered on fatalism. It is far from certain whether he was aware that he was the ultimate target of the Darg. But that fact became abundantly clear soon enough as the Darg dismantled the institutions that were most closely associated with imperial power such as the Ministry of the Pen and the Crown Council. It followed this move with the confiscation of business concerns in which the emperor and other members of the royal family were deeply involved, such as the Anbassa (Lion) Bus Transport Company, the St George Brewery, and the Haile Sellassie I Welfare Foundation. The ruler who had portrayed himself as the caring father of his people was now portrayed as a greedy tyrant. Finally, on the night of 11 September, the ultimate act of vilification was perpetrated as the public was treated to a doctored edition of a famous film on the 1973 famine produced by Jonathan Dimbleby of Thames Televison. A canny collage of royal feast and peasant famine drove home the emperor's alleged callousness to the suffering of his people. The following morning, representatives of the Darg went to the Jubilee palace and read a statement proclaiming his deposition. He was bundled off in a Volkswagen 'beetle' to his place of detention at the Fourth Division headquarters, the very birthplace of the Darg. Thus ended not only one of the longest and most remarkable reigns in Ethiopian history but also a dynasty that traced its origins to King Solomon and the Queen of Sheba.

6.2   *Emperor Hayla-Sellase soon after his deposition and the Volkswagen 'beetle' that took him to his place of detention*

4. Military rule and its opponents

The proclamation that deposed the emperor transformed the Darg into the Provisional Military Administrative Council (PMAC), which assumed full state power. Simultaneously, it suspended the constitution, dissolved parliament, and banned all strikes and demonstrations. What had started as a slogan ('Ethiopia First') now became a creed; opposing it was judged to be tantamount to treason. A child of the popular movement, the Darg now disowned its parent. And that fact became the recipe for collision with the popular elements of the February upsurge, notably the students and teachers. For the Darg and its supporters, 12 September came to be celebrated annually as the crowning moment of the popular movement. For the opposition, more particularly the civilian left, it marked the day when that movement was derailed.

Opposition to the setting up of the PMAC came from the students, the university teachers' group known as Forum, the labour organization CELU, the clandestine leftist organizations, notably those grouped around the two influential underground papers, *Democracia* ('Democracy') and *YaSafiw Hezb Demts* ('Voice of the Broad Masses'), and from sections of the military allied to these forces, such as the Engineers Corps, the Bodyguard, and the Army Aviation. All of them rallied behind the call for the setting up of a 'Provisional People's

Government', as opposed to the military regime that was rearing its head.

The origin of this powerful slogan, which persisted for something like two years with remarkable tenacity, goes back to the early days of the Endalkachaw cabinet. First presented as 'People's Government', it was promoted as an alternative programme of fundamental change in place of the mere reshuffle represented by the appointment of the new cabinet. But the programme's supporters must have realized that the establishment of a people's government in the true sense of the phrase was not going to be easy. Hence, by the time the Darg took the political stage, the slogan had been qualified into '*Provisional* People's Government' (PPG). The Forum group took the lead in articulating the slogan and detailing the projected composition of that government in a letter to the Darg in late July. The supporters of the slogan were far from unanimous on the actual composition of the PPG. Sometimes, it was to be constituted by bringing together representatives of workers, students, teachers, and peasants. At other times, it was to be based on the committees and other organized groups in the forefront of the popular movement since February 1974.

It is of interest that the two main leftist groups – the *Democracia* group which subsequently crystallized into the Ethiopian People's Revolutionary Party (EPRP) and the *YaSafiw Hezb Demts* group which was the organ of *Ma'ison* (the Amharic acronym of the rival All Ethiopia Socialist Movement) both espoused the PPG. Indeed an issue of *YaSafiw Hezb Demts* that came out two days before the deposition of the emperor predicted rather prophetically that a military-led government, however well-intentioned it might be, would in the end deliver the country to one-man dictatorship. This view, which was that of the home-based *Ma'ison* members, diverged significantly from that of the members abroad, which argued that the slogan would only have the effect of diverting the left from the vital task of organizing the masses. After the external wing of *Ma'ison* returned to the country, it prevailed on the internal wing to abandon the slogan. Thereafter, the PPG became one of the fundamental points of difference between EPRP and *Ma'ison*. The debate on the PPG, though couched in lofty Marxist phraseology, appeared in essence to be a struggle for power. EPRP, which had managed to make significant inroads into the mass organizations, was confident that it would be in a position to direct the course of the PPG. *Ma'ison*, on the other hand, which lagged behind in organizational matters, was prepared to let the Darg hang on to power until it itself was sufficiently organized to wrest it away from the Darg. Thus, by early 1975, *Ma'ison* had made a strategic shift from a position of opposition to the Darg to one of critical support.

237

As for the Darg, it showed no sign of heeding the popular clamour and relinquishing power. As the months and years accreted, it came to regard itself as the guardian of the revolution. To return to the barracks was therefore tantamount to betraying it. Once it started shedding blood, it became downright homicidal. It met the popular demand head on with a combination of force and subterfuge. Stealing a feather for its new headdress from popular demand, on 12 September it christened itself the *Provisional* Military Administrative Council. To take the steam out of the idea of popular representation, it also set up a National Advisory Commission whose members represented various government and religious institutions, the fourteen governorates-general, mass organizations and professional associations. To demonstrate unequivocally that it brooked no opposition, it arrested the leaders of dissenting mass organizations and professional associations. Worker protest at the arrest of their leaders was crushed brutally. The confrontation with rebellious military units – the Engineers, the Bodyguard and the Army Aviation – turned equally bloody. While the last two were intimidated into handing over their dissident elements, the Engineers were not prepared to surrender without a fight. On 7 October, troops loyal to the Darg stormed the Engineers' camp, killing five of them, wounding a number of others and detaining hundreds. With that, the illusion that the revolution would remain bloodless was exploded.

The bloody October confrontation augured darker days. On 24 November the Darg announced to a shocked national and international audience that it had shot its chairman, Aman Andom, and executed some sixty people it had held in detention, most of them dignitaries and high functionaries of the imperial regime. The general had died (either killed or committing suicide) after a tank assault on his residence. His crimes, according to the official announcement, included exhibiting dictatorial tendencies, sowing dissension within the Darg and between it and the armed forces, and absenting himself from his post. Unofficially, the general's elimination has been attributed to disagreements between him and prominent Darg members, notably the first vice-chairman Mangestu, over the handling of the Eritrean question, the former urging a more cautious approach as opposed to the latter's hard-line position. In the weeks preceding the incident, both Aman and Mangestu had been canvassing support for their respective positions among various units of the armed forces. In essence, however, it appears that the general had outlived his usefulness and was in fact becoming an obstacle to the Darg's exercise of power. While it needed the popular and charismatic general in the early days of uncertainty, he had become a dangerous rival for power and glory.

6.3   *General Aman Mikael Andom responding to the cheers of the Eritrean public during a rally at the Asmara stadium*

The executed detainees consisted mainly of members of the aristocracy, palace officials, ministers, military commanders, and provincial governors. It took a while to emerge that the Darg had craftily added to the list of victims dissident members from its own ranks as well as leaders of the military units who had opposed its assumption of political power. In the years to come, the Darg was to resort more than once to this canny device of killing two birds with one stone, as it were, thereby baffling and splitting dissent. The connection between the general's shooting and the callous execution of the detainees, which was presented to the public as a 'political decision', is not exactly clear. What is incontestably clear is the fact that the summary execution rendered all the fanfare surrounding the enquiry commission set up to examine the former officials' wrongdoings totally meaningless. It also initiated a cult of political violence that attained its climax in the so-called Red Terror. The event also had an important bearing on the political orientation of the Darg. United by the shedding of blood, members of the Darg realized that there was no going back. The executions provoked international opprobrium and effectively severed the Darg's links with the old regime. Thereafter, it had to seek its legitimacy only within the ranks of the revolutionary movement. Hence the series of radical measures that it took soon after the event.

The first of these was an ambitious programme of rural transformation. This had been aired for the first time a week or so before the Darg assumed full power. Christened the National

Development through Cooperation Campaign, or *Edgat Bahebrat* ('Development through Cooperation') in its more popular Amharic rendering, it envisaged the sending of high school and university students and their teachers to the countryside in order to implement various programmes of rural development under the 'philosophy' of *Ityopya Teqdam*. Although initially the programme might have been conceived with the best of intentions, opponents of the Darg saw it as a ruse to disperse the most vocal elements of the opposition. In the end, the Darg had to make some concessions to its critics before it could carry out the programme. In a move designed to strike a happy compromise between its own creed and the socialist ideology that had deep roots among the intelligentsia, *Ityopya Teqdam* was redefined as Ethiopian socialism or *hebratasabawinat*. The indigenous roots of the new creed were emphasized, an implicit critique of the exotic origins of the students' Marxist ideology. *Hebratasabawinat* was supposed to include a host of principles such as equality, the primacy of the collective will, the right of self-determination within the framework of a united Ethiopia, and non-alignment.

Following a massive rally in late December, in the course of which the Darg leaders made their first public appearance and students singled out Mangestu for chants of acclaim, the *zamach* (as the campaigners were known) proceeded to their various posts of assignment. The experience was to leave an unforgettable impression on both the *zamach* and the rural population with whom they came to interact so closely. The *zamach*'s most significant contribution was to come in the course of the land proclamation that the Darg issued in March 1975. In the initial debate on whether the students should go on the campaign or not, the opponents of the move had demanded such a proclamation as a precondition for their departure. Once that became a reality, they applied themselves to the task of interpreting and implementing it with gusto. Their radical interpretation of the decree, particularly their efforts to inculcate and foster peasant initiative, often brought them into conflict with Darg officials who opted for a more bureaucratic approach. Before long, the campaign centres became a political battleground between the Darg and its supporters, on the one hand, and members and sympathizers of the EPRP with its implacable opposition to the Darg. Opponents of the prolongation of the campaign began abandoning their posts and flocking to the cities, particularly the capital, to engage in the decisive struggle for supreme political power.

The land reform proclamation was preceded in January and February by the nationalization of financial institutions and private commercial and industrial enterprises. It was succeeded by the nationalization of urban land and extra houses in July. The Darg took considerable pride in these measures, presenting them as the

6.4 Zamach *students engaged in one of their daily chores, fetching water*

ultimate proof of its revolutionary credentials. On festive occasions, no speech was complete unless adorned by a litany of these famous 'reforms'. In actual fact, their value to society is far from unambiguous. In essence, what they did was to transfer resources from private to government hands. The state, which had considerable power even before the revolution, now came to assume leviathan proportions. As the ultimate dispenser of rewards and sanctions, its grip on society attained unprecedented tightness. In brief, the nationalization measures constituted the economic foundation of totalitarianism. Conversely, the overriding control that the state came to exercise over almost all forms of economic activity stifled private initiative and ushered in a tradition of bureaucratic management of resources.

It is true that the land reform proclamation represented a positive response to the long-standing demand of all Ethiopian progressives. Intellectuals in the early twentieth century had argued passionately for the amelioration of the condition of the *gabbar*. If rather nebulously, the abortive coup-makers in 1960 had promised the expansion of agricultural production in their manifesto. In 1965, university students took to the streets chanting the revolutionary slogan 'land to the tiller'. That powerful slogan had continued to reverberate, sounding the death knell of the *ancien regime*. After the outbreak of the revolution in February 1974, the land question emerged as *the* prominent issue of public debate. In its policy declaration of 8 April, the Endalkachaw cabinet was forced to address the question, promising that future land grants would be made to

241

6.5 *Partial view of the huge public demonstration that hailed the rural land reform proclamation. Some of the placards read: 'Today is the birthday of the Ethiopian people'; 'Today is a day of great victory for the Ethiopian people'; 'Yakatit 25 [4 March, the day of the proclamation] is a day of victory for the broad masses'; 'Land has reverted to its ancient owner'*

tillers only and that a ceiling of 1000 hectares would be placed on all holdings. The debate continued in official as well as unoffcial circles – in pertinent government ministries and units (such as the Ministry of Land Reform and Administration and CADU), in government newspapers, and in the clandestine leftist press. Issues raised included whether the premium was to be placed on productivity or equity, whether the reform was to come from above or from below, and whether ownership was to be private or collective.

Finally, on 4 March, the Darg surprised the most vehement of its leftist critics by opting for one of the most radical land reform proclamations that any regime has ever issued. The proclamation abolished all forms of private land ownership and prohibited the sale, lease or mortgage of rural land. Peasants were to enjoy only usufructory right over land holdings, whose ceiling was set at ten hectares. Tenancy was abolished. Land litigation, an all-too-common feature of pre-revolution Ethiopia, was terminated. The proclamation provided for the setting up of peasant associations, which would assume primary responsibility for the implementation of the proclamation and the administration of the periodic redistribution of land.

The major historical significance of the land proclamation was that it put an end to landlordism. Its greatest beneficiaries were the tenants and the landless. The latter came to constitute a solid rural mass base for the Darg, particularly in the southern parts of the country. In return for land, the Darg could draw on the vast pool of human resources for the interminable wars that chequered its career. But when it came to improving the lot of the peasant, the proclamation could hardly be judged to have been an unqualified success. Not only did it fall short of making him the absolute master of his plot, but it was also accompanied by a series of unpopular measures that sought to regiment rural life. These measures ranged from state control of agricultural marketing – with the peasant required to supply produce at fixed government price – to forcible resettlement, collectivization and villagization or the relocation of peasant neighbourhoods to new sites selected by government cadres. Rural dissatisfaction with these measures was to be one of the factors for the rallying of the northern peasantry behind the Ethiopian Peoples' Revolutionary Democratic Front (EPRDF) in its campaign to bring Darg rule to an end.

Similarly, the nationalization of urban land and extra houses had more than economic significance. To a certain extent, it dealt an additional blow to the economic power of the ruling élite, for that power had been based on real estate as well as rural property. But alongside the big villas and apartment blocks of the rich were confiscated the hovels of the poor. And that was not only unjust to the expropriated but also uneconomical to the urban dwellers' associations entrusted with the task of administering them. The establishment of those associations – along with the assignment of permanent urban residential addresses – was one of the notable and enduring features of the proclamation. Just as the peasant associations helped the Darg to control the countryside, the urban dwellers' associations helped it to control the towns. In the months of bloody confrontation between the Darg and the EPRP, they became a veritable battleground as EPRP militants targeted their leaders for assassination and the latter, and particularly members of what were known as the committees for the defence of the revolution, orchestrated the so-called Red Terror against the EPRP.

5. The ideological schooling of the Darg

The Darg has passed into history – not without reason – as one of the most doctrinaire Marxist regimes that has appeared in the twentieth century. Well nigh until its demise, it came to pride itself on what it considered impeccable Marxist credentials. And yet, when the one hundred or so Darg members started deliberating furtively in the **243**

Fourth Division headquarters in the summer of 1974, nothing could have been further from their minds than the introduction of scientific socialism into Ethiopia. Their motto of *Ityopya Teqdam* could at best be described as patriotic. Even when it graduated in December into *hebratasabawinat* or 'Ethiopian socialism', this marked only a grudging concession to the socialist creed.

But that concession, grudging as it was, set the pattern for the Darg's ideological orientation. A fundamental feature of the Ethiopian revolution – as regards both its antecedents and its course – was that its tone and parameters were set by the students. Indeed, the soldiers had first entered the February upsurge with strictly economic demands. It was the taunts and derisive comments of the students that pushed them into the political arena. The Darg, too, realized that, if it wished to hold on to power, it had to engage in the prevalent intellectual discourse. For something like two years, the Darg was engaged in a desperate struggle to catch up with the left, which was always a step ahead. It was only when the Darg took the supreme ideological leap and proclaimed the National Democratic Revolution in April 1976 that it could be said to have come level. From then on, it began to see itself through Marxist lenses, appropriating the role of historic vanguard of the struggle of the oppressed and exploited masses.

But, as suggested in the previous chapter, the left entered the revolutionary period in a divided spirit. In particular, the external wing of the student movement had been split into what in retrospect were pro-EPRP and pro-*Ma'ison* camps. Their attempt to forge a common organization having failed, the leaders of the two factions had been busy strengthening their camps behind the façade of student organizations. On the eve of the revolution an acrimonious debate had been raging over the seemingly innocuous issue of whether to form a World Wide *Federation* of Ethiopian Students (WWFES) or not – the pro-EPRP wing advocating and the pro-*Ma'ison* wing opposing the idea. The new structure threatened to make redundant the existing World Wide *Union* of Ethiopian Students (WWUES), which had been controlled by the pro-*Ma'ison* group. The Ethiopian Students Union in North America (ESUNA) had turned out to be solidly pro-EPRP while its European counterpart (ESUE) was divided into two antagonistic camps. Before the outbreak of the revolution, and while they remained confined to the student groups outside the country, these divisions were of little more than academic significance. After February 1974, they became intertwined with divergent interpretations of the nature and course of the revolution. Subsequently, they were transposed onto the national stage with lethal consequences as the ideological debate almost inexorably drifted into a campaign of mutual extermination.

244

At home, Marxist-Leninist study groups had started to grow clandestinely in the early 1970s. When the revolution broke out, they reared their head and began to reach out to the public through their papers. Of these papers, two soon attained prominence – *Democracia* (the organ of the Ethiopian Peoples' Liberation Organization, as EPRP was then known) and *YaSafiw Hezb Demts* (organ of the still undeclared *Ma'ison*). But these were not the only two clandestine leftist organizations. One group claiming to represent the oppressed peoples of the south was (to give it its English name) the Ethiopian Oppressed Peoples' Revolutionary Struggle. Like *Ma'ison*, with which it had a common stand on a number of issues, it was more commonly referred to by its Amharic acronym, *Ich'at*. An organization that was able to penetrate sections of the armed forces, particularly the Air Force, was *Wazlig* (the Labour League), founded by Dr Sanay Lekke, one-time president of ESUNA and an accomplished master of martial arts. He had returned after he lost the big debate on the national question that was held at the 19th Congress of ESUNA in the summer of 1971. Finally, there was the Marxist-Leninist Revolutionary Organization (*Malerid*), a smaller entity formed through the merger of a home-based group and defectors from EPRP.

At the outset, such a plethora of leftist organizations must have put the Darg slightly off balance. But it did not take long before it managed to steer its way into the middle of the debate. An encouraging factor was that not all of the organizations were hostile to it. As a matter of fact, two of them, *Ma'ison* and *Wazlig*, were vying for favour and attention. Leading members of the two organizations were reportedly giving lessons to some members of the Darg on the ABC of Marxism-Leninism. After such early coaching, the Darg, or more accurately its highly power-conscious first vice-chairman, Mangestu, charted his own path on the Marxist-Leninist trajectory by setting up an organization dubbed Revolutionary Fire (*Abyotawi Saddad*) in the summer of 1976. *Saddad*, as it came to be known for short, was born through the midwifery of *Wazlig*, or more specifically its chairman, Sanay Lekke. But much of the subsequent organizational work came to be entrusted to a trusted lieutenant of Mangestu, Corporal (subsequently Captain) Laggassa Asfaw, who like Mangestu had joined the Darg representing the Third Division, based in the eastern province of Harar. Close interaction between *Saddad* and *Wazlig* resulted in recriminations of infiltration and was to prove the latter's undoing.

The first months of 1976 proved of considerable significance for the ideological struggle within the Left as well as in the Darg's graduation into the leftist camp. The Amharic daily, *Addis Zaman*, began devoting a section of its second page to a debate among the leftist groups, primarily EPRP and *Ma'ison*, on the burning issues of **245** the day, notably the contentious slogan of 'provisional people's government'. Known as 'Revolutionary Forum', the debate featured a series of long pieces by some of the leading members of the organizations, invariably writing under a pseudonym, combining liberal citations from the Marxist classics and polemical jabs at opponents. They made for entertaining reading but did not resolve the ideological and strategic differences. If anything, they made them even more irreconcilable.

By 20 April 1976, when the Darg came fully on board the leftist bandwagon with its declaration of the National Democratic Revolution Programme, the debate appears to have petered out. The NDR, as it was known in its celebrated acronym, was the Chinese recipe for socialist transformation in the Third World. It relied on the revolutionary alliance of the proletariat, the peasantry and the progressive petit-bourgeoisie and targeted the trinity of feudalism, imperialism and bureaucratic capitalism as the enemies of the people. The ultimate objective of the programme was envisioned as the establishment of the People's Democratic Republic of Ethiopia, which indeed was what came to be in 1987. The Darg had indeed come very far from its fumbling debut into the arena of revolutionary rhetoric with the slogan 'Ethiopia First'.

To assist in the implementation of the NDR programme, the Darg set up the Provisional Office for Mass Organizational Affairs (POMOA). The move could be considered a victory for those leftist forces like *Ma'ison* who had campaigned all along for just such an office to facilitate what they considered to be essential tasks of conscientization and organization of the masses. And they were to use the office to achieve a degree of influence that their own earlier organizational work had not earned them. *Ma'ison* enjoyed a clear ascendancy in the fifteen-person commission that led the office. This ascendancy was reflected even more dramatically as the POMOA network was exploited to the full to swell its membership. With control of the towns assured by the end of 1976 through the *Ma'ison*-controlled Ministry of Urban Development and Housing, the organization must have felt an understandable sense of complacency. Ultimate state power, it was confidently argued, would be attained not through the strategy of uncompromising opposition adopted by EPRP but by operating within the Darg structure, as *Ma'ison* was doing.

But the Darg was not entirely oblivious to these calculations. If there was one thing it was adept at, it was the mechanics of political power. Moreover, by 1976, its leaders had also mastered the Marxist rhetoric and organizational techniques of the left. So the stage was set for the ultimate trial of strength, which was played out in the second half of 1976 and the first half of 1977. First the Darg allied itself with the malleable left to destroy the EPRP, which had come to be a threat to all through its unstoppable growth and unsparing stridency. The May Day celebrations of 1976, when many labour unions and mass organizations joined the Revolution Square rally bearing banners declaring their allegiance to the EPRP, could be regarded as a watershed in this respect. The Darg and its leftist allies must have concluded then that their survival depended on the elimination of EPRP. The summer months appeared like the lull before the storm; but they were months of preparation in both camps for the inevitable showdown.

The storm broke out in September 1976 and raged unabated for nearly a year. Government execution of EPRP militants went in tandem with the latter's campaign of urban terrorism that claimed many ideologues and functionaries of the regime. Recriminations as to who fired the first shot are futile, as the showdown was manifestly in the making one way or another. What is indisputable is the fact that, once started, the bloodbath escalated in spiral fashion. An unsuccessful attempt on 23 September on the life of the first vice-chairman, Mangestu, was attributed to EPRP. But the first major victim of the EPRP offensive was Dr Feqre Mar'ed, a *Ma'ison* member of the POMOA, who was assassinated later in the month. Vowing to avenge the life of one revolutionary with the lives of a thousand anarchists, as members of the EPRP had now been designated, the Darg hit back by executing already detained members of EPRP and rounding up suspected EPRP members and sympathizers. With the help of a series of search and destroy campaigns, the government was able to sniff out and eliminate or incarcerate EPRP militants who had gone underground as well as to disarm the civilian population. These exercises formed a dress rehearsal for the full-blown Red Terror, in which thousands of the regime's opponents were brutally murdered on the streets. Directed primarily against the EPRP, this licence to kill subsequently engulfed other opponents of the regime like the EPLF and TPLF – as well as, ironically, *Ma'ison*, once a rift was created between that organization and the Darg.

Part of the resentment engendered by the EPRP revolved around its claim to be *the* proletarian party. In the Marxist-Leninist discourse that had prevailed, every organized leftist group was aspiring to be the vanguard party of the working class postulated in Lenin's writings. Partly out of resentment at the speed with which EPRP had managed to penetrate the labour unions and mass organizations, the groups opposed to EPRP began to argue that, in an Ethiopian context, which had been characterized by the total absence of political parties, the proletarian party could not be created overnight. It is indicative of this cautious approach that none of the five organizations that ultimately formed the Union of Ethiopian Marxist-Leninist Organizations (*Imaledeh* in its Amharic acronym) called itself a party; the preferred designation was 'movement', 'struggle', 'league', **247** 'organization', or 'fire'. Such a party, they argued, could only come about after a protracted period of organizing the masses and progressive forces. It was purportedly with a view to achieving this objective that they formed *Imaledeh* in February 1977.

But *Imaledeh*, far from smoothing the process of establishing the vanguard party, became a battleground where each constituent member vied for ascendancy. *Ma'ison* in particular was readily accused of such tendencies towards self-aggrandizement. While the power struggle was going on behind the scenes, an ideological debate faintly reminiscent of the EPRP vs *Ma'ison* debate of early 1976 raged in the columns of *Addis Zaman* between *Ma'ison* and the other members of *Imaledeh*. A recurrent theme of the new debate was the issue of democratic rights, with *Ma'ison*, which felt relatively more confident of its mass base, arguing for the immediate guaranteeing of unrestricted democratic rights. But the logic of the situation worked against it. Just as EPRP was considered a menace because it had grown too powerful, *Ma'ison* had to go because it had become too 'inflated'. Sensing danger, the leaders of the organization hastily tried to go underground. But almost all of them were either captured or killed in August 1977 as they tried to retreat into the countryside in several detachments. That spelt the end of the organization as a viable political force inside the country.

The turn of most of the other members of the union (with the exception of *Saddad*, now more and more steering the course) was not long in coming. *Ich'at*, which was closely affiliated with *Ma'ison*, was crushed almost simultaneously. Then, in late 1978, it was the turn of *Wazlig*, which was accused of infiltrating its members into *Saddad* in order to control that organization from within. Thereafter, the small and not so influential *Malerid*, which itself soon slid into oblivion, could scarcely check the rise of *Saddad* to uncontested supremacy. The soldiers had finally become the sole legitimate custodians of Marxist-Leninist orthodoxy. The Darg had graduated to the status of the vanguard party.

6. Towards one-man rule

The history of the Ethiopian revolution had been linked almost inextricably with the personality of Mangestu Hayla-Maryam. More than any of the soldiers with whom he started the long march to absolute power, or the civilian ideologues who assisted the process, he left his stamp on the revolutionary process. By 1987, when the People's Democratic Republic was inaugurated, he had reached a pinnacle of power that hardly any Ethiopian ruler had enjoyed before. What is more, there was something inexorable about the rise of the obscure major to absolute, not to say *total*, power. Partly, it had to do with the deep-seated authoritarian traditions of the country, which was more conducive to the emergence of a strong man than the collective leadership the Darg aspired to give at the beginning. In the absence of any liberal democratic legacy, it is not surprising that the autocratic emperor was replaced by the totalitarian dictator. Marxist-Leninist orthodoxy, sown on the fertile bed of Christian Orthodoxy, provided the requisite ideological recipe. The parallels with Russia are very striking in this respect. Both countries had a strong Orthodox as well as imperial tradition. And in both instances, revolutions sprouted dictators.

Nor should one underestimate the personal capacity of the man. Unlike his namesake who, in 1960, went about the task of changing the regime in rather cavalier fashion, Mangestu brought ruthlessness to the enterprise. The prevarication of the former contrasted with the dour determination of the latter. While a full biography of Mangestu remains to be written, most observers concur in one thing: his special ability to size up situations and persons. Like his imperial pre-decessor, he also exhibited an uncanny ability to dissimulate his true intentions, thereby lulling his unsuspecting opponents to their doom. Rather charitably, this quality has been equated with intelligence. But it is perhaps nearer the mark to see it as inner-city smartness (or what in local parlance would be called *aradanat*). His passionate nationalist rhetoric, expressed with more than ordinary oratorical skill, also appears to have won him many followers, both among the lower ranks of the Darg (the privates and NCOs) and in the country at large. The Holata *alma mater* (to which most of the officers in the Darg belonged) was an additional asset. His early popularity within the Darg apparently stemmed from the fact that he was one of the very few members who had some sense of direction at a time when the inexperienced appeared overwhelmed by the tide of events that were unfolding in rapid succession.

Moreover, Mangestu hardly forgot the thing that really mattered – military sinew. At first, he relied on troops from his home base, the Third Division, to quell opposition, as was indeed the case with the crushing of the Engineers in September 1974. Then, he set up a force known as *Nabalbal* ('Flame'), which also doubled as a special counter-insurgency force. As he began to concentrate more and more power in his hands, he created the special force that jealously guarded him in his fortress of a palace and played a pivotal role in the suppression of the May 1989 coup. Mangestu also held a tight grip on the security apparatus, both within the Darg and outside. In this respect, two persons (both colonels) were instrumental in his conquest and

249

6.6   *Mangestu Hayla-Maryam, seated third from the left, playing the
meek subaltern. Four of the officers in the photo fell under his ruthless
sword – from left to right: Captain Alamayahu Hayle, Major Sisay
Habte, Lt General Tafari Bante (standing), and Lt Colonel Atnafu
Abata (looking at Tafari).*

consolidation of power: Colonel Daniel Asfaw, the Darg's chief of
operations until he died in the palace shoot-out in February 1977,
and Colonel Tasfaye Walda-Sellase, eventually Minister of National
Security, for much of the period. But Mangestu was no mere military
dictator of the genre of General Idi Imin of Uganda or Emperor
Bokassa of the Central African Republic. He infused the military
apparatus that was his political mainstay with the ideological
flourishes that he had borrowed from the left. The military command
was closely watched by a parallel structure of cadres and commissars,
the latter headed by persons of proven loyalty to Mangestu. While
this arrangement was to have disastrous consequences on the battlefield, as political commissars interfered with and sometimes overruled
the expert judgements of professional commanders, it undoubtedly
reinforced his hold on the military apparatus.

Armed with such an array of favourable factors and attributes –
tradition, personality, and the vital infrastructure of political power –
Mangestu went ahead to eliminate one rival or opponent after
another with nauseating regularity. He overcame his first major
hurdle in late November 1974 when he eliminated Lieutenant-
General Aman Mikael Andom in the course of the bloody storming of
his residence. The calculation of Mangestu and his colleagues to use
250   the popular general as a front figure in the first uncertain days of the

revolution had obviously proved a miscalculation; Aman, who could not himself be said to have been entirely devoid of political ambition, began to carve his own niche of fame and glory. The killing represented a radical break in more than one sense. It marked the end of all efforts at accommodation with the old establishment. Although Aman was replaced as symbolic chairman of the Darg by another general, Tafari Bante, the latter was not allowed the same margin of independence as his predecessor. More significantly, the killing of Aman was immediately followed by the execution of all the prominent representatives of the Hayla-Sellase regime who had been kept under detention. The event also marked the point of no return on the Eritrean question. Thereafter, independence (as advocated by the Eritrean armed groups) and forcible integration (as promoted by the Darg) emerged as two irreconcilable options, with neither side brooking intermediate solutions.

For almost two years after the elimination of Aman, there was no incident. The Darg was probably too absorbed in initiating and implementing radical measures of social transformation such as the land reform proclamation. Whatever inner tensions such measures must have generated did not immediately lead to any significant ruptures. But in July 1976, another major purge claimed the life of one of the leading members of the Darg, Major Sisay Habte of the Air Force. Sisay, who was chairman of the Political and Foreign Affairs Committee of the PMAC, stood out both by his high educational attainment (he is said to have had a Masters degree in engineering) and eloquence in representing the Darg. Such qualities of leadership were more feared than appreciated by a person like Mangestu, who considered him a dangerous rival for pre-eminence. He was brought in front of a military tribunal, charged with conspiring against the revolution and executed. The commander of the Second Division based in Eritrea, Brigadier-General Getachew Nadaw, and two members of the Darg, Lieutenant Bawqatu Kasa and Lieutenant Selashi Bayyana, were declared to have been his accomplices. The general was killed in a shoot-out at his residence that was reminiscent of the death of Aman. The two Darg members managed to escape to their home province, Gojjam, but were later apprehended in their hideout and killed. Another member of the Darg, Major Kiros Alamayahu, who had been leading the Development Through Cooperation Campaign, was also detained and later reported to have died in prison. In characteristic fashion, the Darg also executed simultaneously about half a dozen merchants who were accused of perpetrating 'economic sabotage' by hoarding pepper.

The execution of Sisay apparently sent a clear signal to the remaining members of the Darg that, unless they did something to stop Mangestu, their own days were numbered. In the final months

251

6.7   *Three of the highest officials of the Darg:*
       (from left to right) Mangestu, Atnafu and Sisay

of 1976, the Darg instituted elaborate rules and defined powers and
responsibilities so as to restructure its operations in a fundamental
way. A structure with a congress consisting of all its members, a
central committee, and a standing committee was set up. More
significantly, the powers and duties of the chairman and the two vice-
chairmen of the Darg were clearly defined. The chairman, who until
then had only ceremonial functions, emerged with enhanced powers.
Conversely, the power of the first vice-chairman, Mangestu, was in
essence restricted to the innocuous one of chairing the meetings of
the Council of Ministers. Greater power was concentrated in the
hands of the secretary-general, who, beside heading the Darg's
secretariat, controlled the activities of POMOA, which thitherto had
been working closely with the first vice-chairman. What made the
restructuring even more galling to Mangestu and his allies in the
POMOA was the fact that they perceived it as increasing the influence
of the much-hated EPRP within the Darg. Spearheading the reform
were Captain Alalmayahu Hayle, who now assumed the powerful
post of secretary-general of the Darg, and Captain Mogas Walda-
Mikael, chairman of the Darg's Economic Committee. Both were
suspected of being members or sympathizers of EPRP.

Having clipped the wings of the ambitious colonel in such dramatic
fashion, the reformers continued their activities with a smug sense of
confidence. They clearly underestimated his capacity to hit back.
They left untouched the security branch of the Darg, which was

headed by Colonel Daniel Asfaw, Mangestu's Holata classmate and now his hatchet-man. On 3 February, Mangestu and Daniel finally struck. A meeting of the Standing Committee of the Darg found all the wanted persons assembled in one room. They were readily picked up and summarily shot. Among the victims were Lt General Tafari Bante, the chairman, Captain Almayahu, Captain Mogas, and Lt Colonel Asrat Dasta, chairman of the Darg's Information and Public Relations Committee. Mangestu and his leftist allies had won a clear and unequivocal victory. The revolution was proclaimed to have passed from the defensive to the offensive stage. Marring the sense of complete triumph for Mangestu was the death of the executioner, Daniel Asfaw, and the ideologue, Sanay Likke, both of whom were shot dead by Daniel's deputy, Captain Yohannes Meseker, a partisan of the Alamayahu group.

The coup, for it was nothing less than that, gave Mangestu and his leftist allies the complete freedom to launch a full-scale offensive against the EPRP – the Red Terror. At the same time, it smoothed the way for the consummation of Mangestu's dictatorship. Mangestu now abandoned all pretence of remaining behind the scenes and assumed the post of chairman of the Darg, with the enhanced powers (including commander-in-chief of the armed forces) that his opponents had unwittingly tailored for him. The standing committee of the Darg, which had been designed to act as the chief executive organ, was filled with his supporters or members who did not dare to challenge him. Only one thing remained to make Mangestu's domination of the Darg absolute. That was the removal of the vice-chairman, Atnafu. More of an encumbrance than a challenge, he nonetheless was a source of some discomfort for Mangestu, the more so as he had expressed his displeasure at the way Mangestu had disposed of his opponents in February 1977. Atnafu's political naiveté soon delivered him into the hands of Mangestu and his clique. In November 1977 he was executed following a session of the Darg congress in which he had been provoked by Mangestu's cronies into a rash (if in retrospect somewhat redeeming) challenge to a number of their actions and basic assumptions. The execution of Atnafu, who more than anybody else had symbolized the Darg from its early origins in February 1974, effectively marked the eclipse of that institution. Only occasionally was the atmosphere of total sycophancy dispelled by the fractionally independent disposition of the second man, Captain Feqra-Sellase Wagdaras, whom the coup of February 1977 had elevated from relative obscurity (according to some sources from near execution by reason of mistaken identity!) to the post first of secretary-general of the Darg and then prime minister of the People's Democratic Republic of Ethiopia.

The events of February 1977 were also followed closely by the country's closer alignment with the communist bloc and corresponding rupture with the West, particularly the United States. The communist countries had been quick to express their gratification at the turn of those events, representing Mangestu's triumph as a victory for the progressive forces. Fidel Castro of Cuba paid a personal visit in April, when he mooted the idea of a confederation of Ethiopia, Somalia, and the Yemen Democratic Republic (South Yemen). By this time, relations with the United States had been completely severed; the 1953 mutual defence agreement had been terminated; and American military and cultural institutions had been closed. In May, Mangestu paid a state visit to Moscow, where he concluded with his new patron agreements for cooperation in the economic, cultural and military spheres.

These developments coincided with a shift in international alignments in the region. As America was being estranged from Ethiopia, it was getting closer to the Siad Barre regime in Somalia. Correspondingly, having failed to restrain Barre from his expansionist aims towards Ethiopia, the Soviets found it prudent to back the Ethiopian horse. By the summer of 1977, Castro's rather fantastic idea of a regional confederation had evaporated into thin air under the barrage of a full-scale war between Ethiopia and Somalia. The inter-state war had been preceded by a period of infiltration by guerrillas of the so-called Western Somalia Liberation Front into the Somali-inhabited areas of Ethiopia. Initially, the Somali forces made a quick advance into the Ethiopian highlands, controlling strategic passes and major towns. Soon, however, the attack was repulsed through a combination of impressive mass mobilization on the Ethiopian side (with the raising of a militia force estimated to be 300,000 strong in a matter of months) and the intervention of Soviet command officers as well as Cuban and Yemeni troops. As Somali irredentism was dealt a decisive blow, two more names were inscribed in Ethiopian battle folklore: Tataq, the camp on the western outskirts of Addis Ababa where the militia force was trained, and Kara Mara, the strategic pass in the Ogaden where one of the most decisive battles was fought. On the other hand, the rather equivocal stand that EPRP adopted on the issue of Somali aggression became one of the factors that contributed to the demise of that organization. Conversely, Mangestu came out of the encounter with enhanced stature and the necessary ingredients of the personality cult that was to mark much of his career. The chant of 'Viva Mengistu' reverberated loud on the morrow of the Ethiopian victory.

Thus, by the beginning of 1978, Mangestu had eliminated all challengers, potential or actual, within the Darg. He has silenced all his civilian critics and opponents. External aggression had been dealt a severe blow. Only the Ertirean challenge in the north remained.

Even that appeared to have a short lease of life as the troops victorious in the south-east turned their face northwards with the slogan 'The victory in the east shall be repeated in the north'. What remained for Mangestu was to institutionalize the power that a combination of cunning and good luck had thrown into his lap. The process proved to be a fairly laborious one. Nearly a decade elapsed before the new state structure assumed its final form in 1987 under the name of the People's Democratic Republic of Ethiopia (PDRE).

It started with the vital task of establishing the professedly genuine vanguard party. As we have seen, *Imaledeh* had disintegrated amid mutual recriminations of greed and ambition. The idea of forming the party through a merger of Marxist-Leninist organizations was declared not to be feasible. Instead, it was recommended to assemble genuine and tested revolutionaries around the personality (the *ma'ekal* or nucleus) of the supreme revolutionary, Mangestu Hayla-Maryam. The move culminated in the setting up of the Commission for Organizing the Workers' Party of Ethiopia (COPWE) in December 1979. The commission was endowed with generous government funding and an elaborate organizational structure foreshadowing the party that was eventually formed. For all practical purposes, COPWE evolved almost imperceptibly into WPE (the Workers' Party of Ethiopia, as the party that finally saw the light of day in September 1984 was christened). Chaired by Mangestu himself, the commission had a general assembly, a central committee, an executive committee, committees at various administrative levels, and the primary organization (at the level of *qabale*, association or workplace). All members were carefully selected by Mangestu himself, loyalty being the single most important criterion.

Finally, the big day of the proclamation of the party came. Conveniently, it coincided with the tenth anniversary of the coming of the Darg to power. Rather disconcertingly, it took place against a background of the worst drought in the country's recent history. By one of the many ironical twists of history, a regime that came to power castigating its predecessor for covering up the 1973 famine was celebrating its ultimate triumph on the threshold of an even more disastrous one. Months before the festivities began, reports of people dying from starvation had reached the capital and the Relief and Rehabilitation Commission, set up after 1974 to avert a catastrophe of the magnitude of 1973, had been warning of the impending disaster. But the matter was discreetly ignored by the government, which did not wish its big party to be spoilt. And the party went on, attended by a big international audience of supporters and sympathizers. In the ritual elections that took place, Mangestu inevitably assumed the key post of secretary-general of the party, which was to have a central committee of two hundred members and a politburo of eighteen. The **255** latter body was an interesting amalgam of Mangestu's loyal followers within the PMAC, technocrats and Marxist-Leninist ideologues. The reigning slogan now became: 'Forward with the revolutionary leadership of Comrade Mengistu Haile Mariam!'.

One more significant step remained to complete the institution-alization of power: the promulgation of the constitution and the proclamation of the republic. The task of drafting that constitution was given to a panel of experts assembled under the auspices of the Institute for the Study of Nationalities that had been set up in 1983. The end product was delivered to a formal 347-member Constitution Drafting Commission headed by Mangestu himself. But the real work of finalizing the draft was done in the smaller circle of Mangestu and his close confidants. Completed in early 1986, the draft was formally submitted to public 'debate' both inside the country and among the Ethiopian community abroad. Then, it was ratified by a 'referendum' on 1 February 1987. Pursuant to the provisions of the constitution, elections were held for the supreme body, the National *Shango* (Assembly). In a 'race' that was entirely a family affair, favoured WPE candidates, who were appropriately given the emblem of the invincible elephant, were elected to the *Shango*. In yet another September (1987), that body proclaimed the People's Democratic Republic of Ethiopia. A dramatic act of the transfer of power from the Darg to the PDRE was performed to accentuate the withering away of the Darg and the emergence of the new republic. But the high point of the proceedings was the 'election' of Mangestu Hayla-Maryam as president of PDRE. The obscure major from Harar has finally become Ethiopia's most accomplished dictator.

7. The end

But the fanfare that accompanied the inauguration of PDRE concealed a fundamental internal malaise. Before four years were out, the edifice that had been built with such consummate skill – and so much blood and tears – had collapsed like a pack of cards. The dictator who had outsmarted his rivals within the Darg as well as the urban left fell under the relentless barrage of the rural guerrillas. For over a decade, the regime had launched campaign after campaign to stifle the nationalist insurgencies in the north. Undeterred, the guerrillas surged on to final victory. Mangestu was forced to flee for his life. And EPLF and TPLF (Tigray People's Liberation Front) forces entered, respectively, Asmara and Addis Ababa in May 1991, shifting decisively the regional balance of power and initiating a new political discourse. Having eliminated the multi-national opposition early on in the political game, the Darg was removed by a political dispensation that was determined to revamp its basically centrist political culture.

Ethno-nationalist insurgency

At the outbreak of the 1974 revolution, there was a glimmer of hope among some of the Darg members that the Eritrean dissidents would lay down their arms once the hated old regime had passed away. The Darg chairman, Lt-General Aman Andom (himself an Eritrean) had toured the region in August and September 1974 and presented to the Darg a comprehensive package of recommendations for administrative reform, economic development, and political reconciliation. A possible resuscitation of the federal arrangement might have been mooted as well. But the spirited quest of the general for a peaceful resolution of the problem came to an abrupt end when he was silenced on that fatal November evening.

Nor had the Eritrean fronts shown any enthusiasm for his overtures. On the contrary, they appeared to consider him as more injurious to their ultimate objective precisely because of those overtures. His death was followed by a noticeable escalation of hostilities as the hard-liners within the Darg led by Mangestu got the upper hand. The fronts opened an offensive targeting the Eritrean capital, Asmara. On the other side, a virulent anti-Eritrean propaganda campaign went hand in hand with atrocious executions of suspected infiltrators of the front in Asmara in January 1975. A veritable exodus of urban Eritreans, including some highly placed officials and officers, swelled the ranks of the fledgling EPLF, whose size reportedly increased tenfold. Thereafter, the favoured option on both sides remained total war. Yet another round of negotiations for peaceful resolution, spearheaded by the Darg's Foreign Relations Committee chairman, Major Sisay Habte, was terminated with the execution of that officer in July 1976. These negotiations had taken place in the wake of the Darg's declaration of a nine-point policy to bring peace in the region within the framework of regional autonomy.

But regional autonomy had long ceased to attract the liberation fronts. Although the Eritrean liberation movement initially had the limited scope of restoration of the federal arrangement that had been terminated in 1962, the escalation of hostilities had pushed them into the agenda of independence. The Eritrean problem came to be posed not as a constitutional issue but as a colonial question, with the Ethiopian state cast in the role of heir to a colonial occupation that should have been terminated in 1941 or, at the latest, in 1950 when the UN resolved to federate Eritrea with Ethiopia. A new history was **257** written to emphasize the fact that Eritrea has had nothing to do with Ethiopia. In fact, EPLF and pro-EPLF historiography perceived both entities as having been created in the last quarter of the nineteenth century, in the wake of the famous Scramble for Africa. The struggle of so many Eritreans in the 1940s and 1950s to unite with Ethiopia at all costs was conveniently glossed over. Oblivious to the pivotal role that the Eritrean Unionists played in wrecking the federation, its dissolution was portrayed as outright annexation by the Ethiopian state. What is more, the world came to believe this new story, partly because it was easier to lend an ear to the 'underdog' rather than to the 'bully'.

But before the dreamed-for independence could be achieved, the fronts had to put their own house in order. Throughout the 1970s a bitter struggle for supremacy was waged between the two fronts, ELF and EPLF. The early years of the revolution had found the Eritrean liberation movement internally divided, as the newly emerged EPLF engaged in bloody confrontation with the veteran ELF. At the same time, the two liberation fronts were involved in various manoeuvres aimed at reconciling their differences. General Aman's intervention, by drawing representatives of the civilian population into the peace effort, had the effect of intensifying popular pressure on the fronts to find some form of accord. But the two fronts had clearly divergent approaches to the envisaged unity, the ELF favouring a unity of organization and command while the EPLF preferred a united front of two independent organizations. Far from bringing the two fronts together, the initiatives had the effect of splitting the EPLF even further, as the head of its foreign mission, Osman Saleh Sabby, broke away to form his own organization (the Eritrean Liberation Front/Popular Liberation Forces, ELF/PLF). He took this step after being disowned by the EPLF field commanders for concluding without their consultation an agreement with the ELF leadership in September 1975. Whatever formal agreements the two fronts could be persuaded to conclude by their Arab sponsors foundered on the bedrock of mutual suspicion and rivalry that characterized their relationship. Not even the massive government offensive launched in mid-1978 could bring them together. Finally, in August 1980, the EPLF felt suffciently strong to launch a campaign to liquidate its rival – an objective that it was able to accomplish fully by August 1981.

No sooner had the EPLF established its hegemony in the liberation struggle than it was subjected to the most comprehensive government offensive to date. This was qualitatively of a higher order than the two major offensives that had been launched since 1975. The first was what came to be known as the *razza* campaign of May 1976 when the Darg hoped to drown the rebels under a sea of peasant humanity. To begin with, the government failed to mobilize all the peasant militia from northern Ethiopia that it had intended to deploy. In the end, only some 10,000 militia from Wallo were deployed. Disheartened and disoriented by the military and propaganda offensives of the forces of TPLF and EPRA (the Ethiopian People's Revolutionary Army, the military wing of EPRP), who controlled the approaches to Eritrea in northern Tegray, the ill-fated peasant force was dissipated before it reached its main target. In the summer of 1978, flushed with its victory over the Somali forces and vowing to repeat it in the north, the Darg regime launched a massive offensive that drove ELF and EPLF forces from the areas, including some of the major towns, that they had occupied. EPLF was forced to retreat to its stronghold in northern Eritrea, Naqfa. Some four years elapsed before the government launched its much-advertised Red Star Campaign, which professedly had the double objective of rehabilitating the war-damaged economy of the region and rooting out the forces of secession. In a massive offensive on Naqfa, government forces came very near to achieving the latter objective but ultimately failed. That failure was to cost the regime dearly; thereafter, the initiative could be said to have passed to the Eritrean insurgents.

Meanwhile, south of the Marab river, another major regional challenge to the Darg was unfolding. The TPLF, which was to play a decisive role in the demise of the Darg, was officially launched in February 1975 at a remote and not easily accessible place called Dadabit in the Shere province in Western Tegray. The historical origins of the movement could be traced back to the sense of marginalization that the region and its élite have felt since the death of Emperor Yohannes and the ascent of Menilek to imperial power in 1889. The economic hardships – including recurrent famines – that the region's population had endured over the decades had accentuated this marginalization. Such frustrations had formed the background to the Wayane rebellion of 1943 discussed in Chapter 5. And it is no accident that the university students who launched the TPLF three decades later incorporated that highly emotive term in the Tegregngna rendering of their name (*Hezbawi* **Wayane** *Harennat Tegray*). (Indeed, the English rendering omits this crucial term and thereby blurs the historical continuity.) But the young combatants brought into the struggle an organizational rigour and ideological armoury that their forerunners clearly lacked. They framed their struggle within the Leninist rhetoric of self-determination up to and including secession that had become the creed of the student movement of the late 1960s and early 1970s. More than any other of the leftist organizations that sprouted from that movement, they have stuck to that recipe not only as a matter of principle but also – and perhaps more – for its proven efficacy in mobilizing and organizing opposition.

6.8   Fighters of the Tegray People's Liberation Front (TPLF)

In a process that paralleled the one that was unfolding north of the Marab river, the TPLF spent the early years of its existence establishing its hegemony in Tegray. It had to contend with three organizations, some of which had been established in the region earlier. Probably the easiest to eliminate was the Tegray Liberation Front (TLF), which had developed a close working relationship with the ELF. More serious was the challenge posed by the Ethiopian Democratic Union (EDU), which had securely established itself in westernmost Tegray. EDU and TPLF forces had to fight a series of bloody battles in the years 1976 to 1978 before the former could be expelled from Tegray. Finally, TPLF was locked in mortal combat with the EPRP forces that had established their base in Asimba in the northeastern corner of Tegray. These two leftist forces, both offspring of the radical student movement, differed in their approach to the struggle. EPRP argued for the primacy of class struggle under the umbrella of a multi-national organization like itself, whereas TPLF put the accent on organized struggle by the different oppressed nationalities which would then in due course forge a united front. Moreover, TPLF was committed to a rural-based armed struggle that would gradually move to the towns, whereas EPRP, partly by virtue of the strong influence it had come to exert in the towns, placed considerable emphasis on the urban struggle; its Asimba base in effect served as little more than a safe haven from the retaliatory assaults of the regime. Handicapped by the inherent disadvantage of fighting in somebody else's territory, the EPRP was forced after a bloody battle to move its base of operations to Gondar and Wallo.

Initially, the Darg did not pay much attention to the TPLF. Oblivious to the indigenous origins of the organization, it tended to regard it as a mere creation or appendage of the EPLF. Hence, it was expected to vanish with the Eritrean challenge, to eliminate which the Darg had committed almost all its forces. In actual fact, the relationship between TPLF and EPLF was far from smooth. Indeed, until EPRP was forced out of Tegray, EPLF tended to favour that organization rather than the TPLF. What emerged even after TPLF had established its hegemony in Tegray could be characterized more as a marriage of convenience than of romance. Over and above the deep-rooted antipathies that the two kindred peoples felt for one another, the two organizations diverged on a number of issues. TPLF argued for the extension of the principle of self-determination of nationalities to Eritrea, which itself was a composite of different nationalities, while the EPLF insisted that the Eritrean struggle should be seen as monolithic. Because of the full backing afforded the Darg by the USSR, TPLF took a more virulently anti-Soviet stand while EPLF was more accommodating. Finally, TPLF, which preferred guerrilla tactics, was critical of what it considered to be EPLF's hasty transition to conventional warfare. It was only in the second half of the 1980s that the two organizations patched up their differences to cope with the urgent need of coordinating their operations to deal the final blow to the Darg.

Of the other ethno-nationalist organizations that emerged to challenge the Darg in the 1980s, the one that was potentially most significant was the Oromo Liberation Front (OLF). The origins of the organized quest for Oromo self-identity could be traced back to the setting up of the Mecha and Tulama Self-Help Association in January 1963. According to its statutes, the association had a rather modest objective of expanding educational, communication and health facilities in the Oromo-inhabited areas. Nor was its membership confined to people of Oromo origin only; it had in its ranks some prominent personalities from a number of the southern nationalities. But to a regime that brooked no divergence from its centrist norm, the association represented a threat. It was particularly alarmed when the association managed to win over the commander of the police, Brigadier General Taddassa Berru, who was elected its president. A period of tense confrontation attained its climax in November 1966. The association's audacious attempt to assassinate the emperor on the anniversary of his coronation was foiled by the security forces. This was followed by a bombing incident in one of the downtown cinemas in which members of the association were implicated. The association was disbanded. The general, who had retreated to the bush, was captured and sentenced to death. But the sentence was later commuted to life imprisonment, which remained in force until 1974. Set free soon after the outbreak of the revolution, the general, who had apparently been in close contact with underground Oromo groups, fell foul of the military regime and was executed in early 1975 on charges of opposing the land reform proclamation.

In 1971, an Oromo underground organization had been set up, apparently by a former member of the Mecha and Tulama association, under the deceptively generic label of the Ethiopian National Liberation Front (ENLF). But, it did not seem to make much of an impact. There were few overt expressions of Oromo nationalist sentiment in the early years of the revolution. While *Ma'ison* was sometimes associated with the Oromo by reason of the ethnic origin of some of its leaders as well as a considerable proportion of the rank and file, it was *Ich'at* that came much closer to that kind of association. At any rate, as we have seen, both organizations had ceased to have any political consequence by 1978. Already in 1976, the OLF, which stood quite explicitly for Oromo interests, had come into existence. Enjoying considerable technical support from the EPLF, the OLF waged some isolated guerrilla operations in south-eastern Ethiopia, in the Hararge province, and from across the Sudan into western Ethiopia; but, racked by internal divisions and unable to achieve any meaningful mobilization among the Oromo, it could not pose any serious challenge.

Economic crisis

In the end, the regime's undoing came not only through the military challenge of the northern insurgency but also through its own poor economic record, which in turn was exacerbated by the war economy that the insurgency had imposed on the country. A government that had vowed to free the masses from the clutches of the 'cannibalistic' old regime left the country in a worse state than it found it. In October 1978, victorious over its internal and external forces, the PMAC launched the National Revolutionary Development Campaign. This was one of the many campaigns (*zamacha* in Amharic) undertaken, true to its militarist tradition, by the PMAC. It aimed at mobilizing all available human and material resources for the economic transformation of the country under the guidance of the Central Planning Supreme Council. An outcome of this vigorous exercise was the Ten-Year Perspective Plan (1984/85–1993/94) that aimed at an accelerated economic growth based on the development of agriculture and the expansion of industry. But the anticipated

6.5% growth in GDP and 3.6% rise in per capita income never materialized; as a matter of fact, per capita income declined by about 0.8%.

The ultimate indictment of the regime's economic policy was to be the 1984/85 famine, which affected nearly eight million people and killed about one million. At the root of the problem was the government's predilection for a command economy, which stifled private initiative and overstretched the resources of the state. The capital investment that planned economic growth presupposed was forthcoming neither from domestic nor from foreign sources. Moreover, the government's failure to face up to the impending famine in the early months of 1984 exacerbated the situation. It was only after the festivities of party formation in September 1984 were over that the government turned in earnest to tackle the problem. Thanks to the impressive international response to the disaster, as well as contributions from local sources, the raging famine was finally checked.

As if to compensate for its initial tardiness, the government then embarked on an ambitious project of resettling peasants from the drought-prone areas of northern and central Ethiopia to the relatively fertile provinces of the west and south-west. On the surface, this appeared a logical move. In reality, the forcible nature of the resettlement, as well as the effort to combine it with the government's cherished objective of collectivization, made it a highly unpopular move, both at home and abroad. Over half a million people are believed to have been relocated in this manner. No sooner had the government carried out resettlement than it embarked on yet another controversial piece of social engineering. This was what came to be known as villagization, involving the regrouping of rural households into new villages. The official explanation for the move was that it would streamline distribution of basic services by the government to the rural population. Starting in the south-eastern provinces of Bale, Arsi and Hararge, this massive programme of relocation spread to many other regions of the country. In as much as it involved the uprooting of traditional households, with their cherished vegetable gardens and trees, not to speak of the psychological trauma of abandoning ancestral abodes, the move proved highly unpopular. It thereby contributed to the disaffection of a significant portion of the northern peasantry and the advances that guerrillas opposed to the regime were able to make in the late 1980s.

Global change

In the international arena, too, things were changing at a fast pace in the second half of the 1980s and in a manner hardly propitious to the   **263** regime in Ethiopia. The twin policies of *perestroika* and *glasnost* spearheaded by Mikhail Gorbachev were changing the nature of both the Soviet Union and the global balance of power. In a bid to give communism a human face, the Soviet leader was unwittingly surrendering to the West, effectively terminating the role of his country as a world power. To the Ethiopian ruling elite, which was just beginning to savour the institutionalization of the socialist order, the turn of events came as a bitter pill. But, however reluctantly, it had to be swallowed. Already in November 1988 the regime, while reaffirming its commitment to the building of socialism, had made some concessions to private investment, raising the capital ceiling in joint venture undertakings, small-scale industries and hotel services. But these measures clearly proved inadequate in the face of the fundamental transformations going on globally. Finally, in March 1990, the 11th Plenum of the Central Committee of the WPE resolved to introduce a policy of mixed economy, effectively renouncing its longstanding commitment to socialist construction. In the political realm, too, it provided for a new political party embracing different shades of opinion; it was christened the Ethiopian Democratic Unity Party. But these policy shifts proved to be too little too late. By then, the military balance in the north had shifted decisively in favour of the insurgents and against the regime.

The final offensives

In the military sphere, the turning point came in March 1988, when EPLF scored its most decisive victory to date at Afabet, an important government stronghold north of the Eritrean capital, Asmara. The Nadaw division, which was defending the stronghold, had been thoroughly demoralized after the summary execution of its commander, General Tariku Ayne, following a heated exchange with Mangestu over the conduct of the war. Nearly 20,000 Ethiopian troops were incapacitated and considerable military hardware fell into EPLF hands, with a significant bearing on the future course of the war. For EPLF, Afabet opened the way to Massawa and Asmara.

About a year later, in February 1989, the government suffered another major debacle in Tegray, when TPLF forces scored a major victory at Endasellase in Shere. In addition to superior military tactics and the wholehearted support of the local population that it enjoyed, TPLF benefited from the assistance it got from a mechanized EPLF contingent. By contrast, government forces were beset by poor command and the inherent disadvantage of operating in alien territory. The nearly 40,000 strong 604th Corps of the Third Revolutionary Army, as the force set up to extinguish the revolt in

Tegray had come to be known (on a par with the Second Revolutionary Army based in Eritrea), was wiped out. About 23,000 troops were taken prisoner. The Shere debacle precipitated the withdrawal of all government forces from the region in a move that was ironically dubbed *Zamacha Qetaw* ('Operation Punish Him'). The 'punitive' flight was psychologically debilitating to government forces. Thereafter, panicky and precipitous abandonment of military positions and towns triggered by rumours of TPLF advances became the norm.

Zamacha Qetaw not only delivered the entire Tegray region to the TPLF but also paved the way for the extension of its military campaign further south. An organization which had had its genesis in a desire to liberate a province had thus to think of an agenda that encompassed the whole country. The stresses and strains of adjusting to this change of mission were to endure even after total victory in 1991. It was in these circumstances that the Ethiopian Peoples' Revolutionary Democratic Front (EPRDF) was born. The constituent members were, beside the TPLF, the Ethiopian People's Democratic Movement (EPDM), a group composed mainly of former EPRP members that had been operating in northern Wallo after the collapse of the EPRP in 1978; the Oromo People's Democratic Organization (OPDO), which was meant to represent the Oromo population; and the Ethiopian Democratic Officers' Revolutionary Movement (EDORM), composed of the government military officers who had fallen into TPLF hands. Although presented as such, EPRDF was far from being a united front of national liberation movements waging a common struggle in equal partnership; the predominant position of the TPLF was beyond dispute. Moreover, although EPDM was mainly active in Amhara-speaking areas, it did not at this stage present itself as an Amhara organization. The alliance with OPDO was also an arrangement of second resort, after negotiations to forge a front with OLF had collapsed. As for the EDORM, it barely survived the attainment of victory in 1991.

Afabet and Endasellase marked the beginning of the end for the Mangestu regime. The military crisis generated a political shake-up in the Ethiopian capital. In a bid to stall the impending catastrophe, Mangestu's own generals rose against him. On 16 May 1989, minutes after Mangestu had left the country on a state visit to the German Democratic Republic, the generals, who represented almost the entire armed forces, staged a *coup d'état*. But the generals, even if they had consensus, clearly lacked a sense of direction. Presumably in the interests of secrecy, only four generals in the capital, led by the Chief of Staff General Mar'ed Neguse and the former Air Force commander and Minister of Industry, General Fanta Balay, had been privy to the plot; the others had only discovered the plot when they reported for a meeting to which they had been summoned at the Ministry of Defence headquarters, which had been chosen as the command post. That choice itself, located as the building was in the middle of the city and far from the airport, proved another tactical blunder. More fatally, the plotters had failed to neutralize the special force that was guarding Mangestu's palace. A contingent that had been sent from Asmara to support the coup failed to establish contact and, in the end, the general commanding it had to run for his life. The result was that, within a few hours, the coup had fizzled out and a dazed public came to know of its abortion before it had realized its occurrence.

In Asmara, events assumed an even bloodier turn. Officers loyal to Mangestu and spearheaded by the Airborne Division reasserted government authority in very gruesome fashion. Those implicated were murdered in their offices with lightning speed or rounded up and later executed. Among the victims was the Commander of the Second Revolutionary Army, General Damesse Bulto, whose severed body was paraded in the streets of Asmara. Returning triumphantly, Mangestu administered his own dose of retribution. At the outset the detained generals were brought before a military tribunal to account for their deed. But, as the process dragged on, the dictator developed other ideas. About a year after the coup, twelve of the generals implicated were summarily executed. The net effect of the reprisals was to deprive an already demoralized and disoriented force of some of its best leadership. The new military command that Mangestu was forced to set up was pathetically inadequate for the even greater challenges that awaited it in the military sphere.

After this last desperate attempt from within the regime to avert the impending catastrophe, events moved at a dizzying pace. In February 1990, the port town of Massawa fell to EPLF forces. With the simultaneous destruction of the Ethiopian Navy, the government lost control of the coastline as well as its important lifeline to its forces in the interior, now that the Tegray route had been effectively sealed. Elsewhere, EPRDF forces pushed into Gondar in the west and Wallo in the south. An EPRDF thrust into Gondar in late 1989 was repulsed temporarily and one of the most decisive battles was fought at Mount Guna. EPRDF victory was achieved at considerable cost. But that opened the way to control of the strategic town of Dabra Tabor. Another EPRDF victory at Maragngna, in south Wallo, opened the road to north Shawa. After that, the EPRDF launched the final round of operations that eventually led it to Addis Ababa. Operation Tewodros (named after the nineteenth-century Ethiopian emperor who had left such a deep impression on posterity) brought Gojjam under EPRDF control. Operation Wallelegn (named after the intrepid student revolutionary of the 1960s who was a native of Wallo) drove government forces entirely out of that province. Operation *Bilisumaf walqituma* ('freedom and equality' in the Oromo language) extended the Gojjam victory into Wallaga, an important Oromo-speaking province. Thereafter, EPRDF was comfortably poised for its pincer attack on the national capital from the north, west and east.

After almost everything was lost, the regime began to explore earnestly the avenues for peace. By this time, the fronts not only enjoyed military superiority but also had a clear diplomatic edge. Having been more thorough and more convincing than the Darg in formally renouncing their Marxist-Leninist credentials, they had managed to win considerable sympathy in the US State Department, just as their military successes had impressed on US officials that they should be taken seriously in any future political restructuring of the region. Former President Jimmy Carter assumed the responsibility of bringing together government and EPLF delegations, first in Atlanta, Georgia (in September 1989), and then in Nairobi (in November). But the negotiations became bogged down on procedural issues, notably the question of observers, and nothing of substance came out of the meetings. Likewise, what was described as the third round of preliminary negotiations between the government and TPLF delegations were held in March 1990 in Rome under the good offices of a former Italian ambassador to Ethiopia. But they collapsed when TPLF insisted that the other constituent organizations of the EPRDF should also attend. Beneath these disagreements over procedural and technical issues was the more fundamental reality represented by the military situation. The fronts were negotiating from a position of strength while the government was doing so from a position of weakness.

This reality became even more apparent in the last round of negotiations – if one could call it that – held in London in May 1991. By this time the role of mediator had been assumed by Herman Cohen, US Assistant Secretary of State for African Affairs. An Ethiopian delegation led by the new prime minister, Tasfaye Dinqa, was expected to negotiate a peace deal with representatives of EPLF, EPRDF and OLF. But, by this time, the internal political situation had sharply deteriorated. Mangestu had ordered his last purge of colleagues and made a futile cabinet reshuffle in April 1991. He presided over a desolate political landscape in icy solitude. Finally, on 21 May, he surprised everybody by fleeing the country first for Nairobi and then for Harare. The circumstances of his flight are still far from clear. It now appears plausible that the US might have exerted pressure on him to depart in order to smooth the transition. Whatever the circumstances, the manner of his departure belied popular anticipation that he would follow the example of his hero, Emperor Tewodros, by committing suicide rather than fleeing to the safety of exile. The effect of the flight on the military was instantaneous. The Second Revolutionary Army collapsed, clearing the way for EPLF's entry into Asmara on 24 May. The London negotiations were concluded before they had even properly begun. On 28 May, EPRDF forces entered Addis Ababa. The only obstacle they met was a brief if determined resistance from Mangestu's special force, still guarding the palace.

Sources, Chapter 6

Andargachaw Assaged. *Ba'Acher Yataqqacha Rajem Guzo*. Ma'ison *Baltyopya Hezboch Tegel West* ('A Long Journey Cut Short. *Ma'ison* in the Struggle of the Ethiopian Peoples'). Addis Ababa, 2000.

Andargachew Tiruneh. *The Ethiopian Revolution 1974–1987. A Transformation from an Aristocratic to a Totalitarian Autocracy*. Cambridge, 1993.

Bahru Zewde. 'The Military and Militarism in Africa: The Case of Ethiopia,' in Eboe Hutchful and Abdoulaye Bathily, eds., *The Military and Militarism in Africa*. Dakar, 1998.

Brinton, Crane. *The Anatomy of Revolution*. New York, 1965.

Clapham, Christopher. *Transformation and Continuity in Revolutionary Ethiopia*. Cambridge, 1988.

Dessalegn Rahmato. *Agrarian Reform in Ethiopia*. Uppsala, 1984.

Dunn, John. *Modern Revolutions. An Introduction to the Analysis of a Political Phenomenon*. Cambridge, 1989.

Eshetu Chole and Makonnen Manyazewal. 'The Macroeconomic Performance of the Ethiopian Economy 1974–90,' in Mekonnen Taddesse, ed., *The Ethiopian Economy: Structure, Problems and Policy Issues. Proceedings of the First Annual Conference on the Ethiopian Economy*. Addis Ababa, 1992.

Feqre Bade. 'Tararochu Bawedqatachaw Wazema' ('The Mountains on the Eve of their Fall'), in *Tararochen Yanqataqata Tewled (Ewnatagngna Tarikoch)* ('The Generation that Moved Mountains, True Stories'), Vol. 4. Addis Ababa, 1991 Ethiopian Calendar.

Hezbawi Wayana Harennat Tegray (Tigray People's Liberation Front). *YaHewahat Hezbawi Tegel* ('The Popular Struggle of TPLF'). Addis Ababa, 1992 Ethiopian Calendar.

Kiflu Tadesse. *The Generation. The History of the Ethiopian People's Revolutionary Party. Part I. From the Early Beginnings to 1975*. Silver Spring, 1993.

———. *The Generation. The History of the Ethiopian People's Revolutionary Party. Part II. Ethiopia: Transformation and Conflict*. Lanham, 1998.

Lefort, René. *Ethiopia: An Heretical Revolution*. London, 1983.

Olana Zoga. *Gezetna Gezot* ('Oath and Banishment' – A History of the Mecha Tulama Association). Addis Ababa, 1985 Ethiopian Calendar.

Shumet Sishagn. 'Power Struggle in the Eritrean Secessionist Movement'. MA thesis (AAU: History, 1984).

Teferra Haile-Selassie. *The Ethiopian Revolution 1974–1991. From a Monarchical Autocracy to a Military Oligarchy*. London, 1997.

Tasfaye Makonnen. *Yedras LaBalatariku* ('May It Reach the Protagonist'). Addis Ababa, 1985 Ethiopian Calendar.

Warqu Farada. *Edgat Belo Wedqat, YaWatadar Soshalizem* ('Decline in the Name of Progress; Military Socialism'). Addis Ababa, 1990 Ethiopian Calendar.

Young, John. *Peasant Revolution in Ethiopia: The Tigray People's Liberation Front, 1975–1991*. Cambridge, 1997.

In addition, I have benefited from the following papers submitted to the graduate seminar on the Ethiopian revolution that I have been conducting:

Ahmed Hassen Omer. 'The Endalkatchew Cabinet (28 February – 22 July, 1974'. 1993).
Belete Bizuneh. 'Political Power and the Revolution: The Struggle for a "Provisional People's Government", 1974–1976'. 1997.
Getachew Senishaw. 'The January 1974 Mutiny in Nagale'. 1995.
Medhane Taddese. 'EPRP vs. TPLF, 1975–78'. 1994.
Mekonnen Berhane. 'The Zamacha Syndrome in the History of the Darg'. 1994.
Mengistu Abebe. 'Which Kind of Land Reform for Ethiopia: The Debate Preceding the 1975 Land Proclamation'. 1995.
Oljira Tujuba. 'A History of the Oromo Liberation Front to Early 1991'. 1993.
Shimelis Bonsa. 'From Collective Leadership to Personal Rule: The Emergence of Mangistu's Dictatorship, 1974–1977'. 1997.
Wudu Tafete. 'MEISON: From Opposition to Critical Support, 1974–77'. 1994.

Conclusion

The dawn of the nineteenth century found Ethiopia in a state of political fragmentation. The medieval empire of Amda-Tseyon and Zar'a-Yaeqob had been superseded by a conglomeration of principalities. In the Christian north, doctrinal controversies exacerbated the political divisions. What kept the spirit of unity alive was the imperial throne, which all regional lords sought to control and manipulate. What linked north and south was the long-distance trade routes that traversed the country. It was in such circumstances that the country's second contact – more meaningful and more sustained – with Europe began (the first being the Ethio-Portuguese connection in the sixteenth and seventeenth centuries). As part of the general European thrust in Africa, missionaries came to 'save souls', businessmen to trade, and official envoys to protect both.

These two realities – political fragmentation and European presence – formed the setting for the unfolding history of modern Ethiopia. Successive rulers responded in different styles and with varying degrees of success to the two challenges: the internal and the external. Centralization and unification became the dominant themes of Ethiopia's political history. Tewodros II, Ethiopia's first modern emperor, began the task in a style marked more by vision than by method. Emperor Yohannes IV's policy of controlled regionalism, probably induced by his predecessor's disastrous failure, was hardly any more successful. Of the nineteenth-century rulers, it was Emperor Menilek II who inherited the imperial idea of Tewodros and the tolerance of Yohannes, and whose policy in this regard was crowned with relatively greater success. Not only did he manage to forge the political unity of the core (with the single important exception of the Marab Melash), but he also extended the imperial sway to hitherto unattained limits in the south.

As for the European presence, it represented both a threat and an opportunity to Ethiopia. It was a threat to the cherished independence of the country. Conversely, it generated hopes – bitterly disappointed – of an ally against Egyptian expansionism. At the same time, it opened up new possibilities of introducing western technology, particularly military technology, and of modernizing the country. Thus the attitude of Ethiopia's rulers towards Europeans was marked by ambivalence: they wanted the Europeans' modern technology, but were apprehensive of their ultimate designs. The Europeans themselves were not always ready to take a plunge in the country. The British treated Tewodros's fervent requests for assistance and friendship with what amounted to haughty contempt. The Italians sought to establish themselves in the country with desperate rashness. The first action precipitated the Battle of Maqdala; the second culminated in the Battle of Adwa.

Adwa forms a watershed in the modern history of Ethiopia. It resolved the issue of colonial rule versus independence in favour of the latter. Simultaneously, the results of the Battle of Adwa gave momentum to the creation of the modern Ethiopian empire-state. The era of recurrent campaigns was over. Both internally and externally, post-Adwa Ethiopia enjoyed a degree of peace that contrasted sharply with the turbulence of the nineteenth century. This situation permitted the ruling class to turn its attention to more pacific – and more profitable – pursuits. The extended empire and the relative peace allowed it to enjoy a degree of economic wealth which was unprecedented, and to exhibit a taste for business interests which was not so common in the past. But the basis of wealth still remained land. The growing appetite for land set off a process of transformation of the land-tenure system, particularly in the southern half of the country. Land which was traditionally communal became increasingly privatized, thereby creating the two extremes of land concentration and tenancy. The condition of the *gabbar*, the peasant, rarely good even in the best of times, deteriorated.

Independence did not thus mean development. No one was more acutely aware of this fact than the young Ethiopians whose modern education had equipped them with the intellectual power to analyse the ills of their society. For them, the Battle of Adwa was meaningless if it was not attended by economic development and a rise in the status of the peasantry. By failing to reform, independent Ethiopia would be living only on borrowed time. Their fears were sadly confirmed forty years after Adwa.

The independence that Adwa bestowed on the country was in any case far from absolute. Deprived of the political-military option, foreign elements applied themselves to economic penetration of the country with redoubled energy. Foreign presence and influence in Ethiopia were more pronounced after Adwa than before. Foreigners enjoyed special legal and fiscal privileges. The country's lack of access to the sea made it dependent on the goodwill of the neighbouring colonial powers for the import of such vital items as arms. Its circumscription by colonial possessions created ample opportunities for tension, as well as for foreign penetration. Ethiopia's independence was regarded as an expensive luxury. Its admission to the League of Nations – although eventually of no practical benefit to the country – provoked controversy.

The Italian invasion of 1935 put an end to this precarious independence. Their Eritrean and Somaliland possessions provided the Italians with the bases from which to launch their attack. In other words, Menilek's failure to consummate the Adwa victory ultimately gave the Italians the chance to avenge their defeat. But the memory of Adwa loomed in both camps. Just as it propelled the Italians with a passion for revenge, it moved the Ethiopians with a spirit of defiance and an indomitable will to be free. The result of the latter was a five-year-long resistance which, finally assisted by British arms, brought the Italian Occupation to an end. Yet Italian rule did not pass without leaving some traces. On the issue of national integration, the over-riding problem of the twentieth century, it had mixed results. The network of roads that the Italians left behind, although in a rather woeful state, may be said to have facilitated it. On the other hand, the Italian policy of divide and rule and the redrawing of administrative boundaries emphasizing ethnic and linguistic divisions encouraged centrifugal tendencies. The British, who dominated Ethiopian politics in the decade after the Liberation, added difficulties to the problem.

On the related question of the modernization of Ethiopian society, Italian rule might also be said to have been double-edged. The systematic liquidation of the intelligentsia deprived the country of the agents of social and political change. But urbanization on the whole gained momentum under the Italians. Likewise, the transition to a cash economy was encouraged. Motor transport, one of the distinctive marks of the Italian presence in Ethiopia, also facilitated the circulation of goods and ideas. On a more fundamental level, the under-mining of the hereditary nobility, begun by Emperor Hayla-Sellase before the Italo-Ethiopian war, was continued, so that, when he regained his throne in 1941, finishing the task he had started earlier was relatively easier.

The result was the creation, at last, of the unitary state first conceived in the fiery mind of Tewodros. In this and other respects, the post-1941 period marks the culmination of modern Ethiopian history. The hereditary nobility were finally stripped of their political prerogatives. At the same time, however, a parallel process of greater security in landed property and acceleration of the privatization process enhanced the nobility's economic privileges. These two apparently contradictory processes of the political impotence and economic strength of the nobility became the hallmark of Ethiopian absolutism, of advanced feudalism. The economic strength of the nobility and the rural gentry was achieved at the expense of the peasantry, who were progressively pushed from tenancy to eviction and from impoverishment to famine.

On the external scene as well, the post-1941 period witnessed the realization of earlier dreams and ambitions. Nowhere was this more evident than in the fulfilment of the long-standing quest for an outlet to the sea. Similarly, the search for an external ally, which was so disastrous for both Tewodros and Menilek, crystallized into Hayla-Sellase's partnership with the United States of America. To talk of foreign domination of the Ethiopian economy would be an exaggeration, but there is no doubt that foreign capital enjoyed relatively better opportunities in post-Liberation Ethiopia than at any earlier period.

Yet advanced feudalism, precisely because it was advanced, carried the seeds of its own demise. The forces of change that it generated proved its undoing. Absolutism, because it became a self-justifying credo rather than a vehicle for social and economic development, bred opposition. That opposition was multifaceted. Enlightened members of the ruling class conspired to dethrone the emperor and avert the catastrophe that they saw coming. Peasants rose in rebellion against the growing pressures on their land and on the fruits of their labour. Students waged a sustained struggle for radical reform. Finally, its own soldiers rose against the regime, abortively in 1960, successfully fourteen years later. In the face of widespread opposition, the regime was inherently incapable of reform. Instead, it continued its policy of repression. Opposition and repression mutually reinforced each other until they attained their logical conclusion in the Revolution of 1974.

The Revolution erupted suddenly in February 1974, surprising both the regime and its opponents. It started with the promise and buoyancy of spring. It ended with the sombre darkness of winter. What had looked like an unassailable edifice cracked and buckled under the massive assault of a popular upsurge that involved students, factory workers, civil servants, soldiers and religious minorities. The cabinet reshuffle that the regime initiated as a placatory measure could hardly contain the storm. In the heady atmosphere that prevailed, the idea of smooth transition that the Endalkachaw cabinet could be said to have represented had few supporters. Much as the students and teachers had been the chief inspiration behind the revolution, however, they could not direct it. By fits and starts, the military, which itself was affected by the popular movement, gradually came to assume centre stage. On 12 September, it seized state power, terminating both a reign and a dynasty of remarkable longevity.

That date encapsulated the ambivalent character of the revolution. While it marked the fall of a regime that had failed to deliver meaningful political and economic reform, it also bore the seeds of an even worse dictatorship. As the years progressed, the euphoria that attended the former was smothered by the germination of the latter. To its credit, the revolutionary regime did away with landlordism in **273** a swift move that surprised even its severest critics. It also addressed the question of illiteracy with unprecedented zeal and earnestness. Moreover, at no other time in the country's history has one seen such a scale of mass mobilization, even if that mobilization was not always deployed for constructive ends. Politics, which had been the preserve of the privileged few, came down to the lower ranks of society, albeit carefully controlled and monitored from above. Nationalism has not been new to Ethiopia. But what the Darg did was to secularize and broaden it by dissociating it from the Church and extending it to the economically enfranchised south.

The disaster started when the Darg tried to combine Marxism and nationalism. Desperate to hang on to power, it imbibed the dominant Marxist-Leninist intellectual discourse as the only guarantee of preserving its political ascendancy. But it appropriated the dogma rather than the spirit of Marxism. It followed in the footsteps of Stalin rather than Marx or even Lenin. The result was a reign of terror that became its hallmark and wiped out any salutary aspects of its seventeen-year tenure. The peasants, whom the historic land reform proclamation had appeared to liberate from their centuries-old subjugation, were as distressed as any other sector of society, if not more so. Not only were they denied the legitimate fruits of their labour, but they also came to serve as cannon fodder for the regime's interminable wars.

Those wars ultimately brought the regime to its demise. One of the most nationalist (some would say ultra-nationalist) of regimes in modern Ethiopian history fell under a barrage of ethno-nationalist insurgency. The hour of reckoning had finally arrived: the failure of successive regimes to infuse equity into the country's heterogeneity ultimately put the country's unity to a severe test. The collapse of the multi-ethnic opposition to the Darg in 1976–77 brought ethno-nationalist opposition to the forefront. The élites of the oppressed and marginalized nationalities vigorously pushed the ethno-nationalist agenda both as an effective recipe of mobilization and as a sure guarantee of what they considered to be their legitimate share of scarce resources. Yet, the ethno-nationalist opposition had its own inherent tensions – tensions that were to come to the fore after victory in 1991. The EPLF pushed vigorously the agenda of independence without apparently taking full stock of the economic implications of that independence. The TPLF adumbrated an ethnic federal formula without adequately resolving the dilemma of maintaining its political hegemony in a framework where it was bound to be a clear minority. More or less taking its cue from the EPLF, the OLF toyed with the idea of secession in spite of the fact that the Oromo whom it purported to represent constitute the single largest nationality in the country. The stresses and strains of these contradictory postures were to form the political bedrock of post-1991 Ethiopia.

Glossary

The meaning of Amharic words and phrases not listed in the Glossary is explained in the text

abba	'father (owner) of', the ascriptive word of an Ethiopian horse-name: the horse-name of Emperor Tewodros II was Abba Tataq, meaning 'Gird yourself'; *Abba*, 'father', also form of title for ordinary priests
abeto	a medieval title which came to be increasingly appropriated by Shawan rulers after the sixteenth century
abun	'bishop', the highest ecclesiastical title of the Ethiopian Orthodox Church until the appointment of a patriarch in 1959; *Abuna* when used with a proper noun, as *Abuna* Petros
afa negus	'mouth of the king', the supreme judge of the land under the king
alaqa	head of a church, a learned priest
amba	a steep flat-topped hill, often serving as a natural fortress
aqa	head or chief
azazh	'commander', chief of the imperial court
bajerond	royal treasurer
balabbat	originally hereditary owner of *rest* land; since the nineteenth century, used to denote the hereditary chief of a southern people
balambaras	'head of an *amba*', a low-level administrative title
basha	derivative of the Turkish 'pasha' for low-level government officials
bitwaddad	most favoured courtier, imperial counsellor, often officiating in the name of the king
blatta	a title generally signifying learning, given in the twentieth century to government officials of the director-general level or equivalent
blatten geta	'master of the *blatta*', an exalted version of the title *blatta*, given to government officials of the ministerial level
dabtara	cleric, with attributes of learning, astrology and intrigue
dajjazmach, *dajjach* (contracted form)	'commander of the gate', a politico-military title below *ras*
echage	the highest Ethiopian ecclesiastic until the appointment of Ethiopian bishops (*abun*) in 1929; abbot of the monastery of Dabra Libanos in northern Shawa
endarase	'in my place', viceroy or local representative of a higher authority
fitawrari	'commander of the vanguard', a title below *dajjazmach*, but of higher import when borne by Habta-Giyorgis Dinagde, Minister of War from 1907 to 1926
gabbar	tribute-paying peasant or peasants
gada	an age-grade socio-political system of the Oromo
gasha	a unit of measurement, equivalent to 40 hectares
gebbi	courtyard, generally used in connection with royal and princely palace compounds
geber	agrarian tribute, invariably paid in kind; tax

275

Glossary

grazmach	'commander of the left', a politico-military title above *balambaras*
gult	non-hereditary right to collect tribute, bestowed on members of the nobility and clergy by the king
hakim	doctor
kantiba	mayor, originally restricted to the town of Gondar, but in modern times gaining wider application
kella	toll-post
lej	'child', honorific title generally reserved for sons of the royal family and of the upper nobility
ligaba	royal chamberlain
liqa makwas	official serving as the king's double to divert attacks directed against the king
l'ul (feminine *l'elt*)	'prince' ('princess'), title borne by sons and daughters of the royal family, and by the upper nobility who already have the title of *ras*, hence *l'ul ras*
mahal safari	'those who encamp at the centre', a generic name for the specialized regiments of the imperial troops
makwanent (singular form *makwannen*)	nobility whose rank is earned by service
mar'ed azmach	Shawan title, higher than *abeto* and lower than *negus*
masafent (singular form *masfen*)	hereditary nobility
naftagna	from *naft*, 'rifle', name given to Emperor Menilek's warriors of northern origin, who later settled in the south
naggadras	'head of merchants', originally leader of a merchant caravan, later chief government official in charge of the collection of customs
negus	king
negusa nagast	'king of kings', the official title of Ethiopian emperors
qagnazmach	'commander of the right', a politico-military title above *grazmach*
qalad	'rope', a unit of land measurement, the system of land measurement, measured land
qurt geber	fixed tax
ras	'head', the highest traditional title next to *negus*
ras bitwaddad	a rare title, combining the power of the ras and the imperial favour of the *bitwaddad*
rest	a lineage system of land-ownership, giving usufruct rights to the claimant; in the twentieth century, *rest* assumes the meaning of absolute private property
resta gult	hereditary *gult*
safar	encampment, settlement, quarters
shalaqa	local representative of a higher authority, entrusted with the collection of tribute; in recent times, equivalent to the army rank of major

276

shefta	bandit, rebel
shum sher	periodic reshuffle of ministers or other government officials
tsahafe t'ezaz	head of the royal scribes, keeper of the royal seal; title of the Minister of Pen after 1907
wag shum	governor of the province of Wag in northern Wallo, just under *ras* in status, but entitled to certain royal honours because of his alleged descent from the Zagwe dynasty
Zamana Masafent	'the time of the nobility', the Era of the Princes, 1769-1855

Notes on transliteration

The usual spelling of some common geographical names has been retained, as in Abyssinia, Ethiopia (except in Amharic titles of books or articles), Dessie, Djibouti, Massawa.

Vowel sounds

To simplify printing, only the five vowels in the English alphabet have been used, without accents or other diacritical marks, to signify the seven vowel sounds in Amharic, which are contained in the seven forms of each of the main letters of the Amharic alphabet. It is assumed that readers of Amharic know the correct pronunciation of Ethiopian words. The seven vowel sounds are transliterated as follows:

Amharic forms:	1st	2nd	3rd	4th	5th	6th	7th
English vowel:	a	u	i	a	e	e	o

In spoken Tegregna, the language used in northern Ethiopia, a slight sound of y often occurs before 5th-form e, and is sometimes shown in English spelling, as in *Hamasien*, but is not shown in this work.

Occurrence of two vowel sounds consecutively

Where two different vowel sounds occur together in an Amharic word, they have been printed as in *Mikael, Yaeqob,* and each vowel is pronounced separately. Where a consonant before another vowel appears in its 6th form, however, that consonant is followed by an apostrophe, as in *Zar'a, mar'ed*. Again, each vowel is pronounced, the first as a short intake of breath or glottal sound.

Consonants

'Plosive' or 'glottal' consonants have not been shown, except for glottalized k, represented by q, as in *Qoqa*. The letters g, j and s are sounded as in English *get, jar* and *sun*, respectively. Double consonants are pronounced approximately as follows:

278

ch	gn	ts	zh
as in			
*ch*air	sig*n*or	ra*ts*	vi*s*ion
	(Italian)		

Where it is customary to pronounce distinctly each of two of the same
consonants appearing together, as in *abba, Iyyasu,* the consonant has
been repeated in print; but not all 'geminations' have been included,
as there is a good deal of disagreement on pronunciation, especially
in place-names.

Personal names

Ethiopians do not have permanent family surnames. If an Ethiopian man named by his parents Mabratu ('the light') has a son Tasfaye ('my hope'), Tasfaye adds his father's name to his own personal name, as Tasfaye Mabratu, but he is known as Tasfaye and not by his father's name. If Tasfaye has a twin son and daughter born in 1974, and calls the boy Abyot ('revolution') and the girl Maskaram ('spring'; 'September'), the children's full names are, respectively, Abyot Tasfaye and Maskaram Tasfaye, but they are known by their personal names, Abyot and Maskaram. Maskaram Tasfaye will retain her personal name and her father's name on marriage; she will not change her patronymic to that of her husband.

Instead of a secular name, the church name that a child was given at baptism in the Orthodox Christian Church may be retained as a personal name. These names are most commonly two words, hyphenated in this history: Hayla-Mikael ('power of Saint Mikael'), Walda-Giyorgis ('spiritual son of Saint George'), Walatta-Maryam ('spiritual daughter of Saint Mary'). If Hayla-Mikael has a son and daughter, each will have Hayla-Mikael as second name.

Muslims follow the same system of personal name and father's name, as laid down in the Koran.

In spelling his or her personal name in English, an Ethiopian may of course choose any preferred form of transliteration. We may find the variants Eyasu, Iyasou, Iyyasu; Shawaragad, Shewareged, Shoaregued; Webe, Wibe, Wubay, Wubie, and others.

INDEX

Note that some place-names refer also to the inhabitants of that area
Figures in bold refer to illustrations

Index

283

Index

Index

Imperial Board of Telecommunications, 188

Imperial Bodyguard, **147**, 148, 155, 186, 207, 214

Imperial Highway Authority (IHA), 188

import-export trade, 97-98, 197

income, per capita, 200

income-tax (1949), 199

India, Indian, 8, 9, 97-98, 105, 165, 186, 189

Indian Ocean, and ports, 1, 2, 3 (Map), 4, 51, 161 (Map)

Indo-Ethiopian Textile Mills, 198, 200

Indonesia, 198

Industrial Revolution, European, 24

industry (*see also* textiles), 164, 165 189, 196-201

Institute for the Study of Nationalities, 256

intellectuals, intelligentsia, Ethiopian, 92, 99, 103-111, 168, 212, 278; and Tafari Makonnen, 110-111, 131; targeted in Grazisni massacre, 170-171

investment policy, 199

Iraq, 219

Isayyas Afawarqi, 220

Isayyas Gabra-Sellase (d. 1974), 211

Isenberg, C. W., 25

Islam, Islamic (*see also* Muslim) Aksum's decline caused by, 8; factor in Bale rebellion, 216; in Gibe region states, 19; in Harar emirate 19, 63; Iyyasu's attitude to, 124, 128; in medieval Ethiopia, 9; in Wallaga (western) sheikhdoms, 19, 58-59; in Wallo, 12, 48-49; Yohannes IV's intolerence of, 48-49

Islamization, 19, 20, 61

Ismail, Khedive of Egypt (r. 1863-1879), 50-51, 53-54, 73

Israel, Israeli, 7, 186, 207

Italian East Africa, 161 (Map), 162, 163, 166

Italian Occupation of Ethiopia: administration and administrative districts during, 161 (Map), 162-163, 181; banks established during, 188; brief duration of, 84, 166; collaborators (*banda*), Ethiopian, during and after, 172, 174, 210, 211; colonial settlement during, 165; economic policy in, 165, 230; features of, 160-165, 198; Resistance during, 163, 166-176; significance, historical, of, 187, 197-198, 230

Italo-Ethiopian War (1935-1936) background to, 150-153; Ethiopia's

preparedness for, 147-148; progress of, 153-160; reparations, partial, for, 198

Italy, Italian: Adwa, Battle of, against, 53, 82, 83-85, 229; and agreement with Britain (1925), 152; in Bank of Abyssinia, representation by, 102 British collusion with, 73; colonial boundary delimitation of Eritrea by, 113, 114; diplomatic representation of, 96-97, 111, 152; and ex-colonies' disposal, 180-181, 182; and expedition attacked near Harar, 63; and import of infected cattle into Ethiopia, 72; and Iyyasu, 126-127; May Chaw Battle against, 155-157; and Menilek II, 59, 61, 74-79; negotiations with Ethiopia (1936) by, 166-167; prisoners-of-war (1896, 1941) from, 83, 179; subversion in northern Ethiopia by, 137; Taytu's objections to, 117; territorial encroachment (1880s) by, 56-57; trans-frontier trade with colonies of 96; and treaty of friendship (1928) with Ethiopia, 135, 151; in Tripartite Agreement, 85, 101, 111, 150-151; and Wechale Treaty with Ethiopia, 74, 84, 117; Zula, recommended for cession to, 54

Ityopya Teqdam ('Ethiopia First'), 235, 236, 240, 244, 246

ivory, 16, 22, 93, 97

Iyoas, Emperor of Ethiopia (r. 1755-1769), 11

Iyyasu, *Lej*, ruler of Ethiopia (r. 1913-1916; d. 1936): charge of apostasy against, 121, 124, 127; deposition of, 127-128, 129, 135; and intellectuals, 110; marriages of, **116**, 117, 124; plot (1932) for escape of, 144; reforms attempted by, 92, 121-122, 124, 140; reign, actual and legal, of, 120-128; slaving expedition by, 93; sons of, 174; and succession to throne, 116, 120; and World War One powers, 127; and Ydlibi, 98

Jacir Bey, 166

Janjaro, 7, 16, 17 (Map), 18, 86 (Map)

Japan, Japanese, 81, 92, 97, 110, 196

Jarosseau, André, 130

Jebat, 88

Jerusalem, 28, 33, 43

Jesuits, 9-10, 14, 24, 25, 223

Jijjiga, 126, 157, 190 (Map), 213

Jildessa, 63

Index